The Anatomy of Change

The Anatomy of Change

A MENNINGER FOUNDATION REPORT ON TESTING THE EFFECTS OF PSYCHOTHERAPY

STEPHEN A. APPELBAUM

The Menninger Foundation

Principal Investigator   **Coinvestigator**
RICHARD S. SIEGAL   **IRWIN C. ROSEN**

PLENUM PRESS · NEW YORK AND LONDON

Library of Congress Cataloging in Publication Data

Appelbaum, Stephen.
    The anatomy of change.

    Bibliography: p.
    Includes index.
    1. Psychotherapy—Evaluation. 2. Psychotherapy—Research. 3. Psychological re-
search. 4. Personality change. I. Menninger Foundation, Topeka, Kan. II. Title.
[DNLM: 1. Psychotherapy. WM420 A646a]
RC480.5.A66   616.8'914   77-5382
ISBN 0-306-31002-3

©1977 Plenum Press, New York
A Division of Plenum Publishing Corporation
227 West 17th Street, New York, N.Y. 10011

Printed in the United States of America

To Richard S. Siegal.
A small but significant cruelty of his lot
was not to have been able
to finish this book.

S.A.A.

Foreword

The standard test battery developed by Rapaport, Gill, and Schafer at the Menninger Foundation constituted the most important research instrument (apart from clinical interviews) of the Foundation's psychotherapy research project. The battery's influence on clinical diagnosis and on research in personality assessment and change has been tremendous. In the hands of highly trained and skilled psychologists, the battery, constructed chiefly around projective tests, has been invaluable for diagnosing difficult cases. The complexity of interpreting it, however, and the many dimensions along which its findings can be organized, have made it frustratingly difficult to use in formal research. And its cost, because of the great time investment it requires, has made clinicians reticent about using it on a large scale.

Dr. Appelbaum, an experienced psychotherapist and psychoanalyst, was a distinguished member of the group of highly skilled psychologists who applied this test battery in the psychotherapy research reported here, although his role in this instance was restricted to analyzing the findings of others who administered and interpreted the tests. In recent years, Dr. Appelbaum has been evaluating the mechanisms and effects of various psychotherapeutic approaches.

Drawing on his broad experience, Dr. Appelbaum here presents his searching and open-minded analysis of the psychological test data of the initial, termination, and follow-up evaluations of the patients in the psychotherapy project. His elaboration and analysis of the findings regarding the battery's diagnostic and predictive values represent a significant contribution to both clinical psychology and personality and psychotherapy research. In spite of—or perhaps I should say be-

vii

cause of—the almost overwhelming wealth of Dr. Appelbaum's data, the reader should find this a most instructive and thought-provoking book.

While some of the findings reported here follow expected lines, many more are completely surprising, and still others raise more questions than they answer. Because Dr. Appelbaum has separated his descriptions and summaries of the findings from his own penetrating analysis of them, the reader can carry out his own analyses of these data and take a position regarding Dr. Appelbaum's views. One impressive finding is how strong the predictive value of the initial test reports were—so much so that they overshadowed the psychiatric predictions. The clinical example illustrating how the tests were used sheds a special light on this finding.

The case illustration provides what seems to me truly impressive evidence of how relevant and important in clinical practice is the information derived from sophisticated projective psychological testing. This extensive analysis of one particular case rightly occupies a central position in this book: the entire methodology of psychological testing, including the research psychologist's diagnostic and predictive inferences, are vividly illustrated. This material also lends itself to the raising of critical questions. The patient, a woman with chronic marital conflicts and sexual difficulties, with severe obesity and phobias, was considered (by the psychiatrists–clinicians who initially evaluated her) as having a hysterical personality and good prognosis for psychoanalysis, the treatment she was referred for. The initial test report, however, stressed the indications of ego weakness, the predominance of infantile (in contrast to hysterical) features in her character, a certain degree of looseness in her thought processes, suggesting an occasional breakthrough of autistic paranoid thinking (not in well-structured situations, but in the projective tests), and a predominance of oral-aggressive impulses together with evidence of perverse sexual ideation.

From the vantage point of today's (twenty-years later) knowledge of the structural characteristics of borderline conditions, one would certainly suspect that this was a borderline patient, and raise serious questions to what extent a nonmodified, standard psychoanalysis really would be the treatment of choice. The psychologist who predicted a rather limited outcome of treatment on the basis of his evaluation of the initial test material was considerably less optimistic than the psychiatrists who had recommended psychoanalytic treatment initially. In all fairness, it must be added that the psychologist was also somewhat contaminated by the knowledge that the patient had been in psychoanalysis and that the obesity had not abated. And, more important, he worked directly from the raw psychological test data in contrast to the psychiatrists, who did the predictive study on the basis of the evaluative write-ups of the initial psychiatric teams. The research psychiatrists, then, worked from a different data base. This particular psychoanalysis, as predicted by the psychologists, was of limited effectiveness. The patient's verbal facility permitted her to gain much intellectual "insight," but not to resolve her basic conflicts. There was, however, significant symptomatic improvement at the termination of the treatment. It might be of interest to add that the patient was treated by a candidate in psychoanalytic training with limited experience.

This case material illustrates, by implication, several developments in the theoretical knowledge and clinical practice of psychological diagnosis and treatment indications over the past twenty years, developments that are highlighted (and, to some extent, were initiated) by the Menninger Foundation psychotherapy research project, and reflected in the analyses in Dr. Appelbaum's book. First, careful diagnostic study of patients is extremely important in evaluating indications and progress for psychotherapeutic treatment. For example, the prognosis for a typical hysterical personality with ordinary neurotic structure undergoing psychoanalysis is different from that of an infantile personality with borderline personality organization. Second, high intelligence and verbal facility may mask severe character pathology in patients with common psychoneurotic symptoms (in this case, the sexual inhibitions, the obesity, and the phobias): it is always crucial to supplement symptomatic diagnosis with a characterological diagnosis and, more generally speaking, a structural diagnosis, that is, the diagnosis of ego organization and strength. Third, sophisticated projective psychological testing may fundamentally contribute to the study of the adaptive and defensive function of the ego, predominant defensive organization, level of cognitive organization, and configuration of instinctual conflicts, all of which provide us with a structural diagnosis that separates neurotic from borderline (and also psychotic) structures. Fourth, the clinical sophistication of the particular psychologist is a crucial determinant of how much he can extract from the test data: the research psychologist whose tests and thinking are reported in this book illustrates this issue beautifully. He was an expert clinician, aware of the complications in the psychoanalysis of obese patients, the implications of obesity not improving over years of treatment, and concerned over the prognosis with psychoanalysis for a patient having so severe a pathological ego organization.

I wish to examine further Dr. Appelbaum's findings that the research psychologists who evaluated the test material did better in predicting outcome than the psychiatrists. These studies were undertaken at the time of a diagnostic revolution: the psychologists using the new Rapaport–Gill–Schafer test battery, which stressed structure rather than content, enjoyed a strong advantage over the psychiatrists, who were still stressing descriptive features and psychodynamic "contents" over structure.

This case also illustrates the ambiguous nature of "insight," a point that deserves further comment: Dr. Appelbaum concludes that the development of "insight" may or may not coincide with structural intrapsychic change and improvement, and that, in contrast, supportive techniques may bring about what seems to be structural intrapsychic change. In this connection, the quantitative and facet analyses of the research project data found that, although it was not possible to correlate (because of the small numbers of cases in the various modalities) a specifically labeled modality of treatment ("psychoanalysis," "supportive psychotherapy," etc.) with specific aspects of outcome, there were, however, relationships between the predominant use of expressive or exploratory techniques ("focus on the transference") and outcomes in the case of patients with ego weakness. Thus (with therapists of high skill), patients with ego weakness (borderline conditions) had much better outcomes with an approach that focused more on the transference than with one that did less; and, in the facet analysis, patients with ego weakness who were provided with structure outside the treatment hours had better outcomes than patients whose psychotherapeutic hours became more and more structured, that is, supportive.

My point is that much of what appears to be "insight" in patients with ego weakness has to do with the conscious availability of primitive instinctual material, of primary-process functioning in consciousness. So that dealing with conscious material in borderline patients may bring about structural intrapsychic change *if* the transference is handled in ways that foster an integration of dissociated or split-off thoughts, affects, and behaviors. Therefore, psychoanalysts or psychoanalytically oriented psychiatrists working "supportively" (in theory) with borderline patients may, in effect, by using analytic knowledge and technique in the psychotherapy of these patients and focusing on the transference (insofar as it is conscious material that evolves in the hours) bring about structural intrapsychic change. These same therapists, working in a pseudo-"analytic" fashion with such patients, permitting free-floating, intellectualized, or dissociated fantasy material to fill the analytic hours without confrontation and interpretation of the transference in the "here and now," and without any structuralization of the patient's external life, may fail in their treatment (given the extreme nature of acting out of these patients both in the analytic setting and outside the treatment hours). Regarding this book's illustrative patient, for example, the psychoanalysis, carried out without any modification of technique and without sufficient interpretation of transference and of the acting out of the transference, permitted an endless intellectualized expression of erotic material in the hours, dissociated from other aspects of the patient's behavior and not leading to significant structural intrapsychic change.

Our traditional definitions of supportive versus expressive or exploratory psychotherapeutic techniques need to be reexamined in the light of our newly developing knowledge about primitive types of ego organization. In patients having this type of ego organization, the defense–impulse configurations take on highly "personified" features, where impulse and defense are both expressed in certain primitive dissociated internalized object relations, in alternating and chaotically interacting activations of conscious, affect-laden self- and object-representations. This is in contrast to the predominance of broader, intersystemic conflicts involving ego, id, and superego as overall psychic structures in patients with higher levels of personality organization. The concept of structure and structural change, the relationship between such change and the quality of, respectively, consciousness or unconsciousness of the analytic material, and the techniques that define supportive versus analytic modalities of treatment need to be reexamined and reformulated: this process has barely begun.

One might say that the initial stages of the psychotherapy research project of The Menninger Foundation mark the transition from the traditional diagnosis and treatment of patients with psychoanalysis or psychoanalytic psychotherapies in the light of their predominant symptoms and assumed unconscious conflicts, on the one hand, to the more recent, sophisticated model of psychological diagnosis and treatment based upon the new structural conceptions inaugurated by psychoanalytic ego psychology, on the other. The completion of the project and the findings derived from it initiated, in turn, a new transition from the ego-psychological concepts exemplified by the theories of Rapaport and Knight, on the one hand, and the more recent developments of an ego-psychologically based developmental and object–relations theory initiated by Erikson and developed by Jacobson and Mahler, on the other.

The new theoretical orientation conceives of complex early developmental stages of self and object differentiation predating the stage of object constancy and the overall consolidation of psychic structures characteristic of ordinary neurosis and character pathology, early stages of development that are reflected in the severe psychopathologies, particularly the borderline conditions. This newer psychoanalytic model has been incorporated with clinical psychiatric practice somewhat earlier than with the theory and technique of projective psychological testing, which is in contrast to the revolutionary introduction of psychoanalytic ego psychology, particularly the structural concepts, into psychological testing by Rapaport, Gill, and Schafer. It seems to me that the implications of an ego-psychological object–relations theory for psychological testing still need to be worked out fully, and may have important consequences for the diagnostic and research value of psychological tests in the next generation of research on personality assessment and change.

Among the many issues that may need to be reexamined in the light of such newer models is that of "insight." The definition of insight at severe levels of character pathology may require formulations different from the traditional one reflecting insight at relatively advanced or consolidated stages of structural development. In patients with borderline personality organization, insight, to qualify as such, may require evidence of the patient's concern over contradictory aspects of his thinking, affects, or behavior, and the transformation of such concern into an integrative effort in his work on himself. Conscious memories of the relationship between past experiences and present conflicts can otherwise easily lend themselves to subtle acting out of fantasies of entitlement to compensatory gratifications for past traumas or failure, or of primitive instinctual conflicts in the form of aggressive or erotized primitive fantasies in the transference.

Among the unexpected, and startling findings reported by Dr. Appelbaum is the increase in IQ of patients after treatment regardless of whether the results of the treatment have been successful or not. This finding highlights, it seems to me, the enormous importance of cognitive functions in the patient–therapist interactions. Because in patients with good ego strength, one frequently finds the tendency to use either intellectualization or excessive affect reactions as a defense (obsessive-compulsive versus hysterical pathology), we tend to overlook the intimate connection between affects and cognition at the earlier levels of development and in the more pathological or primitive psychological functionings that retain modes of such early development. In addition, the traditional focus on "catharsis" in psychoanalytic psychotherapies (and the present distortion of these concepts in some psychotherapeutic modalities that naively assume that affective discharge will produce, by itself, fundamental psychological change) has prevented us from recognizing to what extent cognitive clarification and integration are basic and potent psychotherapeutic tools.

In psychoanalysis as well as in the psychoanalytic psychotherapies, the therapist's cognitive formulations strengthen or broaden the patient's integration of affects and internalized object relations concurrently. What Winnicott has described as the "holding" environment—the provision of functioning akin to early mothering by the therapist who empathetically "holds" the patient under certain regressive conditions—involves not only an affective disposition of the therapist, but also, and very fundamentally, a cognitive integration in his mind of fragmented, dissociated, or chaotic information from the total patient–therapist interaction. To formulate interpretations with patients in a state of severe regression is to interpret primitive defensive splitting, to integrate defensively dissociated affects and object relations, and to increase the patient's cognitive capacities, all in one. Not all intellectual knowledge is "intellectualization," and authentic knowledge both fosters and is a concomitant of any emotional growth.

Sophisticated projective testing carried out by experienced, psychoanalytically trained psychologists is an indispensable instrument of psychiatric diagnosis at its best. It is to be hoped that social and financial constraints will not decrease the utilization of a crucial instrument for optimal practice simply because it is expensive, and that our society will not sacrifice optimal psychological care to what is politically expedient. Dr. Appelbaum's book can be considered as closing out an era while at the same time pointing toward a new generation of research instruments and approaches to personality assessment and personality change.

OTTO F. KERNBERG, M.D.

Preface

Through the centuries, when hope for beneficial change has been extended to mankind, mankind has snapped it up. Only those with competing panaceas have raised critical questions. One would think the situation would be different with respect to psychotherapy. Because this major expression and offering of hope in the 20th century came at a time when science was supreme, one might have expected that the scientific method would have been vigorously pressed into service, that psychotherapy would have been experimentally tested in advance of its being accepted. Instead, as with religions, people flocked to be helped, and the arguments have mainly been which religion or psychotherapy was the best one. The growth in popularity of psychotherapy has, in the United States in particular, been phenomenal.

Over 20 years ago members of the Menninger Foundation set out to examine scientifically this cultural phenomenon, this glittering medical specialty, this new hope for the masses. With due regard to the elusiveness of the subject matter, the rule book of science was to be applied. In a systematic and orderly way psychotherapy was to be analyzed into its component parts, and the vicissitudes and ultimate fate of the component parts were to be plotted and traced in the context of the total personality. We were to try to learn whether change occurs over the course of psychotherapy and, if so, how it happens, why it happens, and what the consequences are.

This is a report of that investigation. It is an attempt to supply the answers to these questions. We may have to take certain aspects of psychotherapy on faith, perhaps for a long time, perhaps forever. But in this work we demonstrate an attempt to break with passive, uncritical, and unexamined acceptance.

The Psychotherapy Research Project of the Menninger Foundation began in the early 1950s.* I had a tangential connection with the Project for several years before 1967, which was when I began the work reported here. The circumstances under which I began this work were painful. Richard S. Siegal was dying, but working hard at this research, in some ways better than ever. He very much wanted his years of work to reach fruition, for he was devoted to testing, to exploration, and to carrying out his responsibilities. I worked with him during the last months of his life, both of us knowing and not knowing that I would soon continue alone. He was principal investigator of the testing part of the Project, and his notes and personal communications are incorporated in parts of this book. He was my dear friend—a first-rate person. Death be not proud.

Dr. Irwin C. Rosen made contributions of a high order to the collection, reporting, and analysis of data before he left the Project. Testing of research subjects was done by Irwin C. Rosen and Richard S. Siegal, both expert practitioners and teachers of diagnostic testing. Testing of Menninger Foundation patients, not originally considered as research subjects, was done by Menninger Foundation junior and senior staff psychologists and students in the Foundation's Post-Doctoral Training Program in Clinical Psychology. Their work played an unanticipatedly important role (see Chapter 8). Several contributions to the analysis of data were made by Dr. Rosen and by Dr. Siegal, both by himself and with me.

Dr. Dennis Farrell acted as a judge in the study reported in Chapter 8 comparing the efficiency of tests and psychiatric information. As explicated in that chapter, this was a difficult and demanding task. In addition to making judgments, he creatively contributed to the analysis of the data and to its reporting. He cares about ideas and their implications. Working with him was a pleasure.

Dr. Lolafaye Coyne, the Project's statistician, has through the years been a great deal more. Rather than simply running through the statistical calculations, she helped decide what kinds of analyses to make, and in so doing at times influenced decisively the shape of this work. She demonstrates how the statistical mind at work can be a thing of beauty.

Dr. Ann Appelbaum may be one of the most publicly thanked colleague-editors around. Her combination of psychoanalytic knowl-

* The Psychotherapy Research Project of the Menninger Foundation was supported by Public Health Service Research Grant MH 8308 from the National Institute of Mental Health, by the Foundation's Fund for Research in Psychiatry, and by the Ford Foundation. The writing of this book was supported in part by the Spencer Foundation.

edge, analytical mind, and concern for and expertise in the English language has been of great benefit to me in the preparation of this book, as it has been on my other writings, and to many other colleagues. She did not, however, merely endure my work with wifely forbearance. Rather, she encouraged me by word and by example.

Even though Dr. Robert S. Wallerstein had left the leadership of the Psychotherapy Research Project of the Menninger Foundation by the time this book was being written, he maintained a steady interest in it. Dr. Otto Kernberg, who took over the leadership of the Project when Doctor Wallerstein left and in turn left it, also continued to give aid and encouragement from a distance. His critical reading of a draft of this book was most useful. Dr. Michael Harty and Dr. Sydney Smith, too, helped greatly with their critical reading of the manuscript.

Dr. Karl Menninger weighed the manuscript in his hands and gave a now-discarded title the small-size shrift it deserved. He may have read all or none of the rest. But, no matter, just a few peppery and perceptive remarks from him on almost any subject can make a beneficial difference.

As I grew older at the editing task, Virginia Eicholtz grew younger at it. She was a pleasure to work with, as always.

As secretary to the Project, Mary Patton rescued me on more than one occasion.

Through the years I have been fortunate indeed to have Mary McLin type my manuscripts. With this book she outdid even herself in speed and efficiency. I am most grateful to her.

To Anita C. Appelbaum and Eric N. Appelbaum, thanks for the grace with which they gave to this book time we would otherwise have had together. By the time this work was in its final stages they, too, had become my editors.

When the editorial *we* is used in this report, it refers to the various kinds of collaborative thinking and work involved in the Project. *We* is appropriate in another sense as well. The ways of using tests and thinking about patients exemplified here are part of a psychological tradition associated, at various points in their careers, with such men as David Rapaport, Merton Gill, Robert R. Holt, Phillip S. Holzman, George Klein, Martin Mayman, Roy Schafer, and Herbert J. Schlesinger. All of them worked at the Menninger Foundation at one time or another and have carried on this tradition elsewhere. *We* then refers at times to people, a place, functional roles, and shared beliefs and practices.

Over the long span of years of the Project not only were different people involved in it, but the same people became in a sense different people. One of the consequences of the Project, indeed any attempt to expand knowledge, is that people change. We learned a great deal from the Project itself, from the development of our careers in other respects, and from the burgeoning of knowledge in the professional community at large. Thus, the reader may note in this book different voices from different epochs, at times carrying on a dialogue with one another, criticizing from hindsight, and reflecting new views.

STEPHEN A. APPELBAUM

Contents

Introduction

Each report from the Psychotherapy Research Project of the Menninger Foundation has been eagerly awaited by those interested in research on psychotherapy, in the accomplishments of psychotherapy and how they come about, and in the teaching of psychotherapy. This Project has been several decades in the designing, carrying out, and reporting, and was remarkably expensive of money and time. It is unique in the field in its combination of (1) intensive examinations, including a battery of psychological tests before, after, and two years after treatment; (2) being done with actual patients and actual therapists engaged in long-term psychotherapy under naturalistic clinical conditions; and (3) being carried out by multidisciplinary teams, all according to a relatively homogeneous clinical way of working and theory of personality. It is a landmark in the field, and its design and objectives have been published and debated widely for years, as its findings have recently begun to be.

MAIN OBJECTIVES

When the study was undertaken, more than two decades ago, the tradition of psychological testing was in ascendance. The use of tests at the Menninger Foundation was and is a fountainhead of the influential testing tradition of David Rapaport and was a major feature of the Psychotherapy Research Project. Since that time, this tradition has lost popularity, for a number of reasons: Relatively few people were trained in it, and so as the field of clinical psychology grew larger that proportion grew smaller. The therapeutic *zeitgeist*, in general, has moved more from thought and toward action, toward doing the same things with all people rather than on the basis of a precise diagnosis, and toward placing financial and prestige rewards upon therapy rather than diagnosis.

The intensive use of tests on which this book is based, and the proof of the efficiency of tests used in this way, runs healthily counter to current trends and can provide an impetus to what already is a beginning backlash, a beginning recognition that people are different and need to be treated differently. One of the best ways to do this is to understand them by way of a sophisticated use of psychological tests. (In one section of the book the practical usefulness of tests is compared with that of psychiatric interviews and other sources of data.)

One section of the book includes an extended case example and the meticulous record of the tester's inferences about the test data and its implications for treatment and change. Thus, it demonstrates the way of working with tests used at the Menninger Foundation, a short how-to-do-it course.

It is an open secret that the language of psychiatry and psychology is burdened with jargon, that terms are imprecise and used differently by different practitioners in various institutions and in various parts of the country. These linguistic difficulties are often expressions of underlying conceptual confusion. In this book commonly used psychiatric terms are subjected to conceptual analysis buttressed by data.

Nowadays, with various kinds of therapy, consciousness-raising, and other alleged means of change becoming popular, often in the hands of untrained or self-trained people, it is more important than ever that we survey the means by which people change, e.g., by way of insight, by way of the interpersonal relationship, etc. This book provides a microscopic look at some of the major means by which people are alleged to change.

We address issues of change in the practice of psychiatric treatment, the need for diagnosis and correct match of patient with treatment, the social implications of how best to distribute scarce psychotherapists' time, and the goals in psychotherapy.

The self-conscious evaluation offered here of the Psychotherapy Research Project of the Menninger Foundation as a trailblazing, complex, and ambitious piece of work in a treacherous area of research should enable others to avoid some of its mistakes and benefit from some of its successes.

The objectives of this book and the research that it reports are sufficiently diverse so that different parts of it will be of greater interest to some people than other parts. Those interested in the outcome of psychotherapy and its professional and existential implications will be most interested in Overall Assessment of Change for Better or Worse (Chapter 4), the Follow-Up Study (Chapter 9), and Overview and Conclusions (Chapter 10). Those interested in an atomistic analysis of personality and change, and in the conceptualization of individual aspects of the personality, will be especially interested in Change in Each Patient Variable from Initial to Termination (Chapter 3). Patterns of change among the patients are available in Patterns of Change (Chapter 6) and Profile of Change: Factor Analytic Study of Patient Variables (Chapter 5). Those interested in the relationship between psychological tests and other means of investigation are offered comparisons of Psychological Tests and Paired Comparison Analyses (Chapter 7) and Comparing the Usefulness of Tests with Other Psychiatric Information (Chapter 8). How the Tests Were Used (Chapter 2) offers a view of how inferences were drawn from the tests and how first-order inferences are integrated into succeedingly higher levels of abstraction, as illustrated by case example. Task and Methods (Chapter 1), however, should be read by all in order to get the most out of any section.

The analysis and reporting of the data were carried out without knowledge about the patients except what was available from the tests, without knowledge about the therapists, without knowledge of the kind of treatment that was received by the patient, and without knowledge of the environmental factors impinging on the treatment process. Such information might enrich or alter these findings. That information is or will be available in other project reports (see References, p. 297). This report is solely of the findings from psychological tests.

Rather than using objective measuring instruments, with validity independent of the investigator, the Project's "measuring instruments" were people making subjective judgments. The amount and kind of information they had when they made these judgments, the conditions under which they worked that may have influenced these judgments, and how they were trained are in themselves research data.

Throughout this report, *research testers* refers to those psychologists who administered, scored, and interpreted the tests that were given for research purposes at termination of psychotherapy (when for the first time patient and therapist learned they had been research subjects) and at follow-up, two years later. These test administrations should be discriminated from those tests done before the patient started treatment, at initial. The latter were were done by *clinical testers.* Research testers could not do the initial testing because the naturalistic objectives of the project required that selection, assignment, and treatment of patients be done in the usual clinical manner. (At the Menninger Foundation, most patients are tested before any key clinical decisions are made.) Except where noted, the reports of the clinical testers were not part of the research data. Their test protocols, however, did provide the data for the research test analyses and predictions at initial.

Research psychologists refers to those who analyzed, for research purposes, the documents reporting the collected test data. Usually these documents were the various research forms according to which conclusions based on the tests were organized and abstracted by the research testers. Occasionally, clinical test reports were analyzed.

Nontest researchers refers to those members of the research teams—psychiatrists, psychologists, and social workers—who may or may not have worked with test results in pursuing their own investigations, but who did not collect, analyze, or report test data themselves.

CHAPTER 1

Task and Methods

The psychological test portion of the Psychotherapy Research Project is parallel to and independent of the other examinations. It is parallel in that the test examinations were conducted at the same times and for some of the same purposes—to diagnose the psychological situation of the patient, to make predictions, to learn what changes had occurred, and to examine the possible causes and consequences of such change. It is independent in that the research testers and research psychologists made their judgments without reference to sources of information about the patient other than that which was provided by the tests. Both the testing and nontesting members of the Project judged the patients' intrapsychic processes (called "patient variables"), but the research testers and research psychologists judged only these while the nontest sections judged in addition "situational and treatment variables." (For detailed descriptions and discussions of the overall Project, see *Bulletin of the Menninger Clinic,* Vol. 20, pp. 221–78, Vol. 22, pp. 115–66, Vol. 24, pp. 157–216, Robbins & Wallerstein, 1959, Sargent, 1961; Rosen, 1965; Wallerstein, 1966b, 1968.)

Why were psychological tests used in this research? Tests were used as a kind of control. The overall design of the Project did not include matched control groups, but rather relied on each patient being his own control. By having the test findings independent of other findings, comparability could be interpreted as evidence that various uncontrolled factors having to do with the nontest examinations were not influential. One has greater confidence in the validity of the judgment if that judgment is duplicated by independent means of investigation. Another reason was to conform to the naturalistic design of the study, to change for research purposes as few of the local clinical practices as possible.

Tests have become a routine part of personality assessment at the Menninger Foundation as a result of many years of empirical observation of their utility. One of their uses is to corroborate other clinical judgments, an important though perhaps undramatic contribution. Clinical responsibility demands a high degree of confidence in the making of decisions that may profoundly affect other people's lives, and corroboration of inferences increases the confidence with which inferences and the recommendations based on them are held. Often enough, the tests, or rather the psychologist who interprets the tests, is usually able to extend knowledge of the patient beyond what is available from psychiatric and social work interviews or other sources of information.

At initial, the use of tests by the nontest researchers was, perforce, naturalistic. If for no other reason than to maintain secrecy, "unnatural" research testing could not be added to the usual clinical testing; so initial assessments of variables (Form B) and predictions (Form C) had to be made by the nontest researchers on the basis of the clinical test report. At termination, the naturalistic policy was maintained through making available to the nontest researchers, for use with their termination assessments, a test–retest comparison, based on the initial test protocols and the same test battery repeated at termination by the research testers. A similar report would have been made available in the ordinary run of clinical activities if the clinical issue was whether, how much, and why the patient had changed since his previous testing.

Termination testing conformed to the goal of naturalism in the choice of tests and, in general, in the conditions of testing. Rather than designing or selecting special tests, as is often done for research purposes, the testers chose the individual test battery used in ordinary clinical work at the Menninger Foundation and used it at termination as well as at initial. The research testers knew, however, that they had to assess certain variables specified by the research design—a somewhat different practice from the usual. Yet it is not entirely different since, in order to answer most clinical questions, the psychologist first has to assess a number of psychological variables, most of which are included in the Project list of patient variables (see p. 17).

One way the use of tests did clearly deviate from the goal of naturalism was that the research testers were able to spend as much time as they wished in extracting information from the tests. Case material (offered in Chapter 2 as a demonstration of the making of inferences from tests) provides an instance of leisurely inference-making, rarely possible under the pressures of nonresearch clinical work. Not only is there less time in clinical work, but the sociopsychological context (as we have suggested elsewhere [Appelbaum & Siegal, 1965]) is likely to influence what one learns, thinks, and says about a patient. Such influences were reduced to a minimum in the research context (though this context itself is a source of its own influences).

In addition to the test–retest reports, for some patients the research testers filled out the same systematic assessment of variables (Form Bs) that the nontest researchers did. Such research forms are, of course, not naturalistic. Not only did they require a survey of specific, previously specified variables, but they were filled out with research objectives in mind.

Except for those several cases where by chance the clinical testing had been done by the research testers in their clinical roles (which continued along with their research activities at the Foundation), the research testers at termination had not seen the patient before treatment and thus were usually able to remain uncontaminated from nontest sources of information as well. However, some extratest information did come their way, as is inevitable in a clinical center where people work closely together. The research testers took explicit notice of this contamination in their write-ups, and attempted to minimize its influence on their process of inference from the tests. As with all testers at the Menninger Foundation, the practice and conviction of the research testers were that inferences should be drawn from the tests independent of conclusions based on other information. The tests are done in a clinical context, with which testers are familiar, and from which questions are directed to the tester. But test findings stand alone, to be integrated by others in the final common path of information. When the conclusions match, they are held and acted upon with added confidence. When they do not match, divergences are examined as potential sources of information about divergent aspects of the patient or as evidence of some information being missing or not understood.

One may ask why, in keeping with naturalistic aims, the test information is not simply allowed to speak through the nontest researchers without this separate investigation based on the tests alone. Should not the assessment by the tests correspond to and duplicate the clinical conclusions of which they are a part? Not necessarily. One reason is that there may be slips between test judgments and nontest clinical judgments. Sometimes, when the test judgments conflict with other judgments, the tests are disregarded. Sometimes the test findings are misunderstood. There may be conceptual differences and different inferences from similar phenomena.

It is surely no secret that our "rich" clinical concepts mean different things to different people, sometimes even among people of the
same disciplines, more often when the concepts are derived from different examinational techniques and situations. Anxiety, for example,
may be inferred on the tests from the way the patient uses shaded
areas in inkblots while it may be inferred during a clinical interview
by the perspiration on a patient's hands. The answers to such questions as whether the anxiety is bound, free-floating, averted, attached
to particular contents, or interferes with other functions may be different, depending upon the different means of observation, because
different "things" are being measured though the word we use for
them is the same. So it is possible that test results end up as information different from what was understood and intended by the tester.
Another aspect of this is that information about intrapsychic processes, in this instance gathered by tests, may yield conclusions different from judgments made on the basis of interview and historical
information. Finally, though we at the Menninger Foundation are convinced of the general utility of tests, this research provides an opportunity to subject that assumption to a systematic test.

Our general intentions, then, are to assess the relative effectiveness of the tests with respect to a variety of variables and clinical
questions, and in comparison with nontest judgments and predictions, as well as to make independent assessment of change in psychotherapy as this is reflected in psychological tests.

THE TESTS AND OUR VIEW OF TESTING

Tests provide a standard set of stimuli thus yielding norms; on
the basis of these norms inferences can be drawn about the patient
with reference to theories of personality and to treatment intervention.
By giving a number of different tests, many aspects of a patient's functioning can be studied. By varying the degree of structure of the tasks,
we are able to learn some of the contents of his mind. And we learn
what effects, if any, there are on his formal thought functioning when
thoughts and feelings ordinarily controlled or obscured by the structure of a task and test stimuli are, by degrees, freed for expression. In
principle, none of this is different from the clinical interview. In practice, because the tests are more standard from patient to patient than
most clinical interviews, the examiners can more readily develop
norms. Tests offer a greater variety of tasks than do most interviews,
and the degrees of structure (or projectiveness) are more systematically

altered than with most other interviews. Our method of testing minimizes the patient's self-report. Beyond what may be necessary to ensure an optimal testing atmosphere, or at least a knowledge on the tester's part of the influences in the atmosphere, we do not talk with the patient about himself nor interview him in a formal sense. (We may, however, inquire into the patient's attitude toward his responses, elaborations of them, his feelings about the tester and being tested, all in order to evaluate his test responses.)

The same test battery was used at initial, termination, and follow-up, and consisted of the Wechsler-Bellevue Form I, Rorschach Test, Word Association Test, BRL Object Sorting Test, the Thematic Apperception Test, and the Babcock Story Recall. This battery was used in the pioneering study by Rapaport *et al.* (1945–46; Holt, 1968) and is still in use at the Menninger Foundation. A detailed rationale for selection of these tests, and a description of the particular uses to which each is put, is available in the Rapaport volumes. Suffice it to say here that, practically speaking, for a naturalistic study we had to use tests from daily practice with which we were familiar. And we had ample reason to believe that these tests would tell us what we wanted to know about the patient variables.

The use of the same tests at each specific time raises the question of practice effects. This question is perhaps most pertinent to the variable *intelligence,* and is discussed in detail in that context (see also S. Appelbaum *et al.,* 1969, 1970a). For the rest of the variables the question is somewhat academic. Equivalent forms are not available for most of the tests in the battery, and for our purposes such precision, even if it were possible, would have been unnecessary. As it turned out, change in variables was not uniform, as might be expected from the effects of practice, and the diverse patterns of change were intercorrelated in psychologically plausible ways which seemed independent of uniform practice effects. Finally, the research testers took practice effects into consideration in the making of their inferences from the tests. Such weightings were easier to make in a relatively large group such as this, where patients could be compared with one another, than it might be if one were attempting to assess the attempts of practice on any one person's test performance.

Testers differ a good deal in their beliefs about and their uses of tests. A hoary battle has been waged between the subjective, idiographic, complex, "tender-minded," who feel no need for numerical indices of reliability and validity, and the objective, nomothetic, simpler, "tough-minded," who require numerical expressions of high reliability and validity. This polarity has found pointed expression in

Meehl's *Clinical vs. Statistical Prediction* (1954), rejoinders and exten-
sions of which were made by Holt (1958). In recent years, research and
clinical practice seem to have moved further away from the projective,
global, clinically oriented approach and toward the increasing use of
objective tests, systems of scoring, lists of test signs, and observations
of discrete behaviors. We recognize the difficulties in maintaining the
"subjective" approach (more of this later) and have gone into some
detail in this report about the complex series of inferential processes
by which the psychologist moves from his test data through theoretical and clinical understanding. By careful attention to the inference
process we believe we can minimize inaccuracy and avoid "wild"
analysis of personality, particularly of content. We further believe that
the complexity of people and the processes necessary to learn about
them can be reported, related, and replicated. Rather than limit the
scope of our tools by imposing research strictures upon ourselves, we
have allowed clinical thinking to operate freely in order to demonstrate its full range and penetrating power. We then microscopically
examined the routes we had traversed, and with reference to what has
come afterward in the patient's treatment indicated strengths and
weaknesses of this approach.

SOME CLINICAL ISSUES AND PRACTICES

Since our tests are unlike psychometric tests, which yield mechan-
ically objective responses, we are interested in the process of responding to tests at least as much as in the end products, the test responses.
Similarly, we do not rely upon a sign approach, whether based upon
one or a group of responses, and whether the signs are thought of as
indicators of nosological categories or of personality traits such as passivity, ascendance, aggressivity, and the like. Rather, every piece of
possible test evidence is subjected to the magnet of successively
higher organizing theoretical and clinical abstractions. When a good
many pieces of evidence come together and "stick," much confidence
accrues to the assertion derived from them. At the same time, a single
piece of evidence, evaluated against the examiner's implicit norms and
by his clinical judgment, whether this be normative or intuitive or a
combination of the two, may in and of itself lead to a confidently held
inference. A more detailed explanation of how we used the tests is
available in Chapter 2. There are relatively few such published
records. It is a kind of minitextbook on how to draw inferences from
tests.

Popular habits of language imply that "the tests" have usefulness in one way or another. In fact, the tests have no validity in and of themselves. Rather, the person who in his own way administers, scores, and interprets the tests and communicates his findings is responsible for their value. This value in turn may vary depending upon the particular issues to which "testing" is addressed.

CHOICE OF LANGUAGE AND ITS IMPLICATIONS

As we begin this report, we are faced with the question of whether to call the people whom we examined "patients" or "clients"; whether to call what happened to them "interventions" or "treatments"; whether to describe our examinations of them as "assessments" or "diagnoses." In short, should we seem to embrace the medical model through using its terminology, or should we substitute terms from other approaches, many of which are reactions to, or revolts against, the medical model.

We are aware of many of the ways in which the traditional medical model is inappropriate to psychiatric patients. Psychological treatment does not involve an authority doing something to a passive patient according to a diagnosis which carries with it fixed treatment possibilities that are the same no matter who administers them and under what conditions. Rather than the psychotherapist's doing something to the patient, both of them work together on a task whose psychological field regularly varies and requires varying degrees of activity and passivity. Rather than making a diagnosis of a disease, the diagnostician makes a complex evaluation of structures, functions, and fantasies. These are better thought of as assets or liabilities with respect to particular tasks or goals than as a manifestation of a disease process. Rather than an invariable prescription being made, interventions, derived from the findings of strengths and weaknesses, are tried and evaluated with attention to how well they are furthering original goals and how responsive these interventions are to continually developing goals and needs. Rather than uniformity of treatment, there are differences in treatment, varying to the degree that people, both patients and therapists, are different.

We believe that the impingement of one person on another is most likely to be beneficial when it proceeds according to knowledge of intrapsychic processes as played out in behavior and as empathically understood and used. It hardly matters what one calls this process. Changing the names or throwing away theory and means of observation often seems to us a kind of impetuous "know-noth-ingism," as if simplicity can replace complexity when the subject mat-ter is complex. In our view, souls should be searched as to how much the furor about using such "medical" terms as *diagnosis* and *treatment* stems from political and social antipathies and competitions rather than from sober, analytical recognition of what happens in people's minds and thoughts—intrapsychic processes—and convictions about how to change these. (For an excellent discussion of these issues, see Sarason & Ganzer, 1960; with particular reference to the idea of diag-nosis, see Holt, 1968.) We retained the traditional, or medical, termi-nology, for convenience and because it fits with much social reality and the reality of where we work. When our data stimulated a reexam-ination of some implicit notions about "treatment" or "disease" we have spelled this out. We ask that our work be judged on a substan-tive basis, whether we have remained true to the underlying princi-ples and values of psychological treatment and research thinking, rather than whether it takes sides in an essentially political struggle.

Mayman (1963) has noted three levels, or styles, of language com-monly used in clinical psychology, psychiatry, and psychoanalysis. The first, and lowest in the ladder of abstraction, is the empirical, op-erational, living language of thoughts and feelings, e.g., what the per-son does, thinks, feels, believes. It is a language of verbs more than nouns. The third, or highest on the level of abstraction, is made up of such concepts as libido or superego in psychoanalytic meta-psychology. The second, or "middle language," is that which clini-cians use who share common assumptions and ways of working when discussing patients. It may employ words from the levels below and above it, but it is less systematic than the third order and more general and encompassing than the first order. Some examples are "supportive psychotherapy," "anxiety tolerance," "decompensation." It is a kind of shorthand, useful for carrying an idea, so long as the idea is not carried too far or expected to convey much of the flavor and immedi-acy of the person described. For example, good psychotherapy is always "supportive" and good "supportive" psychotherapy is always "expressive," so the conceptual status of "supportive" or "expressive" psychotherapy is a complex one (Schlesinger, 1969). Yet many clini-cians use such terms usefully to convey and understand quickly a lot of orienting information about the patient and his treatment. The problem arises when this shorthand is used for purposes other than this, or when it has connotations unintended by the speaker or lacks connotations to the particular listener which were intended by the speaker. This happens often and creates much mischief. But it by no means always happens. I would like to have with you, the reader, a clinician-to-clinician relationship, and so I will use the middle language for its immediate utility, when more abstract conceptual precision or more human immediacy is not required. I shall use unflinchingly—well, flinchingly—such words as *psychotic, neurotic, ego,* aware of their unsettled conceptual status and their consequent crudity. I hope, however, to use them only when the situation calls for no more than they should be asked to deliver.

DIAGNOSIS

The concept of diagnosis in psychological/psychiatric contexts has been adversely criticized on a number of grounds in addition to its associations with traditional medical thinking. One criticism obtains in situations where regardless of any individual needs of the patient only one treatment modality is available or believed in. For example, some psychoanalysts possibly still believe, as did many in the past, that classical psychoanalysis is the only intervention that can be considered therapeutic in any substantive, meaningful way. The varieties of psychotherapy are considered by them as superficial, as "merely" counseling and guidance. When large populations are dependent upon few treaters, reliance is placed on whatever treatment can be made available—EST, behavior modification—all more or less freely prescribed by whoever is responsible for the health of greater numbers of people than could possibly be intensively examined and individually treated. In such situations, theory takes a back seat to pragmatic considerations. Workers in these situations may not be antidiagnostic, but adiagnostic. They do not have the time, and may not have the inclination or skill for refined diagnostic assessments of their patients. Implicit in their activities is the proposition that all people, or at least those with a given "clinical syndrome," are the same in relevant aspects so that the appropriate single treatment is as helpful as it is possible to be for any one person.

This implicit idea is elevated to a theoretical position in various explicitly humanistic persuasions. According to some of these, the human condition, being universal, overrides individual differences. All people, for example, have drives toward health, e.g., self-actualization. The therapeutic problem is more or less simply to release these drives. Thus, according to the Rogerians, all people will change in a self-preferred direction if they are given the opportunity in the presence of an accepting other to take notice of what they are and what they would like to be. Some behavioral, conditioning therapists also proceed with a relatively invariable technique on the assumption that all people respond to the same laws of learning. These workers recognize the varying degrees of success which they achieve, that some people benefit more than others. But the relative inflexibility of their techniques continues to make it unnecessary for them to make detailed assessments as a basis for deciding what if anything to do for that person.

While we agree that diagnostic labels in psychiatry do not strictly imply specific treatment procedures, we also believe that there is a good bit of the straw man being argued against in many assumed justifications for throwing out diagnostic thinking altogether. Diagnosis even in medicine is not really as cut-and-dried as the formula—specific disease leads to specific treatment—implies. The problem, in our opinion, is to use diagnosis for the practical good it can do without being a slave to those traditional uses that are inappropriate for the task at hand.

Diagnosis is, first of all, a label that can be useful as a shorthand allusion to the fact that certain psychological characteristics of people tend to be fairly well correlated with one another. For example, if one observes that a patient relies strongly on isolation of affect and reaction formation, then one is in a fairly good position to say that the patient probably relies also on undoing, and to consider as a first hypothesis that the patient's stepping on cracks on the sidewalk in order to avert injury to his children stems from an obsessive idea rather than a delusion.

We also believe that a variety of psychological characteristics can be assessed independently, that they cluster in a configuration specific to each person, and that treatment recommendations and expectations can be made on the basis of inferences drawn from this configuration. Also, we believe that a variety of psychotherapeutic interventions can be made available. These interventions can be changed as the person and his environment changes, from moment to moment and after long periods of time, for people have a repertoire of available and potential behaviors. However, the general configuration of them is quasi-stable. Stemming from all these beliefs is the objective of studying each person intensively and individually for the knowledge that can lead to correct anticipations of his behavior under specified conditions, and to interventions designed on one basis of these anticipations. This knowledge is what we mean by "diagnosis."

The emphasis in this description of our position, thus far, has been on self-conscious processes of induction and deduction, and we are well aware of the criticisms of clinical thinking, especially psycho-analytic thinking, as being mechanistic and unfeeling. But under-standing people systematically, in the ways we have described, does not preclude insight, discovery, warmth, or spontaneity. These are aspects of intuition and empathy which are themselves necessary for the diagnostic process. In actual practice, though elucidation of diag-nosis usually involves a number of steps and judgments, some people synthesize intuitive and systematic thinking with the speed of an "inexplicable" understanding. At certain critical points, when two in-ferences may be equally plausible and evidence for both can be ad-duced, one makes an intuitive decision, in which "feeling," literally and figuratively, plays a part.

SOME RESEARCH ISSUES AND PRACTICES

Stemming from our belief in intrapsychic processes we are inter-ested in the fate of single variables, the clustering or patterns of these variables, and the plausible explanatory interrelationships which make the changes comprehensible according to technical and theoreti-cal understanding. The vicissitudes of such changes are one way of studying the process of change. We are also interested in learning how patients change globally and whether such changes are for the better or worse, the outcome question. Many studies of outcome which cast their findings in terms of goodness or badness, improvement or wors-ening, do so with an implicit belief in an abstract, global concept of mental health, which we do not share as applied to measurement of individual change. What we anticipated we would find, and what we did find again and again in this study, is the need to judge change in each person with reference to himself and his starting point, and with reference to the treatment strategies and objectives derived from and based on the configuration of variables which make up his personal-ity. Our judgments of better or worse refer not to an *a priori* concep-tion of what better or worse should be in terms of how a person should behave or live, but to an assessment of his intrapsychic func-tioning and the objectives which he could, practically speaking, strive for. In this sense people are "closed systems," and there is no use making believe that all things are obtainable by all people, that all things valued by society or by parents or therapists are obtainable by all people, or indeed would be desirable or useful to all people if they were obtainable. For example, in the abstract one might think that an increase in IQ would be desirable. Yet there are people whose IQ is too high in the sense that they expend their energies and focus their attention too much on intellectual development to the neglect of other aspects of life. A result for the better, so far as they are concerned, is a lowered IQ. This would reflect a lessening of the need to struggle to perform at the very height of their abilities no matter what, a sample perhaps of a more relaxed and expanded approach to diverse life experiences. Conscious anxiety, by definition an unpleasant sensation, may seem like something whose diminution in the course of therapy would be desired. Yet, there are some people whose lives are marked by chaos and disaster brought on by their desperate attempts to ward off the experience of anxiety no matter what else the cost—addictive lives, for example. Such people, after successful treatment, may experience more conscious anxiety than they did before treatment, having become better able to tolerate such experiences and consequently less needful of the previous behaviors which brought them to treatment. Individual, internally consistent goals, then, provide the criteria for the outcome aspect of our work.

What use can be made of the outcome aspect? In principle, it would seem helpful to be able to decide how effective psychotherapy was in order to decide whether to use it or not. Implicit in such an expectation, however, are the erroneous assumptions that all psychotherapy is the same and that all people are the same. Any outcome statement which overlooks the falseness of such assumptions is self-deluding. Ideally, one would hope that outcome research would yield a series of conclusions as to what kind of people were helped or hindered by what kind of treatment relative to what kind of goals. The nontest researchers in the Project made statements of this kind. We, too, have made at least implicit predictions and confirmations of what kind of people with what kind of difficulties achieve what kinds of goals. But we were not in a position to know what kinds of treatment were actually prescribed or administered at the time of the writing of this report. Such a knowledge requires an intensive look at the therapists, those who supervised the treatment, if any, and what therapists actually did and felt with the particular patient. We could say, with respect to any one individual in this sample, what changed, and sometimes we could say why. But without knowing the independent variable—the therapy—we could hardly make generalizations for prescriptive use.

There are other reasons why it is not possible in the abstract, or with reference to large and varied populations of patients and psychotherapists, to know from this kind of study whether psychotherapy is good, bad, or indifferent. There was no control group; having the patient serve as his own control does not help answer the question of what would have happened had the patients gone untreated or treated in different ways. The sample is too small to be widely generalizable. Indeed, not all of the 42 Project patients were willing or able to be tested. Because of death, unwillingness to be tested, or precipitous termination of treatment, only 34 patients were tested at both initial and termination, only 28 were tested at both termination and follow-up, and only 26 at all three points. The sample was selected in a nonrandom manner as to degree and kind of disturbance and socio-economic and intellectual factors; it was heavily weighted with wealthy and intelligent people whose varied disturbances are at the extreme, or most serious end, of the range of people to whom long-term individual psychotherapy is ordinarily suggested. The mean IQ at initial of the 26 tested at all three points was 124. They were selected from the neurotic and characterological range of illnesses, specifically excluding overt psychotic reactions, mental deficiency, and organic brain syndromes. Finally, over two decades have elapsed since these treatments were begun, and much has been learned in that time (partly from the Project itself) to increase the effectiveness of selecting, prescribing, and treating patients in our setting.

If, then, one deprives one's self of the audience of readers who want to be told simply whether psychotherapy works or not, who remains in the audience? We believe our audience to be those workers who are interested in microscopic examinations of the process and patterns of change in psychoanalytic long-term individual treatment, in what variables are assessable by tests and useful in planning treatment, in the usefulness and place of the practice of testing in the enterprise of psychotherapy, and in the raising of hypotheses about change and the intrapersonal and social implications of such change. These questions, in our opinion, should be asked, and are answerable by this experimental design.

As with any research, our choices opened some doors and closed others. We recognize that truth can be best approached only by way of adherence to the canons of the scientific method. Ideally, then, variables should have been selected that could be operationally specified, and the reliability between the research testers and measures of the validity of the test instruments should have been numerically demonstrated. But achieving scientific respectability of this rigorous sort could have worked to the detriment of some of the questions in which we were interested. It is just this, the validity of our psychoanalytically derived concepts and clinical practices, that we wanted to test. To sacrifice these in favor of other concepts or instruments which would have had greater *a priori* reliability and validity would have been to forgo the research that we wanted to do in the first place. It would also have been in some ways a travesty of scientific method. After all, scientific method is developed to aid in answering meaningful questions that people are interested in, not to dictate the questions. The fact is that a great deal of scientific and humanitarian work is being accomplished with methods and concepts not yet clearly verifiable. To make believe this is not so by using concepts, instruments, and procedures which we choose not to use in day-to-day work would be to abdicate the scientific and social responsibility to examine what in fact is being done. Our hope is that through such an examination these clinical practices will become amenable to increasing degrees of scientific rigor. In summary, we tried to steer a course between two extremes. On the one hand, we wanted to avoid the uncritical clinical approach which can explain everything to the satisfaction of the clinician no matter how dissatisfied this may leave the logician or philosopher of science. We are well aware of the boom in popularity of psychiatry, and with it the temptations and pressures to solve, through providing service, pressing social and individual problems. We know, too, of the lack of time and inclination to think reflectively and scientifically about what one is doing when under such cultural and moral pressure to act. On the other hand, we wanted to avoid sacrificing, for method, the data we are interested in, namely the effects on people of psychotherapy, as it is actually practiced and understood, and as learned about through commonly used tools.

To exemplify these issues, let us examine the question of reliability. If one is working with rating scales or comparing scores, the assertion of a reliability coefficient is not too difficult to arrive at. In our work, however, reliability is not so straightforward a problem. The subtleness and complications of the inference process, especially when working with unclear concepts, can lead to spurious apparent agreement or disagreement. Agreement on such a variable as, for example, *ego strength* may simply mask a basic disagreement as to what each psychologist would predict under certain circumstances for a patient of particular ego strength. On the other hand, disagreement as to the prediction of what will happen in this patient's therapy should not be taken to indicate that there is no agreement on his ego strength. Reliability would have had to be arrived at through studies of each of the steps in the inference process, an enormous and complicated job. One kind of reliability study which could have been done would have been to have two psychologists do an assessment and prediction study on each of the patients and then compare them. This would, however, have more than doubled the work.

This may be a good time to mention the difficulty any part-time researcher must face in exploring a large complex problem with less than a full commitment of time and energy. The Project members were involved in treatment, diagnosis, and education at the same time we were doing the research. The conditions simply did not permit every potentially useful step to be taken. As a partial substitute for more conventional assertions of reliability, complete records of a psychologist's inferences from the tests and the chains of inferences from the raw data to his final predictions have been included in this report. In this way others can ascertain the degree to which they would make the same kinds of inferences and come to the same conclusions.

The two research testers who read the tests were trained together and worked together at the Menninger Foundation for many years. They can claim, informally, a high degree of general reliability, yet neither would claim perfect reliability for any particular clinical concept. Each has, and recognizes, various degrees of strength and weakness, blind spots and clear spots, and has developed commensurate corrections and exploitations so that the end results of their inference-making can be valid. Validity is a more important criterion for our kind of clinician than is reliability. We assumed this validity for test judgments through most of this study and then subjected it to tests of predictive success (see Chapter 8), which turned out to support this assumption. The accuracy of our predictions, and the effects of utilizing or ignoring these in the overall understanding and treatment of the patient, is, for the clinician, the ultimate sort of validity. For the researchers, it is at least an interim validity, which should encourage and aid future, and more formal, validity studies.

In writing these results we were faced at various junctures with recognizing some deficiencies in design and execution, sometimes those of the research testers or research psychologists, sometimes in the original formulation of the overall design of the Project. (It is always easier to do that through hindsight and when examining another's work than when doing one's own planning and executing over many years.) At these junctures the ideals of scientific conscience required major changes, a new substudy or a new collection or evaluation of the data. We did this sometimes but not always. The reason is simple; we did not have the time and manpower. The decision really was between throwing away the usefulness of what was there, imperfect or limited as it might be, or reporting it for the good it might do.

A good example of this problem came up when we were preparing the report on the patient variable, ego strength. It was clear that differing conceptions of the variable had been used by the research testers. We simply could not go through the original test protocols and rescore this variable according to a homogeneous definition. We did, however, in reporting the data, try to elucidate some of the different conceptions of ego strength in order to provide a rough measure of change in each of these and to try to formulate clinical thinking and research hypotheses. Overall, it seems that the strength of this concept and its referents with respect to the fate of patients was, for some purposes, sufficient to overcome the disagreements (see especially Chapter 8).

For all of its faults (and maybe this is one reason for them), this test study is unusual in several respects. To our knowledge it is the first systematic, clinically intensive study of pretherapy, posttherapy, and follow-up of therapy in which the therapy is of long duration, in which this or a comparable battery of tests was employed, and in which specific focus on the intrapsychic aspects of change in patients was made through the course of treatment.

PATIENT VARIABLES

Since we worked independent of other than test information, our study is of the patient variables, or at least those that can be learned about from the tests. The basic list of the Project patient variables (Luborsky & Sargent, 1956) includes some that are not applicable to investigation through psychological tests: "sex of the patient," "age of the patient," and such reality factors as "presence of neurotic life circumstances," "adequacy of finances to the treatment requirements," "questions about the payment of the fee," "attitudes of significant relatives," "physical health." Among the 22 variables which in principle lend themselves to psychological test analysis, there is considerable difference in how well they can be assessed by way of psychological tests. When nothing could be said about any one variable, the research testers noted this. Consequently, there are different Ns for each of the variables, and the differences usually shed light on the degree to which variables lent themselves to psychological analysis. In addition to the 22 basic variables, the research testers believed that they should analyze two other variables which, in their opinion, were relevant to a thorough assessment of the patient. These were *affect organization* and *thought organization,* and so the optimal number of variables assessed by the psychologists was 24. Some of these variables are taken directly from psychoanalytic theory, e.g., *sublimations,* while most of them are derived from clinical practice integrated with some theoretical ideas, e.g., *self-concept, anxiety tolerance, patterning of defenses.* The 24 psychological test variables are:

Anxiety	Anxiety tolerance
Symptoms	Insight
Somatization	Externalization
Depression	Ego strength
Conscious guilt	Intelligence
Unconscious guilt	Psychological-mindedness
Alloplasticity	Sublimation
Core neurotic conflicts	Honesty
Self-concept	Extent of desired change
Patterning of defenses	Secondary gain
Affect organization	Quality of interpersonal relations
Thought organization	Transference paradigms

Even a cursory reading of this list of variables reveals that, first of all, they are not the sort of discrete factors about which one can say it is or is not there; or, if there, how much of it numerically there is. Second, they are on the face of it unoperational, and can therefore be expected to include surplus meaning, and meanings which vary from person to person and according to methods of investigation. It is not even always possible to tell which is superordinate and which is subordinate to the other. For example, *anxiety tolerance* is obviously related to *ego strength,* but where one leaves off and the other begins, which is a cause or an effect of the other, is difficult to say.

Any participant, or observer, of a conversation between two clinicians will note how these variables, and other concepts, mean different things to different people at different times. This is due in part to there being several psychoanalytic theories as set forth by Freud in his long and consistently self-critical and developing intellectual life, and as set forth by his explicating and extending colleagues and professional descendants. It is further due to the diversity of formal and informal education and differing clinical practices of the students of these pioneers. Also, such differences arise from the variables being observed in different kinds of interpersonal interactions—interviews, tests, psychotherapy, psychoanalysis. In many instances the research testers have used concepts in a way that is quite different from those of the nontest clinicians and researchers. For example, the variable anxiety tolerance, as it was *a priori* defined in the Project's list of variables, was insufficient to cover the range of phenomena that should be implicated and was redefined by the research testers. In turn the analysis of the data done by the research psychologists raised further conceptual issues. In the course of assessing change in patient variables, we took the opportunity to note some of the unclarities, and at times to try to make the variables more operational. (An excellent example of how a concept can be derived and elucidated through the use of tests is provided by Siegal & Rosen, 1962).

SUMMARY OF GOALS

1. Clinical Findings. We attempted to learn by way of the tests alone of the changes in single intrapsychic variables and in patterns of intrapsychic variables.

2. Prediction. We attempted, on the basis of the tests alone, to learn how well we were able to predict eventualities of the psychotherapy. We wished to know whether the tests were more or less effective than the nontest predictions in general, and with respect to what kinds of questions in particular. Thus, we attempted to validate our conviction that psychological test findings can make a crucial difference in choosing those persons who will be most helped by treatment.

3. Clarification of Concepts. Through self-conscious attention to what was meant by various concepts, and to the test findings which give rise to them, we hoped to clarify some of the commonly used clinical concepts and language. A goal ancillary to this one is how to conceptualize variables so that they can be meaningfully understood by way of psychological tests, and to learn which variables lend themselves well and less well to analysis by way of tests.

4. Didactic. We wished to demonstrate how we work with tests, for educational purposes and as a means for the readers to assess reliability and validity informally. In a sense we did two major studies: the first, "patient-centered"—a study of change in psychotherapy *per se;* the second, "basic research"—testing of the tests, exploration of the inference process, and clarification of concepts.

CHAPTER 2

How the Tests Were Used

INTRODUCTION

The following case example is offered to acquaint the reader with how we use tests in general and how they were used in this research in particular. Starting with a brief presentation of the patient we follow with a clinical test report. This test report may be of special interest for purposes of comparison with the research forms also presented here, and with reference to the research use of clinical test reports (see Chapter 7). Notes made by the psychologist (Richard Siegal) while he was thinking about the case demonstrate how he drew his inferences from the tests. Such inferences were recorded on four cases of our research. Something like them occurs in the minds, at least, of all testers trained in the Rapaport-Schafer-Menninger Foundation tradition. This record of inferences and notes demonstrates "face" validity, and offers the reader an opportunity to estimate the reliability between himself and us. The test inference process is also included for its educational value to those who work differently but are interested in trying our way. Finally, we consider it good practice to keep explicit track of how predictions come about. Only if one preserves the route traveled is there a possibility to see later where and why one went wrong or was on the right track.

Although the main purpose in putting together this chapter was to demonstrate how the tests were used, as so often happens with clinicians, the intrinsic clinical issues demanded and got attention. This aspect of the chapter is summarized in a "Discussion and Conclusion" section at the end of this chapter. The reader may wish to turn to these issues and conclusions and read the data with them in mind.

Several issues become immediately apparent from these "notes." First, it is obvious that some kind of insightfulness or intuition plays a part in selecting, weighing, and stringing together one chain of inferences rather than others. Second, it becomes equally clear that clinical inference is not an arcane, simplistic form of art which essentially is unteachable. These notes do offer evidence that the polarization of clinical versus actuarial prediction is erroneous. All through these notes may be seen an implicit actuarial and normative basis for the choosing of one inference rather than another. It is also easily observable that the psychologist is versed in the theory and use of tests, in the psychoanalytic theory of personality, and in the theory of psychoanalytic psychotherapeutic technique, and that his knowledge guides his inferences and conclusions. Sophistication in each of these disciplines is necessary if the test data are to achieve utility for patient care—the chain breaks at its weakest link. Weak links in the form of deficient knowledge of one or another of these disciplines is, we believe, a major reason for the finding of "invalidity" and the current disillusionment with psychological tests. A major weak link, probably, is experiential knowledge of the situation to which tests ordinarily make predictions—to psychotherapy. As is well known, the validity of predictions is dependent upon knowledge of the situation to which predictions are made. Certainly, this is difficult for those psychologists who have not had considerable experience in practicing the range of psychotherapies to which they may be called upon to predict.

An anecdote may help to illustrate some of these issues: Dr. Roy Schafer, one of the originators of the tradition of testing we employ, had occasion to examine independently the test findings of two of our cases. He derived his concepts from the same test behaviors that we used, yet he labeled the patients nosologically different from the way we did. Nonetheless, his predictions about the treatment course and about psychotherapy were the same as ours. One moral to be considered from such an experience is the necessity to carry one's thinking about psychological tests beyond labeling and personality description to predictions and recommendations. This is, after all, the major purpose of the testing, though in many test reports it is not emphasized or spelled out. In addition, it may be that making predictions and recommendations explicit will help clarify the difficulties in terminology and understanding of the conceptual and linguistic links in the inferential chain. The problem of communicating test findings to people with diverse training and theoretical emphasis, especially in view of the increasingly different use of language and concepts, has enormous implications for clinical work. It is a plausible explanation for the differences which this research demonstrated between test finding and nontest findings, and presumably is a source of error in clinical work everywhere (S. Appelbaum, 1970b, 1972a).

Form C includes the formalized predictions made on the basis of the Initial examination by the same psychologist who wrote the "notes."

Following the record of inferences and Form C, done on the basis of the initial test, are the Form B studies done at termination of treatment and at the follow-up point two years after termination. All of these are written by the same psychologist who did the initial documents. Form Bs, written about both by the test and nontest part of the Project, provide the basic data from which the judgments and conclusions reported in this book are derived. These forms were filled out at initial, termination, and follow-up for each patient, except where noted. These research forms obstruct and codify data and inferences relative to each of the patient variables. The initial Form B is not included here since the notes of the inference process cover the same material, and it is retrospectively referred to in the termination Form B.

THE PATIENT

Introduction

The patient, in her early 20s, is married to an architect and they have a baby boy. She referred herself for treatment because of her constant losing battle against obesity and because of her guilt feelings at not always being able to satisfy her husband. She considers it symptomatic, also, that she provokes fights with her husband so that they might make up, which often leads to intercourse in which she has to get hurt physically in order to be sexually aroused. She grew up with both parents and a brother 7 years older than she. Her parents are still living. She graduated from college with a major in English. She married her husband shortly after graduation, became a mother shortly after that, and has not worked at any occupation other than that of housewife. Her medical history is essentially negative.

Psychological Test Report*

This patient is seen through the testing as a person who has never really given up her childish, infantile flouting of reality. She easily

---

* Written by Leonard Horwitz.

slips into a world of make-believe in which fairy-tale characters and science fiction events are given free reign in her fantasy life, often to the exclusion of reality considerations. Her thinking and reasoning are often quite arbitrary and egocentric. She permits herself a greater freedom of indulgence in fantasy than most adults are able to do. In most instances she is perfectly capable of perceiving the distinction between what is fantasy and what is reality, but this distinction is of no great importance to her. Similarly, her affective reactions tend to be rather labile and poorly controlled. Although she attempts to present herself as someone who can keep her emotions well in hand, she apparently is given to affective outbursts, panicky reactions, and possibly temper tantrums despite her attempts at control. She gives evidence of rather intense oral-aggressive drives which would be consistent with a considerable degree of demandingness and possessiveness. Also significant is the patient's tendency to flaunt rebellion in a somewhat immature way. She is intent on demonstrating her independence of mind and spirit and seems to direct most of her rebelliousness and hostility against mother surrogates.

In addition to this patient's characterological tendency to ignore reality, she manifests a moderate degree of loosening in her thought processes which is suggestive of an occasional breakthrough of autistic, paranoid thinking. This loosening is not apparent in well-structured situations but appears in the projective testing primarily under the pressure of intense aggressive drives. These unrealistic thoughts frequently consist of projections of her own enveloping oral-aggressive impulses or at times are based upon a gross denial of her fears of these projected impulses. The loosening of thought processes may also be seen in the breakthrough of material which is ordinarily repressed but which emerges in consciousness. To some extent her talk about "penis envy" is purely intellectualized and based upon psychoanalytic readings, but there is also evidence that such material is pushing past the patient's repressive barriers.

Despite signs of a distinct weakening of her hold upon reality, it is doubtful whether this patient actually experiences distortions in her thinking which reach psychotic proportions. The patient herself is aware of her tendency toward entertaining rather peculiar and paranoid thoughts, and to some extent she is disturbed by the presence of such ideation. There is also evidence of perverse sexual ideation which is undoubtedly upsetting to her. But one gets the impression that her ego is sufficiently resilient to place a definite curb upon the extent to which her autistic and deviant thinking will push her.

As suggested above, one indication of the pressure to which her defenses are subject at the present time is the patient's need to resort to rather gross and transparent denials. To some extent these denials are directed against phobic reactions that are seen quite prominently in the testing. There are indications in the testing of many fears of a hostile, predatory environment based primarily upon the projection of her own oral-aggressive impulses. Her fears often result in panic reactions, at which time she is likely to engage in certain counterphobic maneuvers.

The patient is a woman of very superior intelligence (Verbal IQ 121–122, Performance IQ 125–126, and Full-Scale IQ 125–127). She functions with relatively little impairment in well-structured intellectual tasks. She gives evidence of a great respect for intellectual achievement and shows some aspirations in the direction of intellectual activity. On the other hand, she is much too ambivalent about such interests and too poorly organized in her life goals to be able to accomplish much at this point in her intellectual pursuits.

There is considerable evidence of perverse sexual impulses based upon pregenital fixations. She is preoccupied with sexuality and appears to be quite disturbed by her perverse sexual fantasies. She apparently is unable to find adequate gratification in ordinary genital heterosexual activity and must resort either to fantasy or to behavioral outlets for her perverse impulses. To a large extent these impulses are exhibitionistic and voyeuristic. But, primarily, one can see a fusion of aggression and sexuality, e.g., the patient fears being aggressively assaulted during intercourse and counterphobically finds the prospect of being physically beaten by a man quite stimulating sexually.

Another major conflict is the patient's confusion with regard to her sexual identity. She unconsciously views the world largely as divided into two camps, the weak and the strong (dominating vs. subjugated, devouring vs. devoured, etc.). She is inclined to see the female role as one in which the woman inevitably becomes subjugated to the will of a more powerful male figure. She sees men as being the favored ones, preferred by their parents. Much of the hostility she experiences toward her mother and mother-figures is based upon the view that older women are prim and prudish people who erect barriers against a free expression of sexual impulses. She envies men, tends to compete with them, feels they are favored with superior intellectual endowment, but at times also depreciates them as being ineffectual and weak.

This woman with an acute sense of loneliness is chronically frustrated and suffers from a pervasive sense of deprivation. The patient's externalizations and denials permit her to ward off severe depressive feelings but it is likely that, if she were to give up these defenses in the course of treatment, she will begin to experience increasing depression. Also significant is an underlying sense of discouragement based upon her pervasive sense of oral deprivation about ever finding an adequate solution to her psychological difficulties.

Summary

Diagnostically, this patient is considered an infantile personality who characteristically resorts to ignoring reality in favor of childish and arbitrary fantasies. She also gives evidence of a considerable degree of fluidity in her thought processes such that paranoid thinking and disruptive unconscious material may appear. It is not felt, however, that these deviant thought processes ever reach psychotic proportions, although some of her deviant thoughts, particularly her perverse sexual fantasies, are probably disturbing to her. She engages in rather gross and transparent denials of her phobic reactions and one gets the impression of a tendency toward counterphobic maneuvers. There is evidence of a considerable fusion of sexuality and aggression which colors some of her perverse sexual fantasies.

Tests Administered: Wechsler-Bellevue, Rorschach, TAT, Word Association, BRL Sorting, Story Recall.

INITIAL TEST STUDY

Initial Notes and Inferences from the Test Battery*

I am relatively blind on this case. I know that she has been in psychoanalysis with Dr. X. I know she is obese and if I'm thinking of the same woman she hasn't gotten any less obese. I know she is terminating within the month. Her therapist is leaving during the summer so it leaves some question as to whether this termination represents completion of treatment. That is, both patient and analyst may be using this natural termination point as a way out of an awkward situation;

---

*These notes are pretty much as Dr. Siegal dictated them in keeping with our wish to preserve the making of clinical inferences as they happen. What they may occasionally lack in polish and elegance of language is made up for in verisimilitude.

Depending on the Research Psychologist's availability of time, analysis of the initial tests were done at various junctions between the actual beginning of treatment and after treatment was over. The research psychologist noted what, if any, extra test information he might have gotten inadvertently.

or it may be that the knowledge of his leaving has brought about a completion; or it may be that this represents an interruption with a tacit thought or the explicit thought that she will see how things go. In other words, I don't know anything about the circumstances of termination and that leaves the field wide open for predictions. Other than this I have only the face sheet data on the Wechsler which I will review in a moment. I also have the knowledge that the patient started treatment without tests and was tested shortly after by Dr. H. For all practical purposes testing coincides with the start of therapy. This may have some implications, however: If she started right off in analysis, then she had been in analysis some 2 or 3 weeks by the time testing started and this could have significant effects on the testing. Certainly by this time the testing would be incorporated into the treatment, so to speak. I don't know whether it was easy or not easy for her to begin free-associating, but clearly she must have implicitly or explicitly been facing the questions stimulated by the necessity to "uncover" one's self and the test may have been assimilated to this model. This would be less so had she started in psychotherapy. It occurs to me, however, that her analyst was doing controls and that therefore she would have started with psychoanalysis and not with psychotherapy. This also implies that she was seen as a fairly good analytic case and the fact that she started in analysis without tests would make it seem that she must have been seen as a classical hysteric or something of the sort. From one glance at her self-interpretation of the TAT, I saw that she mentioned snake phobias; I would gather that this places her in the hysterical category, probably as an anxiety hysteric. My immediate association to that is that if she is obese and an anxiety hysteric she may turn out to be a more difficult analytic case, with more infantile oral features than would have been anticipated.

Wechsler-Bellevue

Going now to the face sheet of the Wechsler, I find that she was 22 years old at the time of testing. . . . That's almost 5 years ago so her analysis is certainly of longish duration. She was not working at the time although she was married and had a 1-year-old boy. She had an older brother, her father was an industrialist, her husband was a student, and her religion was Catholic.

Are there any inferences going through the category Section H at this point? If she can afford analysis while her husband is a student and she is not working, either there is money in the family or she is getting a very reduced rate. Probably there is some money in the family and the implication would be that either her family or her husband's family remains in the picture of her life. It is possible that she could have come here by way of student health service in some manner, in which case it might be different, but if she did apply to the Menninger Foundation herself the probability is that her family is in her psychological life space as a live issue. So far I'm getting the idea from all these various things (and it may be wholly wrong) that she's phobic, that the oral-dependent childish infantile features must be strong. I put this together from her obesity, the fact that her parents may still be in her life, and so on and so forth. This may be a wild goose chase and it's certainly premature.

Let us now go to the Scatter of the Wechsler-Bellevue. First I note that her Verbal IQ is 121 to 122; Performance IQ 125 to 126; Total IQ is 125 to 127. The Performance IQ slightly above the Verbal IQ is consistent with the hysterical picture in which alloplastic motoric discharge elements may be expected to appear but probably will not be extremely prominent. If she is hysterical, with her high IQ, one would think of there being some ideational elements (as we know there are anyway from the phobia) and of repression being buried among supporting defenses including some ideational activity. Looking to the Scatter we see that the comprehension is 2 points above information and that digits are not lowered. This would make one think of the phobia as relatively effective in binding anxiety under ordinary circumstances. Next, however, the arithmetic is down to 10, a considerable drop. Is this concentration impairment on the one hand, which is a possibility, or is it avoidance on the other hand? What I have in mind is one could hypothesize that doing arithmetic for her is almost a phobic situation as it is for many people in that she reacts with anxiety, which brings about concentration impairment. On the other hand, one could hypothesize that she doesn't get herself into the situation but achieves the low score by avoiding the arithmetic. This will be, I should think, rather an important thing to determine as it may be some clue toward determining the extent to which she will allow herself to get involved in anxiety. In other words, something relevant to anxiety tolerance may have some bearing on analysis in this case.

I note that the similarities are then elevated to 15 and infer again the prominence of ideational activity. Picture arrangement is a little lower at 11. I would infer from this that she may be awkward in interpersonal relations, not sensing how she is doing or what others think of her. Suddenly I get the feeling that her name is very familiar to me, that it rings a bell as though I once heard something about her but I can't place it. She reminds me a bit of the patient I wrote up with Dr. L. Dr. L.'s patient was also married to a student, was herself a student, and her last name was similar to the name of this patient. Dr. L.'s patient was not Catholic herself but married this Catholic boy really out of rebellion. It was much connected with her sexual role difficulties. This is all incidental but I just wanted to report the vague feeling I have. To return to discussing the picture arrangement subtest, her lowered score may represent an obtuseness picking up cues of an interpersonal nature particularly regarding the way people see her. There may be something specifically sexual in this and I'm thinking of the fact that people often lose points because of their poor performance on the items which have some sexual content. This remains to be seen. There is nothing noteworthy in the rest of the Scatter except to note that the blocks and objects are both high, indicating perhaps some adaptive use of tension. Digit symbol is low but not excessively so. In general, the Scatter is perfectly consistent with an anxiety hysteric. I'm saying that because I know she has phobias.

Turning now to the information subtest, the patient starts right out declaring herself by saying, "I wish I could say Stevenson in answer to who's president of the United States."* So the patient is a liberal. She is also a person who either lets you know where she stands or most preferably she assumes that the tester agrees with her and really in a way she is trying to make an obvious community of interest with him. The wording of her answer to the thermometer question indicates a certain precision and is not consistent with a severe repressor. On the other hand, her answer to "pints" though correct indicates a naïveté and the use of repression. On the "airplane" item, she ends up with da Vinci. There is a touch of the obsessional about her. On the "Paris" item, the way she says "I'm wrong, I know" is characteristic of a self-deprecating person, although it's not intense. On the "heart" item, the way she mentions the lung is atypical. Usually people either describe the oxygenation mechanism for the blood in somewhat more detail, or else they just say it circulates the blood around the body. She is in the middle somehow. I don't know what this means. On the population item she is *way* off, and there is kind of a childish joke on the North Pole item where she says "the Eskimos." There are little inaccuracies here. For instance, it is childishly correct to believe that the Eskimos would have discovered the North Pole, but a more knowledgeable person knows that Eskimos live probably hundreds or perhaps even thousands of miles from the North Pole. There's a funny answer on the Samuel Clemens item where she says, "I like to show off occasionally when I know something," because she

---

*Test items are from the Wechsler-Bellevue, Form 1, still in use at the Menninger Foundation despite its having been largely replaced elsewhere by the WAIS.

had said Samuel Clemens instead of Mark Twain. This is probably illustrative of what I mean about not realizing the impression she may make on people. To spell it out in more detail, she feels as though knowing the pseudonym of Samuel Clemens is a big deal. It's as if answering "Samuel Clemens" will be taken as showing off. Her standards for self-judgment may be off the beam.

On the next item, the "Vatican," she again displays naïveté. She doesn't get too many of the rest of the items but her answer to the Faust item, "I cheated on that," is noteworthy.

I would say this girl's information is vague and shows the marks of some subtle, insidious kind of repression. She's intellectually ambitious but there are indications that she isn't aware of what she doesn't know even though sometimes she professes to feel inadequate. She probably looks less naïve than she is. A possible prediction which might have some application to psychotherapy is that this is the kind of girl who may use words in a way which makes you think she understands them and she really doesn't. The therapist might take for granted her understanding in a certain area when in reality she may have misunderstanding.

Comprehension. On the theater item she says, "It's been drilled into my head." This has the air of a superficially rebellious attitude toward the parents and their moral injunctions and training. She acts as though she rather resents this but introduces it so gratuitously that there must be some satisfaction in it. This is very tentative though. Her answer to the bad company item demonstrates her rebelliousness and the kind of egocentric hedonism. To the extent that this is genuine it would presuppose a kind of narcissism or perhaps self-indulgence. On the shoes item there is a little bit of egocentricity. She's rather sharp when she says it's a by-product of the slaughter of cattle and it would seem to me that this might show a somewhat practical turn of mind. She might be a good practical arranger or understander of everyday affairs. In the land item the phrase "that people think of as desirable" shows an ability to take distance and stand outside of ordinary social conforming behavior. This probably goes with rebelliousness. That is to say, she sees herself as an outsider and thus can look at social processes. It may indicate a readiness to view herself as an object, as it were, and to be able to pay attention to not only intrapsychic contents but intrapsychic processes. This is only kind of tentative, but confirming observations in the rest of the tests would have some bearing on psychological-mindedness. The forest item is noteworthy. First of all she goes on in a somewhat circumstantial ruminative way and ends up with a kind of denial of the anxiety. An implication would be that she can become circumstantial and mildly obsessional in an attempt to defend herself against the conscious experience of anxiety, and the other implication is that she is prone to intense panicky anxiety. Whether it is literally panicky or not I don't know, but she experiences anxiety as such. Her answer to the marriage item, "Man's not basically monogamous but women are," is a funny thing for her to say in this context. She acts as though she feels she is really an expert on human behavior and makes a lot of unwarranted generalizations. Really the same is true in the preceding item, the law item, where she sets forth her view of human nature without any qualifications. In a way she sounds much more positive than one usually does on this test. And of course her answer on the marriage item may have implications about her own sexual life or her view of her marriage and her feminine role, etc. At times, though, she is saying that man is an instinctual, impulsive sort of animal whereas woman is less free to give vent to impulses and is a much more dependent sort of creature. This would be a repressive hysterical and somewhat naïve view of human beings and of women. From the Comprehension, in general, the impression is confirmed that this is not an extremely naïve individual but one who is naïve in certain areas. She is not as sophisticated as she seems, or tries to seem. On the other hand she is rather intelligent, probably has a pretty practical turn of mind, is sometimes more certain about things than she ought to be, but sometimes naïve underneath her sophistication.

Nothing noteworthy on the "digits" except to note that she says twice, "It doesn't feel right" to her, and she expresses herself in terms of feelings—directly, straightforwardly, and economically. She is not an obsessional person.

Arithmetic. Originally I wanted to know whether this patient's lowest scored arithmethic was due to a concentration impairment or some kind of avoidance. Well, from looking over the performance it is pretty clear that it is not avoidance and that it is to some degree concentration impairment and lack of adequate background. She's quite erratic; she gets question number 9 quickly and easily, but she really messes up question number 10. I think what we have is not so much concentration impairment as it is impulsivity. She jumps to conclusions and doesn't wait to check herself. There is a trifle of concentration impairment though. If confirmed in other tests, impulsive action, without adequate forethought or afterthought, may be characteristic of her, particularly when anxiety is aroused. Clearly though, her performance is hysterical rather than infantile or narcissistic.

Similarities. She starts on this test anxiously and impulsively, again saying what comes to her mind; for example, she says she's thinking of an apple rather than the banana. This is akin to the arithmetic. She's pretty good, though, but kind of commonplace on the similarities. She's neither terribly concrete nor terribly abstract.

Picture Arrangement. She indicates a little bit of perceptual unclarity and irritability, as it were, on the "flirt" item where she sees the laundry as a hat, and then says she doesn't think its very funny. This disturbance occurs in a peripherally sexual item. Again we find disturbance on the taxi item, again a sexual item. This is something that she apparently can't joke about. She says as much when she says the first item is not funny and the second item is actually pathetic. One would feel that these are overdetermined responses. The only inference I would make is that she herself has a sexual disturbance of some sort—not necessarily disturbance in sexual functioning but certainly a disturbance in her feelings and thoughts about sexuality, if not disturbance in sexual functioning as well. I would put these together with the response to the marriage item and feel quite confident of this inference.

Picture Completion. On this test she achieves a perfect score and it's very apparent that she is extremely alert. Whether we should consider this hyperalertness or not remains to be seen; there is no indication that it is anything other than characterological. But she sure does note what's going on and what's missing and what's not missing.

Block Design. She seems pretty good on this test, but her behavior, on the sample items for example, would seem to indicate she takes great pains to deny the appearance of anxiety. Probably this goes with avoidance and denial in herself. She apparently does not like to seem anxious but much rather prefers to seem nonchalant and self-assured until she is forced by the experience of anxiety to do something about it. How alloplastically she responds is the question, but it is clear on the block design that she is responding adaptively and effectively.

Object Assembly. Her comment "dexterity is not one of my strong points" seems to indicate that she's ashamed to show any weakness to anybody. I make this inference because she simply fumbled slightly and feels called upon to comment on it. She probably takes anxiety and disturbance as signs of weakness or at least as things she doesn't want to show others.

Vocabulary. Her definition of "diamond" drew a comment from somebody on the test protocol in red pencil which says, "exhibitionistic and obsessive-like." Essentially I would agree with this. Certainly it demonstrates her proclivities for ideational activity. Her joke in response to "fur," although not tremendously funny, is nicely and succinctly put. There is an economy of speech or directness about her.

This same person displayed a very stubborn disposition in her definition of "donkey." On her response to "shilling" she mentions the car-
nival term *a shill.* Either she's been around or she reads a lot and
remembers, but the point is she is not naïve about crime and gam-
bling and so on. In the definition of "nail" she brings in the aggressive clawing aspects of nails. So far in this vocabulary test she is
showing off; she is being a wise guy and showing how much she
knows and how many different sets she can adopt. Implicit in all this
is not only the exhibitionism but the pretentiousness. Being "above it
all" is a defense against anxiety. This has implications, I should think,
of ideational activity used not so much to bind anxiety but rather
partly to bind it and partly to avoid it. This is ideational activity or a
kind of pseudointellectualizing in the service of avoidance. On "afflic-
tion" she betrays that she's been around "the helping professions."
Illness becomes "a problem with which a person has to cope." Probably then, with this ability to use the jargon, there would be some intellectualizing in treatment. She's exact, however, as witness her definition of pewter as an alloy.

The Wechsler-Bellevue in general, then, would suggest a neurotic
individual, a basically hysterical character structure, with hyperalertness, and the ability to use ideational activity in binding or avoiding
anxiety. She does not seem terribly anxious but there is enough anxiety to produce some mild intellectual impairment. She is a sharp hysteric rather than the naïve kind and one might expect, on the basis of
her showing off and "fooling around" in the vocabulary, that she
would be troublesome, perhaps bitchy at times, and so on. Despite
the air of sophistication and knowledge and sharpness there are some
things she is naïve about and things she's disturbed about including
sexual matters.

BRL Sorting Test

Part I*

1. She chooses the ball, makes a loose sorting, and says they are
all vegetable fibers. This response is a lulu and certainly unexpected,
too. The examiner has it scored as a syncretism, but it's not really a
syncretism in my mind. In a way it's the opposite. That is to say, it
goes with her sharpness and hyperalertness. It's more digging into
things, trying to get behind appearances to see what they are "really"

---

*The patient is asked to choose an object from a group, then to put it with things that go
  with it, and tell on what basis they go together.

made of. But it certainly enhances in my mind the probability of ideational symptomatology not of an ordinary phobic kind. Probably there
is some specially intense quality to her phobias and I wouldn't think
only of them being obsessive phobic manifestations. They may be
peculiar or something of this sort. In a way this reminds me of another
Project patient, Mrs. Y., whose early symptomatology I happened to
know. Mrs. Y.'s phobias occurred in an infantile context but the phobias of this patient don't seem to, and yet certain ideational aspects of
them are important. I would predict at this point that she has some
unusual ideation in the Rorschach, either Ms or special sorts of FMs or
maybe small movements of some kind.

2. She gives another overideational answer, "all oral."

3. She shows the kind of intellectualizing she does and it is clear
then that this is pseudopsychologizing.

4. On item number 4, I almost sigh with relief because here we're
back to what one would expect. These items are all found in a hard-
ware store and here we find a kind of a homey hysterical sort.

5. On item number 5 we return to a repetition of number 1.

6. On item number 6 there is a peculiar verbalization, "work
utensils." The idea is okay, but it's pretentious.

It seems to me on Part I that in addition to the capacity for ideational activity there is a good deal of pretentiousness going on. And it
strikes me that even her capacity for ideational activity is somewhat
puffed up or blown up, as if this is what she values or thinks we
value. It's a kind of intellectualizing in the loosest sense of the term. I
say that because it's not intellectualizing based on isolation. It doesn't
seem to me reaction formation. This is not integrated into the character structure, but is rather a more superficial sort of intellectualizing in
the service of avoidance and in the service of pretentiousness. It
strikes me that the exhibitionistic aspect of her impulse life may be
connected not only with obesity but with her use of words. Does she
sing or exhibit herself in some way through the use of words or
sounds or her mouth? I'm getting a little speculative here, but what I
want to say is that the ideational activity which occurs is not typical of
obsessive compulsive intellectualizing.

Part II*

She gives a perfect performance on Part II, arriving very quickly at
the conceptual definitions except, interestingly, for one choice. I forget

*The task is to tell why a group of objects go together.

at the moment if she has children, let me check the face sheet. Sure she's got a child, and it seems funny that a mother doesn't immediately recognize a pile of toys. Shall we list this as a potential problem and see what we happen to think of it throughout the rest of the test?

Story Recall*

The contrast between her hyperalertness in some of the tests and her minor inexactness in the story recall is striking. It seems to me that this shows the repressive aspects of personality structure. The BRL and Story Recall, in general, tend to support the inference of copious ideational activity in the service of avoidance and in the service of exhibiting herself and being pretentious which occurs in a basically hysterical setting. The symptomatology then, it seems to me, would have some unusual or unusually intense aspects perhaps involving both the ideational and the hyperalert aspects of her thought functioning. However, there is no thought disorder in the sense of losing touch with reality, and she is perfectly and very quickly capable of thinking in tune with conventional modes of thought. One thing that occurs to me is that since she has already started treatment and is taking these tests, the intellectualizing and psychologizing about oral gratification, etc., may well characterize the beginning stages of her treatment, particularly so since she is obese and this may well be her problem. It is interesting to wonder whether one can tell from the tests whether this is the problem she comes to treatment for.

Rorschach†

The first thing one notes in the Rorschach is the experience balance of 10 to 4½. Ten movements, all but one of them "plus," stacked up against 3 FCs and 3 CFs, and 2 of the FCs are minus, according to the way it is scored here. If all this scoring is correct and these are all full-fledged Ms, we certainly have a fantasy-ridden person here. We may have some type of hysteric whose repression has or is decompensating, allowing some sort of fantasies into consciousness. Probably this is an inaccurate inference. There are 15 to 17 Ws (about 25%) and there are 10 DRs of various kinds (about 15 to 16% DRs), the rest being Ds. The Ds would amount to a little over 50%. The DRs would

---

*After the examiner tells the patient a brief story, the patient is asked to repeat it from memory.

†The patient is shown "inkblots" and asked to tell what he sees. Scoring symbols denote various characteristics of the responses.

go along with all the other indications of ideational activity including the Fabs, the Fab combs, and the Confabs, etc. In the percentages we have over 50% animals and about 15% humans with 3 or 4 sex and anatomy responses. There is nothing else very striking in the content. What is surprising is the relative absence of the shading varieties. There are 2 (C) responses, 1 FC prime and FCh response. Anxiety binding might be quite successful in view of this. The F percent is 67 to 95, the 67 strikes me as low while the 95 clearly points to some sort of overcontrol. There are 4 FCs and 3 CFs, and even though this is overbalanced by the 10 movements it leaves a good deal of leeway for affective display. Surely this whole face sheet takes us into the category of what used to be described as mixed neurosis. The F+ percent 67 over 70 is rather low, but one doesn't know what to make of that yet. Certainly, however, control over affect seems to be the rule. There may be impulsive breakthroughs or something, but this face sheet would make me revise the suggestion made heretofore of anything in the direction of an alloplastic/impulse-ridden individual. There may be impulsive behavior but one would expect it to be sporadic and while she may be alloplastic it's certainly clear that she is also extremely autoplastic and that ideational activity is very important. Let us now turn to the protocol itself.

Card I. She starts off on an aggressive note. First there is the vampire bat, the oral aggressive response followed by her laugh, and then she puts her next question about turning the cards around in such a way that it is a challenge or a battle. She adds confabulation to the bat, saying that it's ominous, and this seems to be an overvalent kind of labile phobic sort of feeling creeping into fantasy. But the fact that she brings out that it is ominous and foreboding shows that she has the ability to verbalize and describe some of her inner experiences. Is this fearful or depressive or some combination of them?

The next sequence is interesting. First she gives a distorted kind of a man and goes to great pains to justify the distortions, particularly the distortions involving the nose, a phallic element, man need not have noses at all, and so on. She places this clearly in the realm of fantasy, however, which brings up very strongly the question of the sexual role or sexual identity conflict as a characterological or long-standing, much-thought-about concern of hers. This impression is reinforced by the next response, which is a female figure. She goes on to ruminate about whether this is a young curvaceous woman or whether it is a heavier woman. She makes it clear that this is self-referent by saying, "I'm rather figure-conscious." Of course I know she is heavy. Then she describes it as a heavier woman with a dress on. There is all kind of leeway for speculating about the kinds of fantasies she has here. It is almost as though she thinks of herself as a young curvaceous girl encased in a layer of ego-alien extraneous fat. What is clear is that there is a phallic sexual identity conflict aspect to her weight problem. What is also clear from the preceding responses is that her view of the penis and of men is not a wholly benign one, that she is envious and hostile and so on.

The female figure is followed by a childish, counterphobic, denied, grotesque Halloween mask. And then we return to another phallic theme, this time the theme of the phallic woman. Formally this is the first M, although the preceding figure of the woman I probably would have scored as an M or at least a tendency to an M. It's clear that what she's looking at is an M, the ladies are dancing. It's funny how this whole card ruminates around the question of whether women have or do not have penises and whether they are old and young. I'm looking back to see her age. She is 22, which is certainly young.

The first card of the Rorschach gives us a glimpse into her inner fantasy life as follows: She thinks about her weight a good deal and it clearly has connections with sexual identity conflict—some of them near consciousness but probably not conscious. The phallic conflict as to whether she does or does not have a penis, whether she is a man or a woman, ties in with this on a more conscious level. There is some denial, although of a characterological sort, and perhaps there are even some counteractive or counterphobic aspects to this. There is a lot of ideational activity, much of it of a diffuse phobic kind, that is, fantasies or ideas tinged with fear and disturbing affect. She is not scatterbrained but tends toward being relatively well organized. She probably is well-read, and she can talk about herself. She is not defensive in the sense that she is running away from looking at her problems.

Card II. She starts with two old gossips playing patty-cake. It is clear that she sees this very vividly and even adds vividness to it by the expression of "feverishly gossiping." Here is the theme that women are malicious and gossipy. She adds to it red shoes, a kind of integration of affect, quite different from one who might be inferred to isolate. She introduces affect into the next response, the crab, almost inappropriately, and goes on then to see more blood. The whole card is filled with rather heated affect, much of it quite well integrated in the sense that it accompanies her ideas and so on. When she gives the response to men it starts out that they might be dancing, then they might be fighting, that the red might be blood, and then they become cavemen with small heads. Clearly here is a projected hostility toward men reexperienced in the way of most likely denied fears. The last response, the space ship, she is ready to blame on the science fiction movie she saw, thus indicating her kind of externalization although this is not yet a prominent feature of the record. According to this card she is angry at both men and women. She sees women as gossipy, and she seems to have contempt for them. On the other hand, she seems to have a kind of grudging fear of men although probably she doesn't admit this. In her own responses she gives several "masculine" responses—the space ship being one, the pair of pliers being the other. Of course the pair of pliers itself is given to the area generally seen as penis, which she also sees as a hostile or potentially damaging tool. Of course one can speculate that the content of this response is of an oral-aggressive sort, but let's wait and see whether there is anything that comes up to confirm it.

This is along the same line as Card I, but is much more affect-laden. Even the two Ms on this card, which is unusual, do not serve to inhibit or even bind the expression of affect though they do control it to some extent. We would expect a lot of irritability and a fair amount of affect display of one kind or another, not all of it smooth or wholly appropriate.

Card III. On this card she starts out prosaically with two women washing, and gradually as she goes along the whole thing becomes more affect-laden and more phobic and more labile in its content. After the two women there comes an anatomy response, and I think this is misscored because I think it should be a ChF response. However, it is quite clear that the implications are anxiety. It comes suddenly and, although we must wait and see about other anatomy responses, it seems to justify an inference of some somatization in an attempt to bind anxiety which is not successful. And it would seem to me, and this is purely a guess, that this is not an ideational or somatic concern but rather somatic symptoms of some sort. Then comes an evil type of face with horns. Here the projected hostility is reexperienced in the form of phallic fear. Then a red butterfly, to birds falling to earth, to wounded ducks, and this also may have color in it, though she doesn't say so. Then, however, a real phobic response with lability emerges where she says, "Ooh, it's hideous." Here is a loss of distance, in a sense, although this still is to some extent under her control.

As time has gone on, both in this card and in the Rorschach, she has become more disturbed, more anxious, with more outright explanations of her fear, and the figures she sees have become more nightmarish and less intellectualized. But there is also a playful teasing quality about her. Not coyness but as though this is one side of her where she can give vent to these fears. There is another more well-organized, more mature, more "masculine" side, or a more "grown-up" side of her which is not so phobic. That's speculative, but if the speculation has any basis, one would expect alternations or vascillations in the maturity of the level at which she functions. One would expect there would be a great deal of anxiety and fear in therapy hours and then one would expect her to pull herself together and render meaningless those other strong affects. This would be one way, I guess, that she could defend herself against more regressed affects and, although it certainly has its adaptive aspects, it could be a problem in psychoanalysis.

Card IV. She starts out saying, "This looks something like a clown." My prediction here is that this is denial and minimization and that before this card is out she will either rename the same percepts with something more ominous, or someplace in the content of her card there will be a less sanguine, more fearful kind of reversal of this. This implies, on the one hand, that this kind of denial is a shifting one that has been called into play momentarily to help dissolve a sudden extra burst of anxiety or fear. On the other hand, it implies that the defense is not rigid or strong enough to keep the fear completely out of consciousness. Let's go ahead with the card and see what happens. The next statement is, "What suggests that to me is the big feet, oversized feet and big shoes." This implies that the denial here is directed against the idea that men have something big which is either important or has some emotional impact. It's as though she's saying, "Yes, he has a big appendage but it's in the context of him being a clown, a ridiculous human being." So this is partly a denial of fear, and partly a way of expressing her hostility. In the inquiry she says, "Standing in an awkward position with a small head running down the man." Here I consider that my prediction is confirmed because the fourth response is some sort of head like a prehistoric serpent, and in inquiry she says, "Probably thought so because I hate snakes." Let's backtrack a second. The first response was an M response and indicates, I think, that some of her ideational activity is fantasy in the service of attempting to bind or, more accurately, to minimize the impact of this. But after the first response there comes some controlled anxiety, the FCh in the dog response. Then she goes on to see a caricature of a camel's head, which certainly has oral implications of a seemingly diffuse, nonspecific nature. Oh, the dog's mouth is open too, let's not forget that. So there is a mounting of oral responses after this denial. It's almost as if there's a regression to a more infantile level and the content also talks about the prehistoric and then about two bird heads. The camel has its phallic aspect—the long, drooping nose. Anyway we're not going into anymore detail on that card. It seems pretty clear that Card IV represents an attempt to deny or minimize her phobia. To be more accurate, when she looks at the card and sees an obviously threatening phallic male figure of some kind, she immediately demeans it saying, "This is ridiculous," and "I'm not afraid of it." Here is denial and reversal. At the same time there is anger as she describes the man as ridiculous and later on as small-headed, or something of the sort. Incidentally this is by now a theme—small-headed men, dumb men—and it may signify that she feels she can outwit men. This is probably true. Her competition with men probably takes the form of intellectual competition. If she's not pretty enough to use feminine wiles to get men to do what she wants, I bet she outthinks them or outfoxes them in some way, or at least feels that she can do so. After this denial, minimization, and reversal occur, a little anxiety sneaks out indicating it's not wholly successful. It's crumbling as the card goes on. Then there is some attention to oral content indicating a retreat from the self-sufficient, competitive phallic level she has been functioning on to a more infantile, helpless, deprived level. Then here comes the phobia in full bloom again expressed not in terms of fear but in terms of hate. It is clear that her phobic ideas and her phobia of snakes contains anger which is not so well bound as it usually is. She doesn't even experience the phobia of wholly composed fear but says, "I hate snakes."

At this point I'm wondering what this means in an overall way. There is much about her that's very hysterical; there are some indications of oral-infantile features but the picture is, I would say, a neurotic one and not a character disorder, although certainly there are character problems. There is rather a lot of ideation for a hysteric, but I suppose this is not wholly inconsistent with an anxiety hysteric.

Card V. The start of this card demonstrates her familiarity with the Rorschach and her need to control it. This is her reaction to anxiety and although she sometimes does express it, her preference if possible is to get above it. She says it doesn't bother her, this is a familiar situation not an unfamiliar one, she can outwit and outthink men, etc. She likes to keep anxiety from consciousness until she can do so no longer, and so she gives the popular response. She gives the alligator head with the jaws half-open, then she elaborates on her need to deny the anxiety. This is not a terrifying bat at all but it looks like a poor, pathetic creature. This is what she does toward men. When she turns the card over and its character changes, the bat becomes not quite so terrifying, but the two swimmers looked like they were being "enveloped by the bat." On second thought she denies this. Then she gives a buzzard or an eagle, and finally she gives men's heads with exaggerated noses—stupid men to boot. In the inquiry it comes out that the percept is not a very intelligent person. Here we have the same sequence repeated again. She starts minimizing and denying any anxiety and reverts to an oral level of content reversing the roles. It is not she who is the poor, helpless, or dangerously oral aggressive creature, but rather the bat who is poor and pathetic just as she sometimes thinks of men. Then, however, the bat changes character and it is not a phallic sort of creature but an oral incorporative enveloping sort of a creature, and this is followed by another one, a buzzard or an earlier oral-aggressive fear of being devoured or bitten or incorporated. Oral-aggressive strivings within her would certainly be consistent with the picture of the fat woman and her obvious competitiveness and derogation of men. Maybe she feels men get more and she is deprived of what they have. I can't spell all this out explicitly in terms of the unconscious thoughts involved, but on this card there is more oral emphasis than on previous cards, and it is clear that this is connected in some way with the phallic conflicts she experiences. The impulse-defense sequence is interesting. She starts, as she did on Card IV, on a phallic level with the defenses of denial, reversal, and with ideational activity involved. Then some anxiety threatens to emerge, and there is a regression to an earlier psychosexual level. Her failure to control the anxiety is expressed in the form of phobias or phobic ideas. Her last response on the card, if I read it rightly, says it reminds her of an "old shrew" high school teacher, and here the hostility toward women comes out.

Card VI. She starts with Sylvester the cat and in the inquiry she comments, "I'll bet no one ever came up with that before." This is, I think, in line with a comment I made earlier on the Wechsler about her somehow overestimating her knowledge and creativity. This is another example of that. Then, what do you know, a couple of odd-looking men with Vandyke beards and long elephantlike noses. Here we have again the derogation and at the same time probably the envy of men. And another set of odd-looking pugnacious kings with phallic attributes. Then she goes on to give the uterus at the top, which is quite a poor response. Again we are involved in the sexual identity struggle. She starts out overevaluating herself. She thinks pretty well of herself while she's giving the Sylvester response. Then she gives a series of responses, each with phallic significance, ending with a very poor uterus. I can't quite understand the byplay between her and the examiner in the inquiry where she comments, "I know why I saw that," and in response to the examiner's question she says, "I'll tell it to my analyst; I like the idea of being helpless; I think a four-poster bed would be perfect; could be tied to." Perhaps I haven't read this correctly. First of all she's teasing in the sense of saying, "I can interpret this but I won't tell you; however, I will tell my analyst." And then there is quite an obvious reversal where she says I like the idea of being helpless. If there is anything she doesn't like, I think it's the idea of being helpless. This may be her initial reaction to starting analysis, that is, that she should be "feminine" and "helpless." Yet she really feels she can match wits with any man and beat him. In conclusion let me comment that she avoided the experience of anxiety fairly successfully, at least it doesn't show in shading or anything of this sort.

Card VII. She starts with two old ladies whom she mildly ridicules as being prim and proper pious old souls. Then, turning the card upside down, she sees showgirls doing the can-can, and she emphasizes their phallic attributes—the huge hats, long massive hair, and huge pompadours. The rest of the card doesn't seem terribly significant. In fantasy she masculinizes those women she identifies with. The mother is seen as prim and proper and slightly ridiculed. A younger woman is seen as more masculine. This corresponds in a way to what happened on Card I when she obsessed as to whether the figure she saw was young and slim or old and heavy. Young and slim is one unconscious fantasy she has of herself, and it is tied in with the phallic. Old and heavy refers to the part of herself identified with mother and experienced as somewhat ego alien. I have the feeling here that hostility toward mother lies close to the root of the character problem (but perhaps not the neurotic aspects of the illness) and that this is not yet fully represented in the tests. Now, either I'm wrong about this inference or there must be some special reason that it isn't represented in the tests. Perhaps it is and I haven't seen it. Let's wait and see what her comments are in regard to women on the TAT. Let me remark here also that ideation binds anxiety well.

Card VIII. She starts off with a corset which, in this case, must have some personal significance but it isn't clear what, if anything, it is. I've read through the rest of the card, and this is an extremely interesting one. She starts with a diffuse expression of affect: In a very pleasant way, she says, "a valley with a stream and wooded area." This certainly has "mother earth" connotations and seems to be a pleasant place, as does the affect she conveys in the response. Then it changes. She comments, "actually more of a steep canyon in places." The change in the content continues as she gives a very oral-aggressive response as if to say that the thought of pleasant, oral-passive, motherly gratification arouses in her feelings of deprivation and anger and the feeling she has to fight. And then we have a response obviously referring to one level of her self-concept where she talks about "an odd-looking thing like a bloater found in the deep sea." This is followed by a death mask. Boy, I'd like to hear her free-associate about this series of responses! They're all of fairly poor quality perceptually, all toward the "primary process end of the continuum." And I would think that more than any other responses up to now they indicate the deep-seated orality which must be a part of her obesity problem and a part of her character structure. She tries to hold herself in at the beginning of the card, then to give a pleasant picture of oral gratification, then to reveal that she doesn't get enough and blows herself up (as does a bloater) and views herself as a primitive greedy creature, and then the thought of death as punishment probably comes into it. It would seem to me that unconscious hostility and unconscious guilt also are strong. Let's look further in the tests now for signs of unconscious guilt. Confronted with stimuli which elicit affects of oral yearning, she becomes greedy and angry and then guilty. This is a possible pattern that's suggested by this card but we need confirmation for it.

Card IX. She starts with sea horses which then become little Peter Pan sex figures who are "devilish." Then we get the lobster, an oral-aggressive percept, which is rendered ineffectual or castrated; then a man with a walrus mustache, apparently a superego figure, stern and disapproving. Does this relate to unconscious guilt? Then we get something feminine, a dress; and again castration where we get the faces of elephants with chopped-off trunks; then anger; then a response of eyes "glaring vacantly" which stimulates phobic ideas in her and the ideas of death. This almost seems to have a special overdetermined, traumatic meaning. Is her father dead? Apparently from the face sheet the father isn't dead, and I don't know what it does refer to. Perhaps it doesn't have any special meaning or perhaps it is the return of repression from some childhood experience. Then, after this, there is a boxer with a many-times-broken nose. If we take the feelings expressed in sequence, we first have the asexual figure expressing devilishness; then we have oral aggression responded to by the patient with the castration fantasies; then we have a disapproving man responded to by being "feminine"; then more castration; then phobia, anxiety, and the idea of death; then the idea of the boxer, a phallic male, to which she responds by saying, " a pathetic little old guy."

What does she say in this card? Looked at formally, there isn't much affect discharge in terms of color, but there is a lot of ideation and fantasy going on. It would appear that most of her internal struggles take place in fantasy. I think she thinks of herself, bearing on self-concept, as an in-between sex sort of person; and that she experiences greedy feelings, oral-aggressive strivings and guilt over these. She's certainly angry at men, tends to belittle and to castrate them, to devalue them, and in every way to run them down as if saying she's not afraid of them or of her hostile impulses toward them. This is all reversal, combined with penis envy. What is her attitude toward being feminine, toward being a woman? It isn't wholly clear; that is, it is very clear that she feels she can outwit men, that she looks down on some kinds of women, the ordinary women at any rate, but it isn't clear how she considers herself as a woman. Let's drop this now and maybe at some later point there'll be a way to synthesize it a little bit more.

Card X. She starts with a bunch of flowers and immediately changes to evil insects, introducing the phobic elements when she says, "I hate bugs." Then there are a couple of bugs eating the stem of a plant, the oral-aggressive theme; then there is a phallic insect, an insect with many appendages doing a weird dance. This is fascinating because then she goes on to show a rabbit with long hair, and after that a female figure enclosed in plaster. The first response is a labile one thinking of a bunch of flowers, and she reveals this when she says it's a bouquet, which has an implicit oral meaning. But then she spoils it with the phobic aspects and the oral-aggressive content. This is again like on Card VIII, where anything stimulates oral yearnings and the idea that perhaps she would be satisfied by bringing in the oral-aggressive components. Is this related to guilt? Is her oral aggressivity stimulated by unconscious guilt in some way? This is very unclear. She then goes on to talk about the evil-looking eyes and the ballet which is graceful but frightening. Then she starts to mull over in fantasy the nature of femininity and of women. The timid rabbit with the long hair certainly is a feminine figure but is bizarre in a way. Then there is the female figure enclosed in plaster, again leading to the idea that the envelope of flesh with which she surrounds herself is in a way ego alien or the object of some fantasies, and although it may serve a protecting purpose, it also serves a constricting purpose. She gives this response on a higher level, talking about the brassiere; and then she goes to the ovaries, Fallopian tubes, the vagina, and the uterus, and so on. At this point she begins competing with the examiner and trying to one-up him by interpreting before he can, demonstrating some intellectualized insight and probably some real psychological-mindedness, defending herself against anyone else's comments. Her hostility toward women comes out in the discussion of the old maid, who becomes a bald, ineffectual old man. Her fantasy gets arbitrary through here, and the power of her ideas becomes apparent. That is, it becomes apparent that she isn't going to be immediately convinced by any interpretations that any little old man offers her. She's stubborn and arbitrary in her ideas, and is going to be tough to change from that point of view. Her statement about the figures in the plaster cast is that "the outside is a rough approximation of a woman but the inside is shaped." Apparently then, the flesh with which she surrounds herself keeps her from being a woman, keeps men away from her, but inside there is a little girl or a woman. It is very clear that this symptom is intimately connected with her envy of men, which is conscious in an intellectualized way. This is a very overdetermined symptom, one with strong oral roots which are more difficult to spell out and therefore one which may well be quite recalcitrant to analysis. One knows this from the nature of the symptom, and empirically on the basis of clinical experience, but here is the rationale for it. The conflict apparently is a simple one of being a woman or not being a woman, with strong oral roots. The oral roots are more obscure because they are more unconscious and more archaic, but they are strong.

Let's say a few words about organization of thinking and affect. Ideation is extensive in the form of phobias, in the form of fantasies, the form of ruminations and intellectualizing, and there is a particularly stubborn quality to them. She isn't going to give them up very easily, that is her idea. One would expect occasional labile affect, quickly cut off as it were by ideation, and yet she is not at all a cold or isolating kind of person. There must be some alloplasticity—I'm thinking of the orality; obviously she must do a lot of eating. Did she have children yet at this point? Let me check and see. Yes, she had a child. I don't know why that occurred to me or why I asked that. There is more anxiety than would appear from the face sheet, yet she is not overwhelmed with anxiety but tends to defend herself against it. She reminds me a little bit of Mrs. B. because, although her anxiety tolerance isn't low as it is with a character disorder, she doesn't like to experience anxiety. She turns a great deal of it into ideational anxiety, both phobia and fantasy. This makes it less accessible. She has a lot of defensive resources—denial, reversal, ideational activity, and so on—which keep anxiety from consciousness quite well. There is much more that could be said from this Rorschach if I had a chance to discuss it with somebody to clarify it. Here's where working two to a team is helpful in the study. In any case, let's move on to the Word Association Test.

Word Association*

The first noteworthy comment is number 3, *love-*"make" in half a second. Afterwards she laughs and says, "wow." Upon inquiry she doesn't say anything revealing. Somebody has written in red pencil on this, PC, which I suppose means phrase completion, but I don't think this is adequate to account for the response, *love-*"make." Certainly, there is a readiness to sexual associations and a kind of counterphobic or counteractive, even exhibitionistic, aspect. Maybe this comes closest to it: It's an exhibitionistic response which would suggest along with behaviors on the phallic level and ideas about it that there may be some exhibitionistic component.

Book-"cover" is the second noteworthy response. I would take this as a phrase completion. The next noteworthy one is number 8, *curtains-*"draw." On inquiry she says she doesn't know why she said this but associates "privacy, hiding I guess." Again this is related to the exhibitionistic component, and would strengthen the inference that there is exhibitionistic, voyeuristic conflict in this case. *Trunk-*"lid" is somewhat unusual, and she said she had an image of a toy trunk. *Drink-*"smoke" is another unusual response and for a woman I would risk the hypothesis that she is thinking of both of these as socially disapproved activities.

The next word is *party* and she responds "nothing . . . my first one was blocked, after that I think of fun but not the right one." This is a real block. I don't know if she gave it in 1.5 seconds or in 15 seconds, I guess it must be 1.5 though. And in her comments she reveals that she experiences social anxiety. She reveals she tries to take a detached attitude toward it, but feels she has changed. Her response reveals avoidance. This is one aspect that hasn't been commented on. She simply avoids answering this question. This reinforces the notion that she doesn't like to experience anxiety and, although her capacity to experience anxiety is high, there is a conscious, deliberate quality of avoiding anxiety. Here is an interesting distinction. She has the defenses and the capacity to sustain the anxiety, but in a way (and this goes with self-indulgence) she doesn't want to put up with it.

Number 18, *penis,* takes 10 seconds. She blocks and gives "urinate." Her discussion reveals that the word *eat* occurred to her. She goes on to say she is a compulsive eater, and possibly she wants to grow a

---

*A list of words is read with the instructions to give to each word the first word that comes to mind, and to give it quickly. The examiner asks on selected responses about what thoughts or images went through the patient's mind after hearing the examiner's word, and before the patient gives his response word.

penis of her own, and this kind of intellectualizing. What comes to mind is that it is much easier for her to face this intellectualized aspect than it is for her to face the hostility inherent in her symptoms. But she seems to clearly recognize, even though it's in an intellectualized way, that her eating has some relationship to sexual difficulty. The intellectualizing itself is avoidance, and I would say would be a problem in psychoanalysis. Here, then, is a chance to speculate: Should the analyst prohibit this kind of professional reading or not? If he does, will she stick with the prohibition? She is a very stubborn, rebellious person. If he doesn't, the intellectualizing will of course continue, as it will in any case. Anyway, the point is that intellectualizing or psychologizing of this kind is likely to be used as a resistance. What does it mean that eat occurs to her in response to penis? Fellatio fantasies is the first thought one has, but she jumps from this level to the much less embarrassing, much more intellectualized level of Freud's theories. Fellatio fantasies probably for her have the dual meaning of castrating the man in an oral-aggressive way, and on the deeper level must have the unconscious meaning that penis equals breast. Here is the link between the oral-aggressive and the penis-envy phallic aspects of her neurosis and character structure displayed in the Rorschach. Via fellatio she both castrates the man and sucks his strength away while she is gratifying herself. Here, too, is the meaning of her outwitting or outtalking the man. She feels that she can con men into doing things, and this too, I think, must have some oral components in it. Talking people into things, fooling them by means of the way one talks, etc., has a hostile, castrating flavor. Let's leave this response now and go on to *suicide*, that is number 21, where she responds with "homicide." This response is given quickly and is not inquired into so it's difficult to make too much out of it. But "homicide" is an unusual response to suicide, and makes one prick up his ears. Let's keep this in mind on the TAT. On *snake*, she gives the safe completion, "snake in the grass," and again this isn't inquired into, but we know that she's phobic and this is the avoidance of it. Her next response, number 24, *house*-"window," has voyeuristic implications but again is not inquired into. Number 25, *vagina*-"urethra," is inquired into and there is a delay on this of 5 seconds. In response to this she intellectualizes a bit and says that in childhood she's aware that the area "of excitation is around the urethra rather than the vagina." Is she revealing here some of the nature of her fantasy about intercourse or about her vagina? She makes it into a phallic thing, in a sense, by concentrating on one of the most phallic aspects of it, the ability to urinate and project out from the body some bodily product. This also could have some hostile implications. The point is that childish unconscious ideas about the nature of sexuality, sexual parts, and sexual functioning still seem to be alive and influential in her in the form of fantasies, and these fantasies are not altogether unconscious. Some of them come into consciousness but in intellectualized forms. Certainly the generic inference from this and from penis is that sexual behavior is markedly disturbed.

On *tobacco* she says "smoke." I don't know why the examiner inquired, but it comes out that this is a phrase completion. She goes on to say that on *house-*"window" she might have had the feeling of being watched, "the need to hide." This again points up the exhibitionistic/voyeuristic aspects of the conflict. Encasing herself as she does in the "plaster cast" of flesh is her way of also hiding and in a sense may have the further meaning of being a reaction formation against, or compromise formation is more accurate, between exhibiting herself and hiding herself. She makes herself very conspicuous but in an unattractive way which she thinks of as hiding her essential femininity. On *masturbation* she blocks and says she eventually thought of "baby." She owns up to guilt about it afterwards but also comments she thinks her baby does it. Her baby is very young and this would indicate, it seems to me, an overconcern or overinterest in her baby's "sexual" life. Not that children of that age don't masturbate, of course, but mothers aren't usually concerned about it at such an early age. What's striking is that after this no more inquiry was conducted by the examiner. I don't know whether this means that there were no more funny answers or what, but we'll see. The next really noteworthy answer is to number 43, *cockroach*, where she gives a phobic response. The rest of the responses are phrase completions or very close associations which in a way are avoidance. It's as if she revealed so much about herself on the first page that she just didn't feel like saying much about herself after that.

Her response to number 54, *money-*"no," is not inquired into but is an immediate response to a usually not so affect-laden word. She reveals that she "cheated on *mother*," and the first word she thought of but didn't say was "fear." She actually said father. *Mother-*"fear" is a very unusual sort of response, and makes one think of guilt in relation to her mother, as if she fears mother because of the hostile attitudes she has toward mother. On the Rorschach I commented that one would feel that hostility toward mother must be at the root of the oral struggle or the oral conflict but that there wasn't much evidence of it. Here is roundabout evidence of it which is so unusual that I would say it should carry some weight. It certainly demonstrates a great deal of disturbance in her relationship to her mother. The word association *mother*-"fear" (even though this isn't the one she gave, but the idea did occur to her) is most unusual in my experience. The way she "turned herself off" so that she didn't reveal very much on many of the words on the second page is also a little unusual. I think this would go along with the inference made about anxiety tolerance, that she has a good deal of conscious control over what she wants and doesn't want to reveal.

I guess from the nature of the symptom, the outspokenness of her psychopathology, the degree that she reveals herself, and so on, we'd have to think of this as certainly an atypical kind of neurosis. There is repression involved here although there are many other defenses which support and back it up and come along with it. The amount that is actually repressed must be relatively small. But this isn't the usual kind of character disorder, that is, I don't see her as narcissistic or so extremely infantile. It's true that orality is very important and in a certain narrow sense one might diagnose her as having very strong infantile components. Self-indulgence is a part of this, but the self-indulgence seems to be the product of various ego maneuvers having to do with reversal and corrupting the superego rather than with being childish with a nonexistent superego. It does seem to be unconscious guilt, which she overcomes by bribing the superego, rather than the self-indulgence simply being a kind of development which allows her to gratify impulses and prevents her from delaying discharge. Sexual disturbance is severe and maybe she is defending herself against real conscious homosexual impulses. I don't know, that's just a guess and I wouldn't stick by it.

Thematic Apperception Test (TAT)*

Let's turn to the TAT now. The first story is not the most usual theme to this card and has a mild depressed or blue quality about it. The patient leaves the story with the boy being upset. It also has, which comes out on inquiry, a lot of fantasy of violence in it. In this respect it is in line with the various themes in the Rorschach. Here is a boy whose phallic appendage is broken and the boy is deprived. What it really conveys is an overall story with themes of deprivation, mild depression, and dependence, since the boy ends up depending on his

---

*The patient is shown cards on which there are pictures with varying degrees of ambiguity, and is asked to make up a story about each one, telling what's happening, what led up to it, what the characters are thinking and feeling, and finally how it will turn out.

teacher for the violin. But it also conveys that you can't depend on others because you don't get as well fed or taken care of as you want. The boy feels "forelorn" because the violin is damaged. There is also guilt involved here since the boy sows the seeds of his own destruction, so to speak, by leaving the violin carelessly around. What's the *non sequitur* mean where she says, "After many long hours of practice he finds he can afford no new violin"? Certainly it conveys disappointment. Perhaps that's the best overall word to capture the flavor of this story—conveying disappointment.

Story II. Story II conveys her anger and disdain for mothers. They spy on you, they gossip, etc. In this respect she reminds me of a case we wrote up in a natural history of an outcome prediction. The patient conveys, first of all, that she is above responding to this kind of treatment and, secondly, she "understands" the other person and therefore doesn't have to take it personally. This is not a mature statement but it is a way of defending herself against either the anger or the hurt. The mother figure is shocked at sloppiness or messiness. This could conceivably be related to the sloppiness or messiness of her body and her eating habits and could have to do with the idea of shocking someone as one of the meanings in her compulsive eating. This is somewhat strained, however, and we don't need this inference. There is a loss of distance here or an ego simplicity in that she takes the story immediately from her own personal experience. She may be right that this former housemother snooped on her, and yet there is a great readiness to see people as snooping on her and I think this quite probably represents potential for projective thinking.

Story IV. Here is a depressed young man longing for love, and for someone to take care of him, but who ridicules himself. More accurately the patient ridicules him by saying he is so ineffectual that he can't even commit suicide because his room is on the first floor. This is a rational intellectualized solution, which is probably related to one she has tried, that is, becoming an intellectual or seeking knowledge is something she thinks of herself as doing although she really doesn't. She does, however, put great stock in her intellect and feels that she is smart and can outwit people. There is a denial of depression or a minimizing of depression here, and the attempt is to make it appear that she's in control of the situation, of her own feelings. She even does this in her comment on the Rorschach about liking to be helpless. One of the aspects in the conflict must be fear of loss of control.

Story V. Here is an idyllic story, a wishful thought which goes so far to deny loneliness as having both die. There is certainly an arbitrary quality about this; that is, she goes to great lengths to deny even the possibility of loneliness and the possibility of one or the other character having to have the mature strength to go on alone. It's almost like she can't bear any kind of loneliness or frustration, and this too may be related to her eating. This is not a romanticized wish-fulfillment fantasy, but is rather a high-level avoidance. It is a constructed, not spontaneous sort of story, it seems to me. So far in the TAT the quality of avoidance (or maybe that isn't the proper word) strikes me. She seems not to want to say very much about herself in these stories, and so she complies with the instructions, although not in a rebellious or hostile way.

Story VI. Story VI is an unusual story which expresses both the oral and the phallic conflict. She starts out with a story of violence, of deprivation, a story "on the desert," the people passively waiting to be rescued on a lonely road. They cannot survive by themselves, and perish because of their own helplessness and infantile passivity. The other story given as an alternate is a story of phallic attack. Some dreaded monster rises from the past and attacks them. There has been a perceptual distortion here, as the notes reveal. That is, what she saw first as a bridge, she later sees as a serpent and then goes on to alter the story. It almost sounds like a paradigm of her expectations of psychoanalysis: that a landslide will come along, disturb the mountain, and open up a way for the prehistoric monster to come out and kill people. Here she is afraid of herself as a phallic hostile person and I think this is the confirmation I was looking for about the unconscious guilt. That is to say, this has no direct bearing on guilt but she perceives herself unconsciously as dangerous and extremely angry and wishes that she had a penis. So she sees herself as the avenging masculine phallic beast and is afraid that if she lets herself go or something disturbs her enough, this may come out. Here is fear of loss of control and here is a motive for burying herself, as it were, and not letting herself express this aspect of herself. Now it would seem to me that the oral yearnings, the helplessness, the passivity, and all of that regressive business is in response to this percept of herself. She regresses in response to what she senses as dangerous wishes in herself, dangerous because they will involve harming others, perhaps mother. So she identifies with mother in a hostile way and in a rebellious way; at the same time she causes herself to become fat and womanly and unwomanly. It would be interesting to look in the Rorschach at this point to see where oral-aggressive feelings follow the oral yearnings. Is this to be conceived of as a defense against staying with the oral yearnings or a breakdown of this defense? It's a breakdown of the defense, it seems to me, since one doesn't defend against something that's already been expressed. It's easier for her to express the diffuse oral yearnings and the helplessness, as she does in Card VIII with the percept of the beautiful landscape, but she can't stick with this. It doesn't bind the impulses which then break through. The ones that break through are the oral-aggressive ones. The way impulses break through is interesting. "Break through" is not the right expression; she is not shattered by these impulses and they seem to be chronically present in consciousness. It's as though, as she developed mentally, an incomplete resolution of the oedipal situation occurred and the identification with mother is not only a hostile one but also a partial or incomplete one. Either that or perhaps mother was a harsh "masculine" person, and the patient identifies with this aspect of her.

Story VIII. In this story there is something strange about the reason she gives for the man's choice. He stays with the wife and child "because he cannot stand the idea of his son being raised without a father." It is almost as though she is thinking about herself and reversing what she may have felt to be a rejection. That is, here the father loved his son so much that he forgoes all of his sexual pleasure for the son's sake. This is what people do, she is saying, for boys. If I had been a boy, perhaps my father would have done that for me. Here is a clue to the nature of her oedipal situation. She is disappointed she is not a boy because she feels if she had been a boy she could have competed with her mother and attracted her father. This is pretty speculative, but I have a strong feeling about there being something implicit in this story even though the story itself is not terribly different from the usual one. In the story the identification figure for this patient is clearly the man. The older woman is seen as hateful and jealous and completely ununderstanding while the young woman is seen as "lovely" but passive and helpless and deprived. If you're a young woman and beautiful, the patient says, you must be passive and then you don't get what you want. If you are an old woman, a mother, you are wily, quite undesirable, and hateful. Only if you are a man do you get what you really want.

Story X. Here men are expressing themselves in murderous violence only for honor. There is no instance in the tests up to now of women expressing anger in overt straightforward violence, but there is a great deal of evidence of women being angry and castrating in oral-aggressive, biting ways. I can't make anything more of this story at the moment.

Test 19. This is really an unusual fantasy which clearly reveals that the patient has perverse ideas although it doesn't necessarily reveal their nature. The sadomasochistic elements are here brought into prominence really for the first time, as there is a clear intermingling of rapture with death. A couple of other times, in the Rorschach particularly, she has mentioned death. First of all, this is what men are likely to do to innocent young girls. Secondly, this is what men get away with. Thirdly, "if I were a man," this is the kind of sexual pleasure, unusual and violent, that I could permit myself. Any fear or anxiety in this story is hidden. But, she offers the story exhibitionistically in a sense. I mean anyone who gives such a story is in a way showing off, and this is her active way of avoiding the threat of passively experiencing fear. It's counterphobic in a way. Certainly this indicates unusual sadomasochistic sexual fantasies, which must come out in the analysis. Of course this contains the element of hostility toward women.

M 13. Here is the greedy, oral-aggressive woman; here is the phallic woman; here is the sadomasochistic relationship in which the woman has the upper hand. This patient sees herself as being possessive and as smothering love "by demanding too much." She must be quite a handful, this dame. One quality about her that this points up is that she thinks she understands a great deal about herself, and in truth she does. But obviously it doesn't mean a hell of a lot to her. She's not going to be surprised by anything. She's not going to let any man get the upper hand by surprising her. This is one form her resistance will take, that she will know "in advance" the things that her analyst interprets to her. One of the technical problems is going to have to be to point this out and analyze this character trait before any content analysis, so to speak, can be done. This is not only to say that you must analyze resistance before content, but all her analyst's statements say—if he is a man and I know he is and a little one at that—if anything is to have any effect, this problem has to be worked through first, her competitiveness with men.

M 14. I think in a way here she shows an understanding of some resistance. That is, she advances the idea of hypnosis as short-circuiting the problem of resistance. But she sees that you can't get around it in that it is a "long tedious process." Is this the result of psychiatric evaluation? Or the beginning of treatment? Or what? But in any case she tries to scale down her expectations in a way which suggests that really underneath she expects to be "a new man" and that it won't take very long. She is rationalizing that "she knows" it will take a long time, and that "he won't be a completely new man" but will be more able to cope with life. The problem she chooses, "paranoia," is that people are against him, that he feels he is alone in the world and he has no friends. I suppose one thing that she feels is that nobody gives her enough although there are no strong indications of paranoia in our sense of the word. When she says *paranoia* she means she feels like she doesn't get enough. She's pretty sophisticated about the process of psychoanalysis, about herself, and about human behavior. She doesn't give any indication that she's especially sensitive or intuitive, but she certainly has thought quite a bit about herself in an intellectualized way, and yet she is not terribly much of an intellectualizer.

Let's look now at the self-interpretation of the TAT.* She talks apparently quite freely about herself, and starts to say that this story has revealed quite a bit about herself. She said she consciously fears being left alone and doesn't believe in shortcuts. Surprisingly, instead of intellectualizing and overinterpreting the story about the sex pervert, she says that the ending is realistic because sex perverts usually escape and kill again. Then, very naïvely, she talks about the woman being picked up and she says, "That excludes me because I'm a married woman." But she goes on to say, denying this very thought, that she likes the feeling of "helplessness" and the wish to be forceably taken by a man. This is one way of saying that she wishes she could be raped. Or it may be a way of saying that she can't be satisfied sexually except in a situation of violence, probably because of her angry fantasies and maybe because of her guilt about it. There is something very exhibitionistic, however, in talking like this. It couldn't mean a lot to her if she talks that freely about it. Maybe this is an attempt to shock or something of the sort, or maybe this is her provocative attempt to say, "You see you men aren't very strong or anything, you can't even satisfy a woman like me." Then she comments on her phobia and she makes it clear that she has a fear of being left alone and a tendency to be grasping and demanding of love. Here then are the hostile controlling aspects of the phobia. She realizes the implications that he will leave her unless these phobias are corrected. She comments then that she is a conformist, although she doesn't sound much like one. She sees part of her trouble as being due to the inability to discipline herself. She ruminates a bit also about her relations with her husband and the fact that she can't think about him walking out. She comments on her shocking people and shocking her mother and also about her anger against mother. She makes it clear also that her anger toward mother is not fully conscious. In general the self-interpretation suggests that she doesn't know quite as much about herself, or that not as many of the thoughts are conscious as would appear

---

*The patient is asked to think over his stories and tell what, if anything, applies to him as a person (see Luborsky, 1953).

in the Rorschach. I have all along, I think, overestimated the degree to which the thoughts expressed are conscious ones. She describes some of her counterphobic, counteractive attempts to rebelliously shock people, which includes blurting out that she is coming for treatment. Then she intellectualizes further about herself. The self-interpretation also reveals that she has thought of suicide but not as a real intention. The biggest thing it reveals is what I just commented on, that she doesn't know as much about herself as I thought she did. It gives her more of a really hysterical air, although there is so much orality in this individual whether you want to call it infantile or not. The treatment, I think, will be long and hard.

The conclusions drawn from the inferences made from the tests were organized in terms of the patient variable in a research form, Form B. This form is included further on, as filled out at termination and follow-up. The initial Form B is not included here since it is essentially a codification of the just-reported record of inferences. Also, the references in the termination Form B to what was seen at initial give a good idea of the initial Form B. Form C is an extrapolation from the basic data to specific treatment issues and predictions.

INITIAL STUDY

Form C: Prediction Study

I. Treatment Recommendations

I know this patient has been in psychoanalysis. I know she was a control case and I know it has lasted 4 or 5 years. In addition, if I am thinking of the right patient, she is still fat. This, of course, colors the predictions that I will make in that it suggests to me that whatever other problems may have been solved, or whatever other behaviors may have changed, she has not dealt successfully with the oral problems. There seems to be no sense in discussing the indications for various therapeutic modalities in any detail. My overall feeling is that although she has all the requisite characteristics for analysis, that is, intelligence, psychological-mindedness, anxiety tolerance, and a pervasive enough problem, she would be a difficult case. I base this on my feeling that although there are definite neurotic aspects to this, the infantile character structure is very prominent. In my discussion of ego strength, I emphasized that she lacked the flexibility to give up gratifications necessary to succeed in psychoanalysis. I would add to that the strength of secondary gain and the strength of the primary gain she must derive. I am thinking of the oral impulses here and the rather gratifying position she has herself in, in regard to her sexual conflict. That is, in fantasy she seems to feel more powerful and as though she has a bigger phallus than the man. This fantasy is a very important part of her makeup.

II. Nature of the Problems to Arise in Psychotherapy

Although this woman may achieve lots of insights, particularly into oedipal problems, it would be difficult for her to change many of her character patterns. I would say that the transference will develop slowly over a period of quite some time, with the patient being reluctant, afraid, and unable to allow the relationship to mean very much to her. She will compete and in secret deceive and castrate the therapist for quite a long time before she can allow herself to be aware of any genuinely positive aspects of the transference. During this time she may talk as though the transference is positive, but this would be more talk than genuine feeling. In other words, the pattern of transference and resistance would be one in which the basic transference paradigm is competitive, castrative, and so on, based on the penis envy, while she may try to be a "good patient."

This is perhaps a special case of a general problem that should be mentioned, that is, the discrepancy between what she shows externally and experiences internally. I would venture to guess that many times over the course of the whole treatment she will act as if she "gets it," understands things and so on, while in reality either she does not understand it or her understanding is in some way different from that intended.

She will do this perhaps through intellectualizing, but also it would seem to me that it will occur more quietly. That is, the therapist, I would guess, will sense that she is using words that he has used and he will feel that they have a common understanding, whereupon it will turn out that unbeknownst to both patient and therapist, her understanding is different and probably colored in some way by more infantile expectations.

For this reason, and also because of the basic infantile character structure, it would seem to be extremely important that she not be offered content interpretations early in the analysis. While it is a banality that one is supposed to interpret resistance first and so on, it would seem to me that in this case, because of the interesting dynamics that seem to be involved and because of a certain transparency that she conveys (because of the obvious compromise formation of her symptoms), it would be an extra temptation to give her psychodynamic, genetic reconstructions or interpretations. This, however, without prior attack on the character patterns, would be like writing on water. She would assimilate it, quote it, "understand it," talk about it, and use it only in the service of avoidance. More concretely, the more-or-less hidden hostile aspects of her relationship to the therapist, her competitiveness, and her disdain of him must be relentlessly pointed out. And particularly important, the manifestations of her oral-aggressive and oral-demanding attitudes toward him must be pointed out over and over again. At bottom I don't believe that this aspect of the analysis will be successful (cf. acquisition of insight).

It is conceivable to me that toward the beginning of the analysis the entire question of motivation, goals, and extent of desired change might come in for a bit of attention. To take a wild guess, she may reach a point not long after the beginning of analysis where a flight into health of some sort may occur, where her symptoms may abate, or where she may reach some rapprochement with her husband on the basis of her better conscious ability to control her symptoms and, at this point, she may want to settle for this. Obviously, since she has been in analysis for a long time she didn't quit at this point, but it may have occurred.

One of the special problems that may in some way show itself, and this is based on the knowledge of who the therapist is, is his reality characteristics. That is, he is small, and she is a big, fat woman. In what way this may show itself in her fantasies I am not able to predict, other than to hazard a guess that she feels that she is powerful and can deceive men and get them to bend to her wishes. This tendency to be unrealistic in evaluating her own powers may become particularly prominent in some way. The question of possible suicidal attempts or suicidal talk during the treatment occurs. My prediction would be she would talk about suicide and, as frustration and regression mounts, she might threaten suicide, but would not act on these threats. Acting-out, perhaps involving shocking, promiscuous and/or perverse activities, may occur during the course of the treatment. I believe it will be a relatively stormy course, but that the question of the necessity for hospitalization will not be seriously considered, although it is a thought that might enter the therapist's head sometime during treatment. I would bet that the patient does a lot of talking outside the hour about herself, her problems, her therapist, and her therapy. This may be a significant resistance—talking outside the hour rather than in the hour.

Since she is going to be coming in this week for termination tests, let me include a few predictions in test terms. I bet there are fewer Ms on the Rorschach, more colors, including more FCs, and perhaps slightly more CFs. (These things may occur at termination or at follow-up because there is a possibility that she may fall into the group of patients whose termination tests are quite severely constricted.) I'm doubtful about this, however. I bet her TAT will be more open than it was at initial and that she will tell richer stories, but that again they will be consciously self-referent and that she will in this way exhibit herself without any great problem about it. I bet there are content indications in the tests of her disappointment, perhaps mild and denied disappointment with treatment, but surely her disappointment in some area will show. Arithmetic may go up a point or two and digits may come down a few points. Though there will be evidences of exhibitionism, I would think she will tend to be less exhibitionistically shocking in her responses. On the Word Association, for example, I bet it goes smoother without the long delays she had, but I bet there are still disturbances on the oral words, although maybe fewer disturbances of various kinds in sexual words. For instance, she blocked on initial for 10 seconds on penis. I bet she doesn't now. I bet her responses to the phobic words like *snake* and *cockroach* reflect some disturbance, but that they will be given more matter-of-factly, perhaps quicker and less affect-laden.

III. Prognostic Estimate

1. Changes in Symptoms

I know she is still fat. I would think the phobias will abate markedly over the course of psychotherapy, but perhaps not completely disappear. Their influence on her life, I think, will be less and their influence on the life of others will be less. In other words, they will be less obviously or overtly maladaptive, but may still exist at the end of psychotherapy.

In regard to sexual symptomatology, which I thought was present, I would make a similar prediction. She may be better in sexual functioning, but not completely "cured."

2. Change in Adaptive Patterns

a. *Changes in Impulse–Defense Configurations.* The greatest changes here should occur in terms of change in phallic-oedipal configurations of impulses which have had to be be handled through denial, repression, and fantasy. I would predict that fantasy will be diminished also.

In the course of analysis she will have become aware of oedipal features of her illness and these probably will not press her behavior as much as they do.

b. *Changes in Manifest Behavior Patterns.* I believe these will be significant. She will improve generally in her ability to get along with others and in the ability to modulate her demands upon them, although it seems to me that her life will still be colored by oral demandingness and oral anger. Sexual adjustment should be under better control and she should more readily acknowledge her womanly, feminine characteristics. Thus she should derive more satisfaction from her sexual life and from her maternal endeavors and activities.

c. *Structural Changes in the Ego.* I believe some genuine structural change may have occurred in the area of oedipal problems, but that the resolution of the oral aspects of the transference may be very difficult and may never be achieved. It is tough to define this operationally, of course, but this woman may go through life wanting more than she can get and being disappointed. This would reflect not only more controlled and more insightful disappointment in being a woman, but her oral disappointment, which would, I think, be something about which she would have less perspective and less distance.

3. *The Acquisition of Insight and Its Relation to Changes in Attitudes toward the Self, Others, Things, and the Illness*

I believe she will have copious insights, especially into her sexual problems, her oedipal problems, and her relationship to her father, but that her insight in regard to dependency relations will be more limited in meaning to her. That is, it will more likely be partial insight.

I would venture further guesses that she will derive relatively less insight into the sadomasochistic conflicts than into the more strictly sexual or phallic conflicts. That is to say, she may end treatment as a woman with a great many problems solved, but will still be disappointed. The insight she would have into her disappointment would involve the penis envy and the whole Oedipus complex and would be correct insight, but the oral disappointments and the masochistic gratification they may provide her with may not be something into which she has insight. (I use *masochistic* in the loose or broad sense here, as implying the gratification she will get from being deprived and maintaining this deprived position as a constant bribe to the superego, which will enable her to gratify oral impulses and feel that she is making up for what she missed or what she has been deprived of.)

IV. Overall Predictive and Prognostic Estimate

Summing up what I have said thus far, it seems to me that she will achieve significant improvement, some major changes, certainly symptoms relieved to a great extent, but that she will not fall into the category loosely describable as quite successful. She will have remaining problems both internal and interpersonal, but she will be getting more out of life than she was. Some feelings of disappointment, I bet, will be a significant feature.

TERMINATION TEST STUDY

Form B: Reassessment of Relevant Patient Variables

This Form B is being written some 2 months after the patient was tested by Drs. Rosen and myself (Siegal). I remember the patient clearly, her appearance and behavior. This, of course, plays some role in my assessments. As for her direct statements about her treatment, they were confined to her discussion of the TAT, during which she said essentially that she gets along much better with her mother and conflicts between them are not so severe; her husband and she are no longer together; the termination has caused her some difficulty, she feels, in that she has had to "take a vacation from dieting" but hopes to get back to it. She is still obese.

I. Sex and Age

No important inferences fall into this category except to note there is a great reduction in the rebelliousness which the patient displays; the change from 24 to 30 years old can, in itself, contribute to this kind of change in attitude.

II. Anxiety and Symptoms

1. Anxiety

Her test performance in general is smoother, indicating somewhat less drastic effects of anxiety upon her intellectual and performance efficiency. She concentrates better than she did initially. However, even if the effects of anxiety upon her functioning are less, there is some evidence that there has not been a remarkable reduction in anxiety and that, in fact, although it is expressed differently and more adaptively, there is a good deal of remaining anxiety, maybe more directly experienced. That is, anxiety would tend to be experienced and expressed more in rumination now than in phobias as previously. She may experience as much anxiety consciously, however, as she did. She is not as afraid of anxiety though, as she was, and in this sense one may speak of a kind of desensitization, as if she fears loss of control over her impulses and over the intensity of anxiety much less than she used to. She experiences anxiety directly connected with some aspects of the feminine role, perhaps particularly the sexual aspects.

In general, she is now less affected by the necessity to avoid anxiety than she was, and less defensiveness of all kinds is required of her now (cf. "Anxiety Tolerance").

2. Symptoms

The tests indicate a great reduction in phobic symptoms. Phobias now would seem either to be not present at all or only present in a kind of residual form which is not too troublesome to her. The character attitudes mentioned in the initial write-up, which markedly influenced interpersonal relations, are much less in evidence. She is less rebellious, less competitive, less controlling and castrating. In other words, there has been a marked reduction in those aspects of her behavior directly related to conflict over sexual identity (see "Core Neurotic Problem"). Included in this, incidentally, will be a reduction in the counterphobically tinged aspects of her behavior. So far as can be seen in the tests, her attitudes toward sexuality are somewhat less pathological, though there is some reason to believe that inhibition may yet exist in the sexual area. While feelings of inadequacy in general and inadequacy as a woman in particular are still present, they are less intense.

The tests suggest that oral yearnings are intense and that some conflict-laden expression of oral impulses still occurs, though possibly it may be somewhat more adaptive or less maladaptive than previously. This is said not only on the basis of the fact that she is still obese but it is apparent in the test responses involving oral themes.

3. Somatization

This does not seem prominent nor are there any indications of change.

4. Depression and Guilt Feelings

a. Depression. The prominence of the defense mechanism of denial now suggests an underlying depressed mood which is, however, under fairly good control by the patient. She would consciously see this as related to termination, and the tests would suggest that it is related not only to the loss of the therapist but to her uncertainty about what she has achieved and whether she will be able to accomplish the remaining work in creating for herself a satisfactory life. That is to say, more than many terminating patients, this patient is uncertain about her future.

b. Conscious Guilt. The tests suggest that she has experienced guilt more consciously than she did at initial test time and that she would be less prone to evade personal guilt and responsibility and less prone to defend herself against the consciousness of guilt feelings.

c. Unconscious Guilt. Masochistic fantasy and references to masochistic behavior are less. She gives, in this regard, a more "normally feminine" appearance (in line with the shift which seems to have occurred in the direction of a more feminine identification). It is felt that consistent with the less angry, less disturbed aspects of the picture at termination, there is probably less maladaptive behavior; thus one might infer a quantitative reduction in the intensity of unconscious guilt and in the degree to which it influences her behavior.

5. Alloplasticity

Alloplasticity is reduced in the sense that her maladaptive behavior is reduced and thus the secondary gain she derives from it is reduced. The tests indicate that she is still prone to occasional impulsive actions based on diffuse labile affect and that she still has significant tendencies to avoid consciously experiencing anxiety. But alloplasticity, which was not prominent at initial, is perhaps reduced somewhat.

III. Nature of Conflicts

1. Core Neurotic Problem

The biggest change here has been a move in the direction of a firmer feminine identification with less protests against this. All the signs of "masculine protest" are reduced in intensity. The patient says disturbance in her relationship with mother has been reduced and there is test evidence to suggest that this is an accurate appraisal on her part of change based on less intense hostile feelings toward mother. However, she rationalizes about this to some extent, suggesting as do other evidences, that the shift toward a more adaptive feminine identification is one which she experiences with some anxiety or insecurity. That is to say, while significant shifts have occurred in her identifications, one would probably, at this point, be most accurate in describing this as a partial resolution of the sexual conflict pending follow-up investigation as to whether this has become more integrated into her view of herself and the way she lives her life. In any case, there is far less sadomasochistic fantasy and less maladaptive expression in behavior of this conflict.

Strong oral-passive yearnings remain, however. These seem strong enough to suggest that they are expressed in behavior though possibly not quite as pathological as previously. The entire struggle over rebelliousness and autonomy is significantly reduced.

IV. Ego Factors and Defenses

1. Self-Concept

In this area changes are major. She views her treatment, in fact, as an opportunity to more realistically reevaluate herself. And, indeed, she is somewhat more realistic about herself and her ability and her ambitions. At the same time she makes it clear that the underlying fantasies of great achievement, great ability (all of these related to sexual identity struggles) still are present. The difference, however, is that she realizes now these are fantasies.

She feels much more in control of herself, and the fear of loss of control is lessened considerably. She is much more able to see herself consciously as a woman not entirely different from other women, and the passive woman, whom she looked down upon at initial, is much less despised and viewed much more sympathetically.

2. Defenses

a. Patterning of Defenses. Denial and avoidance are still prominent. There has been no radical restructuring of the defensive patterns as far as I can see. The shifts which seem to have occurred involve a reduction in displacement and externalization and a growth in rumination which, in a sense, has taken over the defensive role played by phobic ideation at initial. There is still a good deal of intellectualizing and rationalizing, though this is perhaps not as extreme as it was. In regard to repression, this still seems to play the same role it did and there are hints in the tests that she tends to be more constricted than she was. From the viewpoint of patterning of defenses, the picture is somewhat surprising. That is, there is less change from psychoanalysis than one would anticipate and somehow the picture looks almost as though this patient had been in supportive expressive psychotherapy. As a matter of fact, it is this which suggests that although some conflict resolution has occurred and a great deal of maladaptive character patterns and behaviors have been dispelled, the conflict resolution may either be partial or it is too early to tell.

   b. *Thought Organization.* In sheer quantity there is about as much ideational activity as there was, including a great deal of fantasy. There is, however, a marked growth in awareness of her own fantasies and daydreams. They are not as pathological in content nor as pathological in the influence they exert over her behavior. In other words, though fantasy is still prominent she is a less fantasy-ridden individual. There seems to have been an increase in rumination and a decrease in phobic ideation. The nature of thought organization and the sheer quantity of ideational activity which goes on suggests that she may still be prone to ideational symptomatology.

   c. *Affect Organization.* Here is another place where changes do not seem great; in addition, they are hard to capture. There is a slight tendency, it appears, for directly taking responsibility for feelings which she perhaps experiences more clearly. At the same time, there is the suggestion that there may be some arbitrary aspects to interpersonal relations, especially those involving the patient receiving passive gratification. Also there is the suggestion that at times when affect reaches sufficient intensity it may become diffuse enough to elude her conscious experience. Yet, the overall suggestion is that when affect is within certain limits of intensity it is probably experienced and expressed more adaptively; but beyond these limits, maladaptive expression may still occur.

3. Anxiety Tolerance

   She is less frightened of anxiety, thus she defends herself less against the experience of anxiety and may even experience more and more intense anxiety. There are grounds to infer, then, a perceptible increase in anxiety tolerance.

4. *Insight*

There are less evidences of insight than one would expect, and there are suggestions that some insights are rather intellectualized, though they do have some meaning to her. It would seem accurate to say that a certain "middle range" of insights (in terms of levels of depth) is the most meaningful for her. That is, insights based in her conscious experience of wanting to be a man and insights involving her responsibility for her behaviors and the ways in which she provokes certain responses would probably be the most meaningful for her, while insights on a "deeper" level involving more unconscious material might be somewhat intellectualized. The implication here, and of course this is highly speculative, is that regression in psychoanalysis may not have preceded to as deep a point as it often does or that if it did she may not have been able to utilize the insights gained. This is in line with a feeling that it's almost as though this has been an expressive psychotherapy rather than a psychoanalysis.

5. *Externalization*

Externalization, unequivocally, is reduced a great deal. This can be seen not only in the reduction of phobias involving displacement but also directly in her greater willingness to take responsibility for her own feelings and problems.

6. *Ego Strength*

While clear changes have occurred in her adaptive behavior, the prominence of denial and avoidance, and of ideational activity, the lack of striking change under patterning of defenses and affect organization and insight would suggest that the change in ego strength is limited. I am, of course, using this as a catchall to describe an overall estimate of her change. While changes have been significant they are not dramatic and the implication is that they might not be as stable as one would want. So, while her adjustment will unquestionably be better than it was, remaining conflicts may play some part.

V. Capacities Factors

1. *Intelligence*

Her IQ at termination was 136–137, with Verbal IQ of 128–129, and Performance IQ at 139. The largest rise, and it is a significant one, is in the Performance IQ, which went up from 126 to 139. This is largely accounted for by the rise in one test which suggests her increased capacity to perceive what others expect of her and, in general, to function much more smoothly and adaptively in a social way. In addition, her greater efficiency and smoothness of functioning contributes to this rise. Specific mention was made at initial of her difficulty in accurately sizing herself up, and she has clearly improved in this regard as well as in being able to size up other people and what they expect of her (cf. "Self-Concept").

2. Psychological-Mindedness

There has been no great growth in this. Unlike many analytic patients, there doesn't seem to have been any tendency toward an increased interest in what makes people tick and so on. Clearly, however, she does understand herself much better.

VI. Motivational Factors

1. Honesty

There is far less need to shock others exhibitionistically and thus the patient seems much more honest with herself and with others.

3. Extent of Desired Change

The patient conveys the impression that she is, to some extent, trying to convince herself of all the changes which have occurred in her. While it is clear that many changes have occurred, she seems to be somewhat disappointed in their extent or somewhat dubious about them. On the other hand, she conveys the feeling that she feels she can "make it" on her own and there is certainly no great indication of a desire to continue treatment or anything of the sort.

4. Secondary Gain

This is markedly reduced but there are indications that some gain from neurotic patterns still occurs. This can be seen mostly in her reaction to termination. In fact this is probably the place to say that the patient feels her reaction to termination is influencing her behavior markedly. This is very difficult to assess because there is some feeling conveyed from many aspects of her current functioning that she tends to use this.

VII. Relationship Factors

1. *Interpersonal Relations*

The striking change in this area has been in her relations with both men and women. She is less competitive, less controlling, less castrating and, in general, the sadomasochistic orientation (particularly in regard to relationships with men) has been much reduced. In regard to relations with women, these seem somewhat less conflictual and therefore she needs to maintain less distance between herself and other women. She can see herself as being more like them and can sympathize with them more than she did.

2. *Transference Paradigms*

She says she feels the termination deeply. There are indications to suggest that she is going through a relatively severe termination disturbance. However, one is forced to ask the question, is she using this, in a sense, to cover some disappointment she experiences about the treatment?

FOLLOW-UP TEST STUDY

Form B: Reassessment of Relevant Patient Variables

I have heard nothing of this patient since her termination. Dr. Rosen and I (Siegal) administered tests to her during the month of June. She seems to have reduced significantly since she was last seen. She is more attractively dressed and her figure is better. In her contacts with me she made it clear that she feels troubled and is as a matter of fact contemplating resuming some form of treatment. She also implied that the program of weight control and the professional contacts stemming from this program are important to her. She told me, for example, that she was late to our appointment because she had to stop and see her doctor.

II. Anxiety and Symptoms

1. Anxiety

There seems, from the tests, to have been a significant increase in experienced anxiety. She probably experiences more intense anxiety more of the time than she did 2 years ago. This does not seem to limit significantly her ability to perform intellectual and perceptual motor tests since she has maintained the increase in her Performance IQ visible in the last set of tests. It isn't clear to what ideas or circumstances she attaches her present anxiety, but that it may reach proportions of great intensity does seem evident. There is also test material which suggests that the process of averting affect discharge is a longer and more complicated one these days and this, which depends upon certain realignments in defensive functioning (cf. "Patterning of Defenses"), may lead to an increase in anxiety. Anxiety tolerance is strained.

2. Symptoms

There are still some evidences of phobic symptomatology, though phobias do not seem to be terribly disturbing to the patient. There is evidence which suggests the greater prominence, greater importance, and more disturbing quality of sexual symptoms. The salience of sexual identity conflict is increased, the allusions to sexual dissatisfaction are increased, and the rebellious, pseudoassertive nature of her ideas about sexuality is more apparent. The tests would suggest, speculatively, that alloplastic expression of her sexual conflict may imply homosexual impulses. That is, though they may be heterosexual liaisons, even so, homosexual elements will be seen.

Oral-aggressive impulses are still prominent, and one would expect them to be expressed not only in her interpersonal and sexual relations but presumably in her struggles over her obesity.

3. Somatization

There is no additional material in the tests which bears upon this.

4. Depression and Guilt Feelings

a. Depression. There is a significant change in moods since the last time. While on the one hand the patient seems less overtly depressed, gayer, quicker, less inhibited, and with fewer depressive thoughts, on the other hand there is a much greater prominence of denial of a strained sort which makes it now appear that she is trying to laugh off the difficulties in her life and trying to minimize serious depressive feelings. In addition, affect in general seems more diffuse and more labile than it was 2 years ago. It may well be that one of the things she is struggling with is the threatening emergence of depression.

b. *Conscious Guilt.* Conscious guilt over sexuality seems to be present, although she rationalizes it and tries to overcome it by simply asserting to herself that her life is her own. There seems to be less inhibition concerning sexuality and conscious guilt is more likely to appear.

c. *Unconscious Guilt.* It's difficult to infer anything about changes in this variable since termination. In some elusive indefinable ways she seems less masochistic than at termination. (Perhaps it is her directness in relating to the tester and her assertiveness about her own values which contributes to this impression.) There is material in the TAT stories, also, to suggest that she is less locked in sadomasochistic personal relationships. For example, what was previously seen as a bad mother figure in one of the stories is still seen as a bad mother figure, but the present telling of this story implies a good deal more empathy for this bad mother and a good deal more perspective and distance from her. Perhaps this implies a corresponding change in her own life. Is she more distant, more objective, and somewhat more sympathetic to her own mother, and does this represent a diminution in unconscious anger and guilt toward her?

5. Alloplasticity

The present tests would suggest that inhibition is less, and alloplasticity is increased. This means there must be more frequent discharge in behavior of sexual and homosexual impulses and conflicts. Autoplastic resources are also called upon (see "Patterning of Defenses").

III. Nature of Conflicts

1. Core Neurotic Problem

The shift toward firmer feminine identification described in the termination test report has not been maintained. There is a marked increase in signs of sexual identity conflict amounting almost to a full recrudescence of the homosexual conflict. Or it may be that growth, taking her farther from more infantile, oral conflicts has vivified sexual conflict. In this sense she is now more like she was at initial than at termination.

Although there are indications that there is a growth in assertiveness and that this is based upon a genuinely greater feeling of autonomy, one must also infer that the whole struggle over autonomy is a live one, although it is taking a different form than at initial. It is a more internalized struggle now, more of a struggle with her own values and feelings of guilt than with projected, distorted, or real parents or parent surrogates in her environment.

IV. Ego Factors (and Defenses)

1. Self-Concept

The change described in the termination report in regard to her ability to evaluate herself more realistically is maintained. However, there seems to have been a regression in her self-concept which may be a product of some current struggle she is undergoing. In any case, whatever its source, she now seems to be viewing herself preconsciously as though she were a less mature, younger, more girlish person. There is almost an adolescent quality to her self-concept.

2. Defenses

a. *Patterning of Defenses.* The tests suggest that repression is less effective now than it was at termination, although in certain areas she is still a markedly repressive person. Since repression is no longer as readily available to her, there is a greater use of ideational activity as a defense. In the termination test study the prominence of rumination was mentioned. At follow-up, rumination and particularly fantasy seem central in her defensive makeup (along with denial, which will be commented upon in a moment). The process of control over affect and control over impulse expression is a longer, more complicated one, and more of a struggle. That is, neither does she passively give in to impulse pressure nor does control occur automatically, but she engages, it seems from the tests, in long and complex defensive struggles with her impulses. This keeps her anxious.

Denial of a strained and particularly flagrant kind is more promise now than at termination. The denial is directed particularly against recognizing the significance of her disappointment and of her anger.

In general, her defensive organization gives the impression of someone who is struggling against some ego decompensation. (Decompensation refers only to greater strain and pressure upon her ego and the overworking and partial ineffectiveness of some defenses, not to psychosis.)

From the standpoint of defenses, the partial resolution of conflict which was inferred at termination has not continued or been maintained and become a more stable conflict resolution, but rather has receded so that conflicts are again somewhat active in her.

b. Thought Organization. There is perhaps a slightly greater tendency for thinking to be a little distorted, projective, arbitrary or, in general, in line with the needs of her defensive system. Ideational activity is, as was mentioned, central in her defensive struggles (along with denial), and its centrality has been increased by the fact that repression is no longer as effective or useful as it once was.

c. Affect Organization. The arbitrary aspect of affect expression in interpersonal relations (mentioned at termination under this heading) may have increased. The tests now suggest that there are clear arbitrary troublesome aspects to her interpersonal relations. In addition she seems more labile, less inhibited in affect discharge, and more troubled than she was at termination, although her overt mood was lower then.

3. Anxiety Tolerance

She is more anxious now, yet the fact that even despite the mild decompensation anxiety still seems to be within manageable bounds suggests that she has maintained the increased anxiety tolerance inferred at termination.

4. Insight

There is still some indication of an intellectualized character to some of the insights she has achieved, but there is no noteworthy lack of insight. Insight into some aspects of her sexual problems seems present, yet the fact that these continue to be a problem to her suggests that only partial insight has been achieved.

5. Externalization

Externalization remains less than it was at initial. The change noted at termination has been maintained.

6. Ego Strength

She is hard put to maintain her equilibrium without further decompensation into a more disturbed, depressed, or a more maladaptive affect and impulse expression. The fact, however, that she continues the struggle without any definitive yielding or being overcome suggests that ego strength is fairly good in the sense of her ego capacity to continue to struggle, even when very hard pressed.

V. Capacities Factors

1. Intelligence

She has maintained her gains in this variable and functions quite well despite the anxiety she experiences and her self-depreciation. It is possible that work may have become more meaningful to her if one is to judge by some of her remarks.

2. Psychological-Mindedness

Once again, she does not seem remarkably psychologically minded and although she seems to continue to attempt to understand herself psychologically, she does not feel great success in this nor do the tests suggest any growth in the capacity for useful understanding of herself.

VI. Motivational Factors

1. Honesty

The patient seems normally honest.

3. Extent of Desired Change

The patient's perception of her treatment, at least on one level of consciousness, is that she was helped to delineate and circumscribe the areas of her problems but not to "solve" them. It was remarked that she seemed disappointed in some ways at termination, although hopeful that changes would continue for her. The changes she thought or hoped would occur or would continue to occur have not. At one point in the tests she voiced significant disappointment that after "5 years" she should still have this much difficulty. This wasn't said bitterly nor is there any bitterness conveyed in her tests, but there is disappointment in the amount of change she has achieved.

4. Secondary Gain

There isn't much to be inferred about this from the tests at this point. She seemed to gain gratification from her contacts with the physicians who are supervising her weight reduction and she also said directly she would like, were it possible, to return here for treatment. There may be secondary gain tied up in this statement, but it seemed more like direct requests for help rather than attempts in some way to secure secondary gains from her symptoms.

VII. Relationship Factors

1. Interpersonal Relationships

While there is some basis to suggest that sadomasochistic aspects of relationships are less disturbing and less prominent, there is test evidence to suggest disturbed and deviant aspects of interpersonal relations. One would suspect that she is not entirely appropriate in her demands and expectations in interpersonal relationships (though no gross inappropriateness of a social sort is meant here). Rather, subtle arbitrary demands or expectations or disappointments probably occur. The recrudescence of sexual conflict might suggest that this kind of interpersonal difficulty may occur both with men and with women.

2. Transference Paradigms

I take this as an opportunity to comment on any unresolved or still-present features of the transference relationship. She mentioned she had seen her former therapist and spoke of him warmly and in an appreciative way. On the other hand, she mentioned her disappointment with treatment. That she does not in any way try to relate the one to the other (though of course we did not talk much about this) might suggest certain unresolved aspects of the transference. Specifically, she may never have been able to come to adequate grips with her hostile or negative transference feelings.

CONFIRMATION STUDY SUMMARY

The following is an overview of the entire data of the case done by Drs. Ann Appelbaum and Leonard Horwitz (1968) as part of a study primarily designed to learn the fate of specific assumptions. The results of this study were the criteria used in comparing tests and psychiatric diagnoses and predictions in Chapter 8.

The Initial Study Group predicted that this patient would emerge from psychoanalysis with an excellent treatment result. It was anticipated that her major conflicts around sadomasochistic impulses and her difficulties with femininity based upon a hostile identification with her mother would be significantly modified. It was predicted that her obesity would abate somewhat. This optimism was based upon what turned out to have been an overestimation of the patient's ego strength, which was described as "excellent." They recognized that it was "in the area of incapacity to delay or to modulate certain impulse gratifications (particularly food intake) that her chief deficiency in regard to ego strength is manifest. Other than this diminished tolerance for tension, the things that go into appraisals of ego strength like motivation, determination to change, intelligence, psychological-mindedness, capacity for insight, etc., are all high." The termination and follow-up teams* expressed strong disagreement with the initial team's assessment: "She lives out her impulses, sexual, masochistic, as well as oral-aggressive, in an immediate way without guilt feelings or any effort at control." Her lack of real insight, her externalization, her low self-awareness on a conscious and preconscious level together with her poor control over impulse expression indicated a severe lack of ego strength both at the time of initial and at termination. The termination team added that the lack of information about the patient with which the initial team was handicapped determined their inaccurate assessment. The termination team also thought that the patient's lack of anxiety and depression, rather than indicating good ego functioning, was the result of her immediate living out of in-

---

*Senior Project clinicians who interviewed patient, therapist, and therapist's supervisor, if any.

stinctual impulses. The other factor cited by the termination and follow-up teams as inhibiting a more favorable outcome was the therapist's countertransference, which disposed him toward overemphasizing the patient's positive erotic feelings, which were often used to defend herself against sadistic impulses.

The treatment result provides a mild strengthening of the general assumption: "To the extent that a resolution of unconscious conflict occurs via the expressive aspects of psychotherapy, there is at least a proportional change in symptoms, character traits, and character structure." The research teams judged that little, if any, conflict resolution occurred and there was indeed no substantial change in the patient's obesity, impulsiveness, sadomasochistic orientation, etc. While the judgment about conflict resolution was undoubtedly influenced by the lack of change in symptoms and character traits, the decision was probably mainly influenced by the research team's analysis of the treatment process in which the sadomasochistic paradigm did not emerge clearly in the transference nor was it interpreted and worked with fully enough. Psychological tests also indicated the presence of the same major conflicts.

A fairly significant finding concerns the relative effectiveness of psychoanalysis and supportive psychotherapy in relation both to dealing with specific symptoms and to the stability of change in symptoms which are resolved by conflict resolution as opposed to a "transference cure." We have postulated that certain specific pieces of symptomatology can be more easily alleviated by means of the wish to please the therapist than by the resolution of the underlying unconscious conflict. This proposition was partly strengthened by the fact that during the follow-up period, in anticipation of going to visit the analyst, the patient lost a considerable amount of weight, in contrast to her failure to lose any weight during the course of the analysis. Motivated by transference wishes to impress the analyst with her accomplishments, she was able to achieve something she had been unable to do during the analysis itself. We have also assumed that the transference cure tends to be unstable and this was confirmed by the fact that shortly after her visit she proceeded to gain back all of the weight she had lost before that. Similarly, the patient's hostile relationship to her mother, the aspect which she was most able to improve upon in treatment, was not altered by strictly interpretive means, i.e., by uncovering the patient's introject of the hostile, sadistic, and depriving mother. Rather, the therapist's suggestion to the patient that she was contributing to the poor relationship between the two of them and that her life would be more satisfying and harmonious if she made an effort to become more congenial with her mother contributed to the change. The fact that this change continued to be stable over the follow-up period may perhaps be based upon the greater stability of introjection as a curative agent in contrast to a strictly transference cure. That is, she spent a year or two working specifically with the therapist's suggestion and probably made this her own, while the weight reduction was more of a circumscribed wish which she experienced during a part of the follow-up period. Another facet of the greater stability of her changed behavior with her mother was that she got prompt gratifying responses from the environment when she became more reasonable with her mother and this encouraged her to persist in her efforts to improve her behavior. With her weight reduction, on the other hand, the gratifications accruing from her change from marked to moderate obesity must have been slight in comparison with the severe deprivations dieting constituted for her.

DISCUSSION AND CONCLUSION

This chapter was designed to offer a view of how we use tests in general, and in this research in particular. In the process, this illustrative case raises a number of other issues.

The tester was less optimistic about the gains the patient would achieve than were the other clinicians, who had at their disposal psychiatric, social work, and clinical test report data. This is an instance of the general finding of greater accuracy in such predictions when made from the tests alone than when made from other data, as demonstrated in Chapter 7. One might gather from the initial test write-up that the patient should have been recommended for expressive, even supportive-expressive psychotherapy, rather than for analysis; in any case, an analysis would be difficult and limited in effect. Indeed, if one is constrained to try for sufficiently limited goals, and rely on suggestion, introjection of a benevolent figure, any variety of "transference cure," and probably intellectualized insight, then brief psychotherapy could also have been considered (S. Appelbaum, 1975).

Stemming from his initial understanding, the tester specifically pointed out traps awaiting the analyst, and made suggestions to him: the seductive possibilities of her seeming to be insightful which would lead to content interpretations in advance of resistance interpretations; the need to point out relentlessly the hidden hostile aspects of her relation to the analyst, her competitiveness, and her disdain—in short, her oral-aggressive and oral-demanding attitudes. Even so, the tester says, "At bottom, I don't believe that this aspect of the analysis will be successful." So, one does not know whether this was a patient who, by nature, could not be expected to work through such difficulties in analysis, or whether the analyst had not fully heeded the admonitions of the psychologist, whether through lack of skill or through being unpersuaded by them. The independent overview of the treatment based on interviews with the patient and the therapist suggests that the analyst was bemused by the positive, oedipal transference and never did attend sufficiently to the negative, pregenital, especially oral-aggressive aspects of the relationship.

Another issue raised by this case is the difficulty in judging results at termination. Overall, this patient was thought to have improved at termination; but perhaps it was the flimsiness of her improvement, more or less apparent at termination, that was fully revealed at follow-up. The stress of terminating an important relationship might result in a patient's appearing more troubled in some ways at termination than he would 2 years later, or a patient may achieve a high point at termination while still relating at least temporally to the analyst, which would later give way to less adequate functioning. (This issue is dealt with further in Chapter 9.)

This case also illustrates some of the dangers of insight (S. Appelbaum, 1975, 1977). This patient had achieved partial insight and partial conflict resolution, which apparently served to help lull the analyst into a partial analysis. By the time of follow-up, with projections and other externalized distortions lessened, she was assaulted with increased anxiety, guilt, and imminent depression, along with an exacerbation of sexual, especially homosexual, conflicts. In some respects, at least, she had been ill-served by her capacities to use partial insight as an avoidant defense and to get others to conspire in this avoidance as well, to become somewhat, but not enough, aware.

As noted in the analysis of the single variables (see Chapter 3), those patients who did best of all achieved the greatest amount of resolution of core neurotic conflict in the context of increased insight and psychological-mindedness. Yet, as we shall see in the follow-up study, there seems to be a class of patients (of which the present examined patient is one) for whom a little knowledge is a dangerous thing. Every behavior is a defense; that is, every behavior can be looked at from the point of view of defense as adopted instead of some other behavior and thus wards off the disadvantages of the other behavior. For example, one might surmise that the finding with this patient of less sexual inhibition might be a good development (assuming that sexual inhibition was a complaint in the first place). Yet, as we have seen, along with a lessening of sexual inhibition at follow-up, the patient had more conscious guilt, more anxiety, more sexual symptoms, had lost the gains she had apparently made in resolving problems of sexual identity, and had become more alloplastic. Regressive impulses were achieving more freedom of expression. The whole organization of the personality was under severe pressure. Despite her exaggerated and strained denials, the patient acknowledged all of this in experience; she felt bad, and indeed seemed to be considering going back for more treatment.

Too often, it seems, we speak, and perhaps think, in simplistic, linear terms. These data give rise to a view of the personality as one of interlocking, reciprocal elements—an interdependent structure. When one removes or rearranges one piece of such a structure, then all the rest are rearranged as well. One cannot judge whether the removal of the one piece was beneficial overall until the new structure has been similarly assessed. Nothing in the human personality is, by definition, good or bad. Such a judgment depends upon what the goals are at any given moment, what the disadvantages as well as advantages are relative to the various goals and needs of the person, including the price paid by the environment.

Like a parody of an Ernest Hemingway character, this patient had "seen too much." She had achieved partial insight, partial conflict resolution, and had exposed herself to new intrapsychic, and possibly extrapsychic, changes. To the extent that she had given up or relaxed defenses, particularly her externalizing ones, she was to that extent defenseless. Apparently she was unable to replace these losses with more adaptive ones. Yet she could not go back to her previous organization. *Why* she could not go back is an interesting question with this patient as with many other patients. It may be that there is something progressive or, as some people call it, "actualizing" in people which prevents their going backward. There may be something about a new perspective which invalidates the old, no matter what travails the new one brings. It may be that the "suggestion" implicit in having completed a treatment, the categorical imperative that one *should* be different, prevents the resumption of pretreatment patterns. And it may be that a kind of loyalty to the therapist prevents it—the therapist may have come to be perceived as disapproving of the past ways. After all, he was hired on the proviso that he help the patient overcome the past ways, the complaints which brought the patient to treatment. The patient might experience her backsliding as an attack on this steady, benevolent, seemingly helpful figure.

Whether the treatment is psychoanalytically based, behaviorally based, or humanistic, the dangers of interfering with the homeostasis of personality, no matter how maladaptive that homeostasis may appear to be, should not for some patients be underestimated. Provoking psychosis or suicide is merely an extreme, an obvious example of more subtle dangers. The latter may be so subtle as to masquerade as successes, especially if one is oriented toward removal of symptoms, ameliorating complaints, rather than an existential appreciation of the patient's overall personality and life circumstances.

CHAPTER 3

Change in Each Patient Variable from Initial to Termination

In this chapter the fate of each patient variable will be traced and clarified. The basic data are individual statements about each variable made by the research testers solely on the basis of their reading of the tests. We went over these statements and abstracted from them statements of presence or absence of the variable, increase or decrease in the variable, change for the better or change for the worse in the variable. Until this book was completed, we had no knowledge of the patient other than what we got from reading the test write-ups. While the objective in this portion of the study was to study each variable singly, the compellingness of patterns and relationships led at various points to at least rudimentary connections between one variable and another. This was partly due to the essential artificiality, if not impossibility, of rigidly restricting clinical thinking, which is characteristically based upon correlations and patterns, and partly because of the overlapping nature of many of the variables themselves. Thus, for example, in writing about the variable *patterning of defenses*, it was difficult to avoid commenting upon other variables such as *ego strength, affect organization, thought organization,* and *alloplasticity*—all intimately related to patterning of defenses. These interrelationships are demonstrated later by intercorrelation figures.

Throughout this report the importance of making judgments on the basis of the fullest possible knowledge of the particular person is stressed. Isolating a single personality variable is a little like taking a single piece out of a painting. Usually one is hard put to tell whether that particular piece is a "good" part of the painting or a "bad" part of the painting. Only when it is seen in context can one judge whether it contributes to the benefit or detriment of the whole.

Why could not each patient be known individually, so that an encompassing clinical judgment could be made in each instance? The reason is that the individual variables were first done with the object of tracing changes in them singly, independent of halo effects and their interactions with other variables. This part of the task was facilitated by the research psychologist's not having seen the original test data and not having known about all the variables while he was judging a particular one, although obviously by the end of this task he had seen all the others. However, having seen previous variables had limited practical effect on the analysis of later ones. The work was done over a long period of time, the data were voluminous, and the task all along of the research psychologist was to forget and disregard anything except the variable being investigated at the moment.

In the absence of other information, the research psychologist judged and wrote in an "average expectable" way. That is, all things being equal, such and such variable would be expected to be related to such and such other variable, or have such and such effect. There were occasions, however (usually specified in the write-ups), where even with the limited data available the immanent configuration was so convincing that not to indicate that the conclusion was specific to this patient or group would have been artificial. To return to the painting analogy, sometimes when one knows that the painting is representational and knows what the isolated piece is supposed to represent, he can decide whether the way that piece is done is likely to contribute beneficially or harmfully when it is put into the picture.

PSYCHOLOGICAL-MINDEDNESS

Introduction

Psychological-mindedness is defined by Wallerstein and Robbins (1956) as "the patient's capacity—and readiness—to see some relationship between his symptoms or behavior and his emotional state. To what extent is he able to see significant relationships between his thought, feeling, and action? To what extent does his ego have the capacity to split into an observing (introspective) and experiencing part?" (p. 246). This definition, serviceable as it often may be, suffers from the same restrictiveness as the clinically frequent question, "Is the patient motivated?" (A. Appelbaum, 1972). Both of these fail to attend to (a) the individual intrapsychic factors which taken together make for psychological-mindedness (or motivation) as if these were discrete things that people have or do not have, and (b) whether the person might *have* these capacities, but be able to use them only on other people or on characters in books and plays. Such persons might be psychologically minded enough, but be inhibited in using this capability for analysis of themselves.*

The research testers implicitly redefined the variable by attending to the intrapsychic components that would be expected to make for psychological-mindedness—ideational richness, reflectiveness, control over emotions and affects, etc. They also recognized that, while the psychological-mindedness available to a person only with respect to others could not be considered in and of itself a treatment asset, it does suggest a potentiality for psychological thinking about one's self which might be exploitable in the treatment.

Findings and Discussion

A good many of the judgments of this variable, while clear about the general tendency of change, are somewhat inexplicit about the degree of change. Maybe this is too difficult a variable to judge minutely. At any rate, we have somewhat limited confidence in the fine discriminations.

All patients ($N = 34$) were commented upon with respect to psychological-mindedness. The patients were judged as to the degree of change on a 4-point scale with 3 referring to greatest change, 2 to moderate change, 1 to slight change, and 0 to no change. While in principle there seems no reason why a patient should not become less psychologically minded, it did not occur with any of these patients. The data are:

Change in Psychological-Mindedness
+ = increase

++++ = 4; ++ = 4; + = 12; same = 14

Since psychological-mindedness is defined with reference to basic capacities and functions, it may not be surprising that a large number of

---

*A conceptualization of the component parts of psychological-mindedness and an application of this understanding to a psychoanalysis is available (S. Appelbaum, 1973).

people should remain unchanged in this respect. It is, however, noteworthy that in treatments geared to stimulating whatever capacity there might be to think psychologically so many subjects remained untouched by these efforts.

In assessing these findings, one should keep in mind the level of psychological-mindedness the patient had to begin with. Obviously if a patient was quite psychologically minded at the start, he need not, or perhaps could not, increase psychological-mindedness much or at all. Thus, we categorized the patients as to their degree of psychological-mindedness at initial. Only 2 of them were considered highly psychologically minded. Seventeen were considered moderately psychologically minded, and 15 were considered low in psychological-mindedness. The 2 persons of highest psychological-mindedness increased at termination an average of 1 scale point; the 17 patients of moderate psychological-mindedness increased an average of 1.3 apiece; and the group of 15 people with low psychological-mindedness increased an average of only .5 each. The greater gain in psychological-mindedness of those high to begin with, according to analysis of variance, is significant ($p < .05$). It seems, then, that persons with low psychological-mindedness, though they have the greatest room for improvement, are the most difficult to improve in this respect, achieving around 60% less improvement than those who are at least moderately psychologically minded to begin with.

Numerically the most important drawbacks to psychological-mindedness were externalization, projection, and low anxiety tolerance. Seven patients were noted as being inhibited in psychological-mindedness through externalization with 1 noted as having increased in the use of externalization, 3 having decreased in its use, and 3 simply with a notation of its presence and with no comment about its increasing or decreasing. Projection was noted in 5 instances: Two were noted as having decreased in projection; with 3, projection was noted as being present. Taking projection and externalization together as a focusing outward which inhibits psychological-mindedness, the combined instances of 12 is clearly the quantitatively most important reason noted for lack of psychological-mindedness. To the extent that the research testers were influenced by the Project definition's emphasis on being inclined to look inward, this finding is circular. But it makes good clinical sense, and must have to the research testers, to see such outward deployment of attention as inimical to psychological-mindedness.

Six persons were noted as showing an inhibition of psychological-mindedness due to their difficulty in tolerating anxiety, with no judgment having been made as to an increase or decrease of this with any of them. Four persons were noted as being inhibited in psychological-mindedness through little control over affects, with the threat or emergence of stormy periods interrupting the possibilities for self-reflectiveness. One person improved in this respect and there were three notations of the presence of this problem. There were five instances of intellectualization inhibiting psychological-mindedness, with no judgment of change one way or the other. There were five instances where weakness in basic ego functioning inhibited psychological-mindedness, with no indication of change one way or the other. Denial was noted twice: One increased in denial; one simply of the presence of denial. Self-deception was noted twice, with no judgment of change being made once, and decreasing once. Narcissistic self-absorption was noted twice, with no judgment of change noted. Self-esteem was noted three times—twice decreasing, once simply being noted without judgment. A concrete nonintellectual, nonideational turn of mind was noted three times, without judgment as to change. Avoidance was noted once as decreasing. Alloplasticity was noted once with no notation of change.

No notation of change, it should be remembered, is not the same as saying there is no change. It simply reflects the fact that though the issues in question were mentioned as contributing to the inhibition of psychological-mindedness, no judgment was made as to change or lack of change presumably because of the difficulty of making such judgments confidently. The characteristic highlighting of these inimical influences to psychological thinking should contribute to the analysis of process underlying such discrete-sounding terms as *psychological-mindedness,* which may conceal as much as they reveal.

Summary

1. Psychological-mindedness, often discussed as if it were a somewhat homogeneous talent that people have or do not have, was assessed with respect to the intrapsychic components that would be expected to help or hinder thinking psychologically.

2. A substantial number of people (41%) failed to change in psychological-mindedness.

3. Those who had high psychological-mindedness before treatment increased in psychological-mindedness significantly more often than those who had low psychological-mindedness before treatment. Evidently psychological-mindedness builds on itself.

4. Focusing outward by way of projection and externalization was the major way (35%) patients inhibited their psychological-mindedness.

INSIGHT

Introduction

The research testers defined *insight* as "a change in some aspects of the patient's functioning brought about through and related to some increase in self-awareness." Insights, then, involve new self-awareness that results in change. This is a different and broader definition than the Wallerstein and Robbins (1956) one, which includes whether the patient sees his disturbed functioning as "maladaptive and as the proper object of therapy" (p. 245), whether it corresponds to the way others see it, the degree to which the discomfort is acknowledged as being an internal problem, and whether the patient is aware of some connection between "symptoms, behavior, and underlying conflict" (p. 245). As noted with respect to psychological-mindedness, the Wallerstein and Robbins definition tends to be narrow, having reference only to one particular insight, whether the patient knows he has a problem. Such a definition is more fitting at the beginning of treatment; the Rosen and Siegal one is more fitting for the time of termination.

Findings and Discussion

Degree of Insight Achieved

This refers to the amount of insight developed during treatment regardless of how much insight the person had at the beginning. Thus, this is a presumed measure of the effectiveness of the treatment in enabling the patient to develop insight. Data are:

Degree of Insight Achieved
++++ = considerable insight; +++ = moderate insight;
++ = little insight; + = minimal insight

++++ = 11; +++ = 8; ++ = 9; + = 6

Extent of Insight at Termination

This refers to the absolute amount of insight the person had at termination of treatment (regardless of whether he developed it during the treatment or not). Data are:

Extent of Insight at Termination
++++ = 8; +++ = 12; ++ = 10; + = 4

Comparing insight achieved during treatment with total insight available at termination offers an indication of whether insightful people gain relatively more in treatment, presumably because of their natural bent, as compared to those who are less insightful naturally. All eight of the persons who had a considerable degree of insight at termination also had developed a considerable degree of insight during treatment. Analysis of variance revealed a positive relationship between amount started with and amount ended with ($p < .001$). This suggests that people with a natural bent for insight use psychotherapy effectively to gain more insight. Only two patients judged as having a moderate amount of insight at termination and one judged as having little insight at termination developed a good deal of insight during treatment. At the other extreme, four patients who developed a minimal amount of insight during treatment had very little all told, while the remaining two who developed a minimal amount were considered as having only slightly more all told. Again, this suggests that natural inclinations strongly aid or inhibit the development of insight. Occasionally, however, it may be possible to aid a person to develop insight even though it has not been natural for him to that point. And this corresponds to clinical lore. Insightful patients are often offered psychotherapy on the supposition that they will "use" it better than those who are less insightful. And yet, as many clinicians will attest, every so often a patient who seems not to be insightful to begin with develops a good deal of insight in treatment. In principle, however, it should be possible to predict who these people will be on the basis of amount and quality of ideation and tolerance of anxiety.

Qualities of Insight

Range. Range refers to the number of areas of conflict, or other aspects of the self, about which insight has or has not been achieved. Four patients were described as having achieved a wide range of insight, while one was pointed out as not having achieved more than the narrowest kind of recognition, namely, that he was helped to recognize his loneliness. To say that someone has achieved a wide range of insights is not necessarily a ringing endorsement of his insightfulness. For example, the statement about one patient was sharply qualified with comments about the lack of depth in the wide range of insights he developed. With respect to another patient, it was recognized that the possible usefulness of his wide range of insights was diminished by his propensities for intellectualization.

Depth. As described by one of the research testers, depth is the degree to which insight is connected with its genetic roots. However, one might wonder whether the dimension of depth might still not be a meaningful one even if it did not extend as far as genetic roots. That is, certain behaviors could be understood as being connected with various unconscious aspects of the personality, e.g., defense mechanisms and character attitudes, without connections having been established through the full recovery of infantile memories and other genetic antecedents. Two persons were considered to have achieved considerable depth, 4 people were considered to have achieved partially deep insights, and 3 people were specifically pointed out as not having achieved depth of insight. The question of depth with respect to 1 person's wide range of insights remained equivocal. That only 10 patients were written about in this respect suggests that depth of insight is difficult to ascertain from tests. Again, depth of insight is not necessarily all to the good or by itself can hold the day; for example, one patient who apparently achieved deep insights could not manage to stick with the treatment in the face of the discomfort generated by such insights.*

Inferences about the Treatment. With seven patients, comments were made about the kind of treatment that was likely to give rise to the particular insights observed or absent. In two instances, the insights were considered to be expectable from expressive psychotherapy rather than from the psychoanalysis which these patients had. In two instances, the insights were considered to be those expectable in supportive treatments, which was the kind of treatment these patients had. In three instances, comments were made about the direct support received from the relationship with the therapist which, through design or not, limited the amount and depth of insight.

Insight Accompanied by Affect. Affect is, of course, an important aspect of insight, and the fact that affect was commented upon in only one instance surely does not imply anything to the contrary. It was most likely implicitly assumed to be included in the comments about range and depth of insight. By the definition used here, insight brings about change and, according to theory, useful insight must include affect. The one instance which was noted was an increase in the affect accompaniment to insight.

Durability. Another characteristic of insight is durability. In principle, something could have been said about durability in each patient. But only two direct references were made: One person showed

---

*This is an example of the occasional extratest information which found its way into the test write-ups.

an evanescent, unstable grasp of her insights; the other showed even less grasp, the suggestion being that his insight was simply mouthed rather than believed or experienced. Implicitly, those insights considered of considerable depth would be expected to be more durable, and those based on a noncritical attachment to the therapist might be less durable. But this is inferred from theory rather than being based on particular comments made about particular test performances.

Insights That Overwhelm. Three people were noted as having developed insights which proved too much for them to tolerate without having to leave treatment or being driven to increasingly maladaptive behaviors.

Insights Unaccompanied by Affect. Six persons were considered to have developed insight which was unaccompanied by affect. This was prominent with four of them and fairly prominent with two others. The insights of six others were considered as being heavily intellectualized.

Seeing Difficulties as Coming from One's Self. A particular aspect of insight, one which is central to the Wallerstein-Robbins definition of both insight and psychological-mindedness, is the degree to which the patient looks into himself for the causes of his difficulties. Eight persons were commented upon in this respect: Five of them developed insight into this way of explaining behavior, one developed a partial insight along these lines, and two failed to develop this way of viewing themselves. A variation of this quality is when the patient develops insight into his behavior as maladaptive, in effect seeing himself as "sick." Three people were mentioned in this regard. One developed a partial insight into this way of viewing himself, and two were not able to see themselves in this way.

Insight into Phallic-Oedipal Issues. Three patients were mentioned with respect to insight into phallic-oedipal issues: One was judged as not having developed any insight into his oedipal difficulties, one as having developed insight into her oedipal difficulties, and one as having developed insight into phallic-oedipal difficulties with a bit more emphasis on the phallic aspect than the oedipal.

Insights into Oral Dependency. Six persons were commented upon with reference to insight into oral-dependent issues: Four of them developed partial insight, one developed relatively full insight, and one failed to develop such insight.

Insight into Hostility. Five persons were commented upon with respect to insight into their hostility in general: One developed relatively full insight in this respect, three developed partial insight, and one failed to develop insight.

Hostility to Particular Kinds of Persons. Eight people were commented upon with respect to the insight they had developed in regard to their hostility toward a particular person or persons. One person achieved a partial insight into her hostility toward men in general and her mother in particular; one person developed relatively full insight with respect to his hostility toward his father; one person developed relatively full insight with respect to her hostility toward her mother; one person developed relatively full insight with respect to her hostility toward men; one person developed relatively full insight with respect to his hostility toward women; one person developed partial insight with respect to his hostility toward his father; one person failed to develop insight into his relationship with his father; one person failed to develop much insight into her hostility toward both men and women and mother in particular. Thus, eight people contributed 11 entries in this category.

Homosexuality. Insight into homosexual difficulties was noted in two cases, with both of them developing relatively full insights.

Sexual Identification. Insight into difficulties establishing sexual identifications was noted five times: Three persons developed relatively full insights into this problem; two developed partial insights.

Depression. Insight into depression was noted twice: One person developed relatively full insight, and one person developed partial insight.

Independence. Two persons were noted as having developed relatively full insight into conflicts over their need to be independent.

Alloplasticity. Three persons were commented upon with respect to developing insight into alloplasticity: One achieved partial insight with respect to this style of behavior; two failed to develop such insight.

Character Traits. One person failed to develop insight into her character trait of pseudostupidity while one did develop relatively full insight into her character trait of arrogance.

Relationships with Mother and Father. Relationships with mother and father were probably an object of insight with almost all patients, to a greater or lesser degree. However, this general issue was commented upon with respect to only three of them: Two developed insight into these relationships; one failed to develop insight into a relationship with father.

Loneliness. One person developed relatively full insight into his loneliness; one seemed unable to develop such insight.

Passive Masochism. Four persons, all men, were commented upon with respect to developing insight into passive-masochistic styles, with two of them having developed relatively full insight into this problem, and two having developed partial insight into it.

These categories include too few instances to offer proof or to indicate trends. They are mainly included to indicate the kinds of issues that occurred in the psychotherapy and which were judgeable from the tests.

Summary

1. Different people mean different things when referring to insight. The original Project definition of insight emphasized whether the patient knows he has a psychological problem. The research testers thought of insight as a change in the patient's functioning brought about and related to an increase in self-awareness.

2. Insights can be analyzed according to such formal qualities as range, depth, durability, whether they are accompanied by affect, are overwhelming, and of a kind likely to occur in supportive or expressive treatment.

3. Those who had more insight before treatment developed significantly more insight than those who had less insight to begin with. As with psychological-mindedness, insight seems to reflect capacities which psychotherapy can build upon, but not create. In short, "the rich get richer."

4. Insights were noted with respect to the following content: Phallic-oedipal, oral-dependent, hostility in general, hostility in particular kinds of persons, homosexuality, sexual identification, depression, independence, alloplasticity, character traits, relationships with mother and father, loneliness, passive masochism.

CORE NEUROTIC CONFLICTS

Introduction

The research testers felt they had a good deal of evidence for making comments about this variable, and felt comfortable and adequate in assessing it. This is hardly surprising as tests lend themselves easily to making dynamic or content inferences. In fact, many testers make only such inferences which, in our view, is an inadequate and constricted way of using tests.

The research testers advisedly categorized their inferences on the

basis of empirical salience for each patient rather than on *a priori* theoretical basis. The following categories were so derived:

1. Oral-dependent
2. Oral-aggressive
3. Oral-symbiotic with allied problems establishing ego boundaries
4. Anal
5. Phallic
6. Oedipal
7. Pseudo-phallic-oedipal (this category refers to superficially phallic-oedipal behavior which is better understood in pregenital terms)
8. Exhibitionism-voyeurism
9. Castration of males by females
10. Castration of self by males (the latter includes such inferences as humbling one's self with respect to authority, male masochism, avoiding activity in favor of passivity for purposes of avoiding situations felt as potentially castrating)
11. Homosexuality
12. Sexual identity in general
13. Female masochism
14. Hostile identifications with mother
15. Character problem more than neurotic conflict
16. Neurotic conflict verbalized more than lived out
17. Neurotic conflict revolving around the management of hostile impulses

These conflict categories are not necessarily precise and delimited theoretically; they are simply classifications of what the research testers
chose to highlight. For example, there are separate categories for "sexual identity," "castration of men by females," "castration of the self by
males," and "homosexuality." Obviously these are conceptually related—one can hardly think of homosexuality as being independent of
conflicts about and concerns about sexual identity or castration.

According to the ideal in psychoanalysis, core neurotic problems
would be resolved through their coming to consciousness by way of
verbal symbols with accompanying emotions. If "resolved" is used in
an ideal sense, such an ideal is often not achievable even in psychoan-
alyses considered generally as "successful." It certainly was imper-
fectly applicable to our population of patients, most of whom were far
less than ideal for strictly expressive treatment.

Findings and Discussion

Every patient tested at termination ($N = 34$) was written about
with respect to core neurotic conflicts. Of the 109 comments made

(more than 3 per subject), 81 noted change in conflicts brought about one way or another, and only 28 were considered to have come about through conflict resolution. Even these are stated tentatively and in terms of a modest degree of change. Different patients were judged as to the number of conflicts they had.

Degree of Resolution and Number of Conflicts
$+++$ = considerable resolution; $++$ = moderate resolution;
$+$ = slight resolution

$+++$ = 4 conflicts, 3 people; $++$ = 9 conflicts, 3 people;
$+$ = 15 conflicts, 8 people

Although the term *conflict resolution* has a definitive, all-or-none ring to it, these data fail to confirm such a way of thinking about it. Rather, conflicts are written about as being "somewhat" resolved, "fairly well" resolved, "considerably" resolved. Mastery over neurotic conflicts is likely to be partial rather than complete, and judgments are relative to the original severity of the conflict. Rather than a *state* of completeness, there seems to be a *dimension* of completeness. This dimension is presumably based upon the degree of connections between past and present and the adequacy of verbal symbols in comprehending the ramifications of the conflicts. A further complication is that neurotic conflicts are subject to vicissitudes of life, and may be activated from situation to situation. Conflict resolution seems best thought of as relative.

Change in the status of conflict, though without resolution, was possible through bringing conflicts into awareness.

Increased Awareness in Consciousness
34 conflicts, 13 people

Nineteen instances of change in core neurotic conflict came about through a variety of means other than through insight or through bringing conflicts into consciousness.

Miscellaneous Means of Change in Conflicts
$+$ = degree of change

$++$ = 15 conflicts, 8 people;
$+$ = 4 conflicts, 2 people

Other means of change in dealing with conflicts include: controlling effects of conflicts through increased defensiveness, development of an addictive relationship to the therapist, exhortation and direction by the therapist, gratification of orality through the treatment, becoming orally giving as a way of dealing with conflicts over orally taking, increased symptoms replacing phallic struggles, living out conflicts in a less self-damaging way through the creation of a particular identity or role, and changing the conflict terms from phallic-exhibitionism to oral.

Finally, 28 conflicts contributed by 12 people showed no change.

No Change in Conflicts
0 = 28 conflicts, 12 people

Notations from Table 1 are of number of conflicts converted to percentages (of the total of 104). A = no change; B = increased awareness of conflict in consciousness; C = resolution, with subnotations of 1, 2, 3 corresponding to small, moderate, and considerable degree of resolution; D = change other than through resolution with subnotations of 1 and 2 corresponding to small and moderate degree of change.

As can be seen from these data, the largest number of changes in conflicts occurred through patients developing an increased awareness in consciousness of neurotic conflicts. Two possibilities present themselves. Since emergence in consciousness would seem to be a necessary first step toward conflict resolution, it may be that these patients will build upon this awareness and demonstrate greater resolution of conflict as time goes on. Or this finding may suggest that conflict resolution is indeed a difficult thing to achieve, and even though many patients such as those studied in the Project can bring their neurotic conflicts to awareness, they may not be able to resolve them. If that is true, one would expect to see increases in anxiety, depression, and guilt—all affects that should be experienced more intensely as neurotic conflicts—become conscious. And, indeed, as the write-ups of these variables show, this was largely true with respect to test indices. There might also be increased "acting-out" as a means of dealing with conflicts which have become conscious but remain unresolved but we

Table 1. Percent Change in Conflicts

$$
\begin{aligned}
A &= 26\% \\
B &= 34 \\
C_1 &= 14 \\
C_2 &= 8 \quad\Bigr\} \quad = 26\% \\
C_3 &= 4 \\
D_1 &= 4 \quad\Bigr\} \quad = 18\% \\
D_2 &= 14
\end{aligned}
$$

have no data bearing on this. Finally, there might be instances of persons benefiting simply from their conflicts coming to consciousness despite the painful affects brought along in the process. This would be true particularly with those people who have warded off such knowledge and affects through alloplasticity.

Another piece of information supporting the idea that conflict resolution is much more difficult to achieve than bringing conflicts to consciousness is the fact that of the 26% notations of conflict resolution more than half are of the minimal variety, and only 4% of the conflicts were considered to have achieved "considerable" resolution. Eighteen percent (D_1 and D_2) achieved change, most of it of a moderate degree, through means other than conflict resolution and the coming to awareness of conflicts. If people whose conflicts changed in these ways could be demonstrated later to have achieved stability of change, and if they were rated high as to the success of their treatment, one would have to hypothesize that considerable therapeutic good can come about, at least in a population such as this, without conflict resolution and, in some instances, even without the patient's becoming more aware of his conflicts than he was previous to treatment. An analysis of this possibility is available in "Conclusions from Analyses of Single Variables" at the end of this chapter.

Analysis of variance comparing global change in neurotic conflicts with conflict resolution, increased awareness of consciousness, and other kinds of change revealed no significant difference, while all three together were significantly different from those who showed no change in neurotic conflicts. Thus, these data do not support the claim that one or another of these changes determines global change in neurotic conflict. Rather, these data suggest that all three kinds of change have an effect in bringing about change in neurotic conflict.

As to the kind of neurotic conflicts noted in this population (Table 2), 28% were oral-dependent, 12% were oral-aggressive, 4% were oral-symbiotic, a total of 44% for oral conflicts in general. If one takes castration of men by females, castration of self by males, homosexuality, and sexual identity difficulties in general as a group, then sexual difficulties account for 30%. Clearly, with a combined total of 74%, oral and sexual difficulties predominate in this population. Little massing of conflicts is noted along the other dimensions, and especially noteworthy is the finding of only one anal conflict, three phallic ones, and one oedipal one. Some of the great disparity between oral issues and those of other psychosexual levels may be caused by differing "response pulls" in the test material. Or it may be due to the ease with which people can express these kinds of difficulties (it is easier

Table 2. Percent Tabulation of Kind of Conflict
and Kind of Change in Conflicts

1. Oral-dependent
   $A = 36\%$ $C_2 = 4\%$
   $B = 25$ $D_1 = 4$
   $C_1 = 18$ $D_2 = 16$

2. Oral aggression
   $A = 50\%$ $D_1 = 8\%$
   $B = 16$ $D_2 = 16$
   $C_1 = 8$

3. Oral symbiosis
   $A = 50\%$
   $B = 25$
   $C_3 = 25$

for most people to say "milk" than "feces"). But even with such allowances it is likely that this population is weighted with oral fixations.

Notation: $A =$ no change; $B =$ increased awareness in consciousness; $C =$ conflict resolution; subnotations 1, 2, and 3 correspond to small, moderate, considerable; $D =$ change other than through conflict resolution; subnotations 1 and 2 correspond to small and moderate degrees of change.

Thus, for each of the three oral categories, no change occurs in the greatest number of instances, followed by increased awareness but not conflict resolution in the oral-dependent and oral-symbiotic categories, with change other than through resolution occurring second most often in the oral-aggressive category. A similar relationship holds when one combines all three oral categories: Forty percent of the notations do not change; 23% show increased awareness in consciousness; only 18% resolve conflicts, with 14 of these at a minimal degree; and 11% change without conflict resolution. The 40% "no change" in the oral categories suggests the resistance to change of orally fixated conflicts. Taking as a group notations of castration of men by females, castration of the self by males, homosexuality, and sexual identity difficulties in general (N of 30), it turns out that only 16% show no change, 60% show greater awareness in consciousness, and 23%, 20%, and 7% show conflict resolution of mild, minimal, and considerable degree, respectively. Sixteen percent show change without conflict resolution, 3% mild, and 13% moderate. Thus, as compared to oral difficulties and the group as a whole (which of course includes itself), sexual difficulties are less resistant to change than oral difficulties, and particularly likely to be brought into consciousness. They tend also to be more amenable to conflict resolution and to change without conflict resolution. Thus, with respect to all kinds of noted change, sexual difficulties seem more amenable to change than do oral ones. This finding lends some implied support to the general principle that the earlier the fixation, the more resistant it is to change.

Summary

1. Resolutions of neurotic conflicts were small in number and limited in degree.

2. Increased awareness of conflicts in consciousness was the most common kind of change. Since emergence in consciousness would seem to be a necessary first step toward conflict resolution, it may be that these patients will build upon this awareness and demonstrate greater resolution of conflict as time goes on. Or this finding may suggest that conflict resolution is indeed a difficult thing to achieve, and even though many patients can bring to awareness their neurotic conflicts, they may not be able to resolve them.

3. Some patients can achieve change in neurotic conflicts through a variety of means other than through conflict resolution or bringing conflicts to consciousness.

4. The greatest number of conflicts involved some variety of orality (44%). The second greatest number of conflicts involved some variety of sexuality (30%).

5. Sexual difficulties are less resistant to change than oral difficulties (16% "no change" as compared to 40% "no change"). This finding implies support for the general principle that the earlier the fixation, the more resistant it is to change.

AFFECT ORGANIZATION

Introduction

Affect organization is something of a wastebasket term. "Organization" suggests that it refers only to formal, structural properties of affects. Yet a mixture of formal and informal, structural and content statements are usually subsumed. Most often affect organization simply refers to what patients' feelings are and whether and how they are expressed.

Findings and Discussion

How much did affect organization change in these patients between the time of initial and termination testing? How much of this change was for the better? How much for the worse? Patients were ranked on a 7-point scale. Zero on this scale stands for no change or same (S). An ascending scale of $+1$, $+2$, and $+3$ stands for magnitude of change for the better, while a descending scale of -1, -2, and -3 stands for magnitude of change for the worse. Because affect organization is multidimensional, some patients were scored more than once, e.g., $+2$ for greater expressiveness, -1 for awkwardness of expression. These were summated algebraically for general categorization of better or worse, e.g., $+2$, -1, $= +1$. One patient, for example, achieved a $+1$ (mildly improved) on the basis of such statements as "greater overall affective responsiveness," and "the range of so-called acceptable affects seemed to have somewhat broadened." She also achieved -2 scale units on the basis of such statements as "inferred increase in affect breakthroughs and the inferred increase in irritability seemed particularly significant." Irrespective of whether the change was for the better or worse, 60 scale units of change occurred in these patients. Every patient except one ($N = 33$) was scored with respect to affect organization. The mean change for each patient, again irrespective of direction of change, is 1.7.

Change in Affect Organization
$+ =$ change for better; $- =$ change for the worse

$$+ = 12; \; ++ = 7; \; +++ = 2$$

$$- = 3; \; -- = 6$$

No change $= 3$

Change in affect organization tends to be all or none. Only seven patients were scored as being better in some ways, worse in other ways, and thus necessitating an algebraic summation for categorization of the above data as "better" or "worse."

A like amount of scaled change in people need not have the same consequences for each person, and may come about in different ways. For one thing, the people start at different points. For some people a little change represents a high proportion of the total and may make a lot of practical difference, while for other people a lot of change may represent a small proportion of the total and may make little practical difference. Thus, the scale units of change mean quite different things depending upon what personality organization the affect organization takes place in. Limited as they are in these ways, these data suggest that the major change in these patients was a small change for the better. In summary, affect organization seems highly amenable to change of one kind or another (in at least 97% of patients), and usually for the better (in 66% of the patients), the extent most often being judged as mildly improved (in 42% of the patients).

Turning from the amount of change, we ask *what* changed? Gross categorizations of affects included hostile, depressive, sexual, fearful, and passive-yearning ones. ("Depression" is referred to by such descriptive words as *abandonment, helplessness, dejection, weakness, desolation, futility,* and *loneliness.*)

How Different Kinds of Affects Changed
+ = change for the better; − = change for the worse
Hostile
+ = 11; − = 3;
No change = 1
Depressive
+ = 9; − = 9
Sexual
− = 1
Fearful
+ = 2; − = 5
Passive-Yearning
+ = 6

Only hostile affects and depressive affects are represented in numerically large terms. The relatively few references to the subtler affects, and to sexual affects, may reflect the unclarity and inadequacy of the theory of affects or the emphasis of the research tester, or, more likely, it may simply reflect the fact that hostility and depression are the most prominent affects in patients such as these.

The qualitative comments about 12 patients gave rise to a concept analogous to anxiety tolerance which might be called "affect tolerance." One patient tolerated affects rather than acting upon them; 3 patients could better modulate affective experience; 6 patients were more affectively responsive; 4 patients showed an increased range of affective experience; 2 patients were more adaptive in their expressions of affects. What these patients had was a newfound ability to experience and to use affects efficiently rather than to be frightened of the emergence of affects or to discharge them diffusely and awkwardly.

A hard-and-fast positive relationship between improved affect organization and the patient being rid of disturbing feelings does not appear, since three patients were judged improved in affect organization while showing at the same time an increase in depressive feelings. It may be that the "structures" improved sufficiently to allow the emergence of these feelings to be used perhaps as signals rather than acted upon. Of the eight patients who were judged to have worsened in their affect organization, however, only one showed a decrease in disturbing affect while the rest, as one might expect, showed an increase in disturbing affect.

Let us consider how some of these changes came about and what kinds of people showed what kinds of change. Affect organization was related to ideation-intellectualization 4 times, to isolation 2 times, to reaction formation 5 times, and to a pattern of denial-avoidance 10 times. Of the 10 patients with whom denial-avoidance was an issue, 5 showed improved affect organization and less denial-avoidance. One would think of this as the hoped-for pattern in expressive therapies, as these therapies tended to be. With the other 5 patients there was improved affect organization with increased denial, a pattern which one might expect from especially troubled and disorganized people for whom the rather primitive defenses of denial-avoidance might be all that was open to them in order to bring about improvement, and this seems to have been the situation with these patients.

Thus, for some people improvement in affect organization came about through their becoming more free and expressive. With other people improvement came about through their affects becoming more controlled and in the lessening of expressiveness. Patients likely to be labeled "neurotic" would be in the first group, and patients likely to be labeled "behavior disorders" would be in the latter group. The next question, then, is whether one or another of these groups changed for the better or for the worse with respect to affect organization. The Ns for the two groups came out to be almost identical ($N = 15$ for those who loosened control over affects and $N = 14$ for those who tightened control over affects). Four other patients were not considered as fitting in either group. Almost the same proportions and numbers of people in the two groups improved or got worse with respect to affect organization. In the "loosening" group 6 got worse and 12 improved. In the "tightening" group 5 got worse, and 11 improved. Put another way, about half the patients who improved in affect organization did so on the basis of loosening of affects, and the other half on the basis of tightening of affects. This is also true for those who got worse with respect to affect organization.

Was severity of difficulties with affects related to the degree of change for the better or worse in the tightening–loosening groups? The tightening group was split into three degrees of increasing severity of difficulty in affect organization, as judged at the time of initial testing. Of six patients in Group 1 ("mild"), four were better, one worse, and one at zero on the scale. (Remember, the zero refers either to no change, patient remains the same, or to worsening and improving changes which algebraically balance each other out to zero.) Of three patients in Group 2 ("moderate"), three improved and two worsened. Thus, in those patients who tightened their control over affects, there seems no substantial relationship between improvement in affect organization and the original degree of severity of affect difficulty. In those who loosened control over affects in the course of treatment, however, the rich seem to have gotten richer while the poor broke even. In Group 1 ("mild"), seven improved and two got worse. Among the more troubled patients in the "loosening" group, four improved and four got worse. (Only two groups were used since this group seemed too homogeneous to be scaled into three groups.)

Turning now for a qualitative look at how the patients did in treatment in general and in affect organization in particular, one can see certain groupings. In one group of 4, there was general improvement but the price of this improvement was troublesome affects, that is, patients were more aware of distressing feelings after treatment than they had been before. In another group of 13, general improvement coincided with better affect organization, described by such terms as *greater spontaneity, adaptiveness, appropriateness, modulation, positively toned experience.* In another group of 5, the patients generally got worse, and their affect organization got worse at the same time. In 3 patients the improved affect organization was probably heavily dependent on introjection of the therapist, and for 4 patients the change in affect organization was possibly unstable, in that there was a general air of flux about the situation.

Summary

1. Affect organization seems highly amenable to change (at least 97% of patients) and usually for the better (66% of the patients) most often judged as mildly improved (42%).

2. The major kinds of affects noted as changing were hostile ones and depressive ones.

3. Approximately one-third of the patients were described as having increased in their ability to experience and use affect efficiently

rather than being frightened of the emergence of affects or discharging them diffusely and awkwardly. This gives rise to the concept, "affect tolerance," analogous to anxiety tolerance.

4. Improvement in affect organization does not imply that the patient is necessarily rid of disturbing feelings, and in fact, troublesome feelings may increase as affect organization improves. Such a finding is consonant with some patients showing improved affect organization along with less denial-avoidance, an expectable pattern in expressive therapies. Another pattern was improved affect organization with more denial. Thus, for some people improvement in affect organization came about through their becoming more free and expressing, which could be called "loosening," while with others it came about through their becoming more controlled, "tightening." The proportion of patients in these two subgroups of tightening and loosening were almost identical, with half the patients improving in affect organization through loosening and the other half on the basis of tightening, and a quarter of the patients getting worse with respect to affect organization through loosening and another quarter through tightening. In the "tightening" group there was no substantial relationship between improvement in affect organization and the degree of severity of affect difficulty at initial. In the loosening group, however, those with relatively mild affect difficulty at initial tended to improve, while among those with more severe affect difficulty as many got worse as improved. In this group, as often ocurs in these analyses of data, the more serious the difficulty, the less amenable it is to change.

THOUGHT ORGANIZATION

Introduction

Thought organization is also not included in the original list of patient variables (1956), but the research testers considered it not only an important variable of intrapsychic change but one that can be assessed particularly well by psychological tests. Indeed, one of the major uses of psychological tests is to discern subtle disturbances in thought organization, which are often difficult to obeserve in other ways.

Many implications can be drawn from the way a person thinks—as many implications as there are people, since everybody has some kind of thought style. And particular thought styles have long been observed to correspond to various nosological categories. If one were to take the way a person thinks as an indication of the kind of person he is, *thought style* might be a more suitably encompassing term than *thought organization*. The latter, however, seems to have been chosen advisedly since most of the research tester's comments about this variable center around the organization of thought as this may reflect the organization or disorganization of ego functioning. Thus, in the data, most of the references to such dimensions of thought as abstract–concrete, rich–impoverished, slow–fast were inferred with a view toward the overarching question of disorganization of basic ego functions. Thought organization, like "decompensation," is often, therefore, jargon shorthand for psychosis.

Findings and Discussion

The gross distinction of "loosening" and "tightening," used in several of these test data analyses, is used here as well. While these distinctions do not stand up to highly precise logical analysis (as with much categorization of psychological functioning), they do reflect a way that clinicians, at least initially, organize their thinking about patients.

Loosening

"Loosening" refers here to a great number of ideas coming to mind, often at high speed, and often with distant, imprecisely linked associative ties and cause and effect relationships. Of the 33 people commented upon, 13 were considered to have loosened in their thought organization over the course of treatment. These 13 were divided as follows:

With Formal Disturbance. "Formal disturbance" refers to breaches of the "rules of secondary process thinking," such as: violations of logic; faulty observance of the boundaries between concepts or percepts; poor fit between the language symbol and the object as in dreams; or put to adaptive uses as in humor, art, and other creative thinking. Assuming the waking, relatively unaltered state of consciousness, the difference between adaptation and pathology is one of control, the ability to use thinking to achieve the appointed goal. Thus, the category of loosening with deviant formal properties is broken down with reference to the task at hand (the tests) into two other categories: (1) inadequate control, and (2) adequate control. The category, looseness with inadequate control, includes people who would be labeled by most clinicians as showing one or another variety of psychosis. Eight persons were included in this category. This is not meant to imply that these people necessarily got "worse" in a global way. One patient, for example, though his difficulties in thinking were more obviously expressed, nonetheless showed a greater encapsulation of it which, all things considered, could well have been a benefit for him. Another patient seems to have changed in the manifestations of his thinking but, on balance, seemed not to have necessarily worsened in this respect over the way he was before treatment. The third patient was described as so much in flux, so variable in his functioning, as to make a judgment of improvement or worsening extremely difficult. Another patient, though described as showing violation of formal properties of thinking, nonetheless showed these to a relatively mild degree, and there is some evidence to suggest beneficial consequences of this change for her total behavior. Four of the eight patients, however, showed a loosening of thinking judged as generally detrimental.

The category of loosening, along with added control, includes only two persons, both judged as having changed for the better in this respect. The research tester noted about one of them that with the diminution of repression both content and formal properties were more deviant but that "his grasp of reality seems to be even more sure than it was at initial test time, and the deviant ideation which does occur is more sporadic and circumscribed." It was expected that by the time of follow-up testing he would be using more conventional patterns of thinking. The other patient showed a loose thought organization, not necessarily any more loose than it was at the beginning, but now offered with much less anxiety which, unsatisfactory as it might be from one point of view, shows his acclimatization to it. Being less anxious about himself, he was, plausibly, less likely to indulge in anxiety-driven behaviors.

Without Formal Disturbances. In four patients, a loosening of thought organization was noted, but without a violation of formal characteristics of thought. Since the expressive aspects of psychotherapy involve, by definition, a loosening of thought by way of overcoming repressions and other inhibitions, this would seem an expectable and probably desirable development. In fact, it was considered desirable for expressive purposes in three of the four cases. In the fourth case, the loosening was so frightening to the patient that there was in response to it a secondary constriction. This did not hold and she terminated the treatment. Thus, for expressive purposes, loosening is desirable, but its pace and extent requires consonance with the patient's ability to tolerate new thoughts without undue discomfort (S. Appelbaum, 1977).

Loosening—14
+ = change for the better; − = change for the worse
1. With formal disturbance
   a. Inadequate control:
     − = 4; ? = 4
   b. Adequate control:
     + = 2

2. Without formal disturbance
   + = 3; − = 1

Tightening of Thought Organization

This refers to lessened productivity, lessened conceptual distance between ideas, and firmer boundaries between concepts and percepts. Twenty of the 33 patients were considered to have become more tight in their thought organization. These 20 patients can be divided into two major subgroups:

With Formal Disturbance at Initial. Thirteen patients showed a formal thought disturbance at initial. These can be divided, again, in a gross way which is nonetheless used clinically, into nonschizophrenic and schizophrenic looseness. A precise delineation of these two types would be difficult, lengthy, and require some arbitrariness since the term *schizophrenic* is used in different ways by different people. What is meant by this breakdown is that one category includes people variously labeled as schizoid and borderline whose basic ego functions are undependable and inefficient. Three patients were included in here. In the second subcategory are patients who would be labeled by many people as "infantile." Again, speaking quite grossly, these people become disorganized in their thinking in a way which seems more closely related to sweeps of affect and impulse than to dereistic, autistic fantasies and fundamentally distant object relations. Nine patients, clearly and unequivocally loose in infantile, nonschizophrenic ways before treatment, changed through tightening of their thinking. The 13th patient in this group was loose at initial in both nonschizophrenic and noninfantile ways, and he, too, showed tightening. His disorganization was due to an excess of anxiety to the point that the possibility of organicity was considered.

Tightening-20
1. With formal disturbance at initial-13
   a. Schizophrenic-borderline: + = 3
   b. Nonschizophrenic: + = 10
     (1) Infantile: + = 9
     (2) Noninfantile: + = 1

Without Formal Thought Disturbance. Six patients were not loosely organized before treatment and at the end of treatment were still more efficient and less symptomatic in their use of their ideational abilities. The research tester noted tighter connections between the activity of thought and the use of thought—between the means and the ends.

Changes in Thought Organization

These were judged on a 5-point scale with respect to "better" or "worse." The midpoint refers not to "no change" but to people whose change is of such a nature that it is difficult to say whether it is for the better or for the worse. On this scale $++$ refers to considerable change for the better, $+$ to a moderate change for the better, $-$ to a moderate change for the worse, and $--$ to a considerable change for the worse.

Changes in Thought Organization
$+ = 17; ++ = 7; 0 = 3; - = 4; -- = 2$

Of the three patients difficult to judge in this respect, one diminished in his use of projection in favor of greater denial, and increased in alloplasticity, which was described as an aid in his struggle against deviant autoplastic thinking. Yet the disorganization of his thinking was even more prominent than it had been at initial, though it was in some respects "encapsulated." Another patient showed evenly balanced but contradictory changes, a gain in IQ points, and a tightening up of expansive and syncretistically tinged approaches, along with increased looseness, fluidity, and paranoid thinking elsewhere on the tests. This variability was considered as evidence of his being in a state of flux at the time of testing, which precluded judgment of whether changes could be considered for the better or for the worse. Another patient also showed a mixed picture which included less depression and other discomfort, but more constriction in some respects along with more evidence of a loosening of thought processes in other respects.

In summary, then, 58% of these patients tightened in their thought organization after treatment, and 42% loosened. Except for the six patients whose loosening was unequivocally accompanied by lessened control over their thinking, and the one patient who was apparently made more anxious by the loosening than she could tolerate, these changes in thought organization, different in direction as they were, were generally favorable developments.

The degree of change for the better seems strongly related to the degree of disorganization to begin with. Of the 7 considered to have changed considerably for the better, 4 had a pronounced "infantile" disorganization of thought and 1 of them was considered to be brain-damaged as well; 1 thought in a disorganized way as a result of intense anxiety; and 1 showed depersonalization and estrangement experiences at least suggestive of the profound weakness in ego functioning often labeled as "borderline." The 17 people who showed moderate change for the better were less disorganized to begin with than these 7, except perhaps for 2 cases who had a long way to go but still improved only to a moderate degree.

From the preponderance of patients whose thought organization changed for the better (73%), one may conclude that thought organization is among the more modifiable intrapsychic variables, especially when it is a pronounced problem to begin with.

Summary

1. While in general thought style might be a more suitably encompassing term than thought organization, these analyses centered around the question of organization or disorganization of ego functioning.

2. "Loosening," referring to many ideas coming to mind, often at high speed, with distant, imprecisely linked associative ties and cause and effect relationships, was found to have occurred in 42% of the patients.

3. When loosening occurred with formal thought disturbance, this was generally considered as a worsening in thought organization, although occasionally it was not so considered, and even at times was associated with the assertion of new controls.

4. When loosening occurred in the absence of formal disturbance, it usually implied that a desirably expressive process had taken place, although in one instance the loosening had frightened the patient into a secondary constriction.

5. "Tightening" of thought organization, referring to less productivity, less conceptual distance between ideas, and firmer boundaries between concepts, occurred in 58% of the patients.

6. Of the 13 patients showing a formal thought disturbance before treatment, whether of an "infantile" or "schizophrenic" nature, all improved through tightening.

7. Of six patients who showed tightening without a formal thought disturbance before treatment, all improved through tightening.

8. Except for six patients whose loosening was unequivocally accompanied by less control over their thinking, and one patient who

was apparently made more anxious by the loosening than she could tolerate, changes in thought organization, whether in the direction of loosening or tightening, were generally favorable developments.

9. People most disturbed in thought organization before treatment changed more than those who were less disturbed in this way before treatment.

PATTERNING OF DEFENSES

Introduction

Judging whether patterns of defense have improved over the course of treatment or have become less efficient requires specification of the purpose of defense functioning. While one purpose of defense, by definition, is to minimize anxiety (or other affects), this is not always the criterion by which improvement is judged, especially during and after psychotherapy. For example, one would think of tightly organized, constricted patients as having their "goals" of stifling impulse achieved, according to one set of internal rules. These patients may come to treatment for an apparently unrelated complaint, or because life seems dry and meaningless to them. One treatment goal, then, is the loosening of defenses, with consequent increase of anxiety or other affects. Thus, according to the patient's old rules, the defenses are less efficient. According to the new rules—the treatment goals which may or may not at any particular time be shared by the patient—defenses are more "efficient." An additional complication is that defenses may allow too much impulse too quickly, as judged by an excess of anxiety and possible impairment of ego functions, a situation often called "decompensation" or "regression." Thus, "improvement" or "lack of improvement" requires judgment with respect to the overall clinical situation. The therapeutic process, designed for whatever speed or direction may be considered strategically best, is the overriding value; and defenses are considered to be efficient or inefficient with respect to how well they aid or hinder this process.

For the most part, the research testers did not know what the patient's and psychotherapist's goals were. What they did know was the outline of the patient's personality, the details of his intrapsychic assets and liabilities, and from these, in conjunction with their clinical know-how, they derived implicit psychotherapeutic strategies and goals. All other things being equal, the psychologist's understanding of therapeutic goals presumably should be similar to those of the therapist. This would be because of equal clinical sophistication, similar clinical frames of reference, and because the therapist's plans are based, at least in part, on the test findings.

Findings and Discussion

All 34 patients received test analyses of their *patterning of defenses*, which implies, not surprisingly, that the research testers felt tests are well able to shed light upon this variable.

Using the testers' overall understanding and judgment as the criterion, 26 of the 34 patients showed improved defense functioning.

Change in Defense Functioning
+ = change for the better; − = change for the worse
+ = 13; + + = 13; − = 5; − − = 3

Patterning of defenses showed a considerably greater incidence of improvement than did most other variables. In fact, more improvement was shown in defensive functioning in general than overall improvement through treatment. However, in a number of instances, the improvement was noted as being rather small. Further, improvement was probably more easily noticeable in those patients who were quite sick in loose or disorganized ways to begin with.

Loosening or Tightening

One general dimension by which patients can be categorized is whether their patterning of defenses requires "loosening" as in expressive treatment, or requires "tightening" as in supportive treatments.* Patients were placed on a scale of 1 to 4, corresponding to how "loose" (1 on the scale) or "tight" (4 on the scale) they were *before* treatment: Three patients were at #1 on the scale; 17 patients were at #2 on the scale; 11 patients were at #3 on the scale; 3 patients were at #4 on the scale.

Change in Loosening and Tightening
+ = change for the better; − = change for the worse
Loosening: + = 8; − = 7
Tightening: + = 17; − = 2

*Readers with psychotherapeutic experience will recognize the implied gross distinctions between the respective goals and methods of "expressive" and "supportive" treatment. Just as surely they will be able to think of finer distinctions and exceptions, e.g., a patient who under certain conditions is expressive, at other times requiring support, the expressiveness possible at the same time support is given, and the support possible at the same time expressiveness is encouraged. The terms are used here as general tendencies which for the practical purpose at hand is sufficient. For a conceptual discussion of these issues see Schlesinger (1969).

On this dimension the total improved is 25, and the total worsened is 9. The fact that, of the patients who loosened in their defensive functioning, about half as many worsened as improved calls attention to the fact that loosening of defenses can be a dangerous procedure. On the other hand, almost all instances of tightening of defenses resulted in improvement for the patient. Thus, considering this group as a whole, the major gain was in tightening loose defenses. Contrasting this with the relative lack of conflict resolution by design or inadvertently, most of these treatments were in significant respects "supportive psychotherapies." To that extent they succeeded rather well, at least with respect to defensive functioning. This is further supported in that 14 of the 17 patients benefiting from tightening were originally scaled at #2, or quite loosely organized, before treatment.

Flux

One tester noted that observable changes were unstable—in flux. Nine such instances were noted. Of the nine patients, five were in the scale #2 and in the category improved through tightening.

Decompensation-Regression

Originally comments about decompensation and comments about regressive lapses were kept separate, but the incidents under each was quite small and identical: Three patients improved from their "decompensation" and one patient worsened; the same was true for "regression"—three patients showed less regressive lapses and one showed more. Thus, by combining these two, six patients improved in these respects and two patients got worse. Actually, there seems little of value in this category except for the fact that the little value itself may tell us something. What it may tell us is the rather imprecise use of these terms so that quite dissimilar patients can be characterized by a comment about regressive lapses, and other dissimilar patients can be characterized by a comment about decompensation of defenses. That *only* eight people got either kind of comment is probably happenstance. Technically speaking, decompensations of defenses, character, ego functions, and regressions from libidinal levels could be remarked upon in all people who have gotten to the point of becoming psychiatric patients. And one cannot say that the terms were used here only in instances of severe difficulties because some patients with quite severe difficulties were not commented upon in this respect while some with less difficulties were.

Kinds of Defenses Used

Here are listed a variety of defense mechanisms, patterns of defenses, and other defense processes (Siegal, 1969). Unlike the previous category where change was described with respect to improvement or worsening according to the overall clinical understanding of the patient, in this category change is noted below with respect to an increased use of the defense or a decreased use of defense irrespective of whether this change is for the better or not.

The single most used defense was denial ($N = 26$): Eleven showed increased denial, 15 showed a decreased use of denial. Approximately half as many, or 14 as compared to 26, used avoidance. But of the 14 persons who used avoidance, 12 also used denial, which supports the clinical notion that avoidance is an extreme of denial. Of the 14 persons using avoidance, 4 showed increased avoidance, 10 showed decreased use of avoidance. Taking avoidance and denial together as a unit gives us a total of 38 instances. Adding regression and constriction to avoidance and denial (all four of them being considered clinically as highly correlated ways of blotting out ideas) gives 54 instances of 149 instances of defense. This is the greatest cluster of defense patterns or groupings. Eight persons were noted as relying extensively on repression, with 3 increasing in this use over the course of treatment, 4 decreasing in its use, and 1 remaining the same in this respect. Eight persons employed constriction as a defense: 5 showed increased constriction after treatment, 2 showed decreased constriction, and 1 remained the same in this respect. It might be well to note that surely repression is operative in all of the cases. That these 8 were singled out in this respect is to some extent happenstance. They do not, in fact, seem to be the most "repressed" of the patients. With respect to constriction, it is unlikely that the 5 patients considered as becoming more constricted were considered to have become so *in toto,* but rather there was a shift in the impulse-defense configuration resulting in greater constriction in some respects.

The next most commonly used single defense was projection ($N = 20$). Of these, 13 came to rely less on projection while 7 increased in their use of projection. All but the latter 2 are people who in a number of ways seem to have gotten worse during the course of treatment, and so their increased use of projection is probably on the basis of greater recourse to what is ordinarily considered a fairly primitive defense. The latter 2 evidently increased in their use of projection as part of intrapsychic shifts without its implying worsening or ego regression in general.

The next grouping of defenses, 41 instances, are those ordinarily considered in the general category of obsessive-compulsive defenses ($N = 41$). These include: reaction formation ($N = 7$), with 1 person relying upon this more, 4 persons relying upon it less, and 2 persons remaining the same in this respect; isolation ($N = 8$), with 3 people showing increased use of isolation, 3 people showing decreased use of isolation, and 2 people remaining the same in this respect; intellectualization ($N = 10$), with 5 people showing increased intellectualization, 3 people showing lessened intellectualization, and 2 people remaining the same. The use of fantasy in ruminations and obsessional thinking occurred 6 times with 2 people showing increased reliance on this defense, 3 people showing decreased use, and 1 person remaining the same. This "pure-culture" use of ideation for defense purposes was kept separate from changes in ideation in general of which there were 10. Six people increased their use of ideation in general; 4 people decreased in this respect. Adding use of ideation in general to reaction formation, isolation, ruminative-ideation, and intellectualization results in a total of 41 instances as compared to the 54 associated in the repression-constriction-avoidance-denial grouping. These two clinically familiar clusters of defense, adding up to 95, account for 64% of the 149 instances of defenses mentioned. Projection with 20 instances accounted for 14%. The remaining 34, or 23%, are spread over eight categories. These latter categories include: autoplastic, with 3 people becoming more autoplastic and none less so; externalization, with 2 people increasing in this respect and 4 people decreasing in it; suppression and conscious deception, with 3 people using such devices more and 2 using them less; somatization, with 1 showing an increase and 1 remaining the same; alloplasticity, with 3 becoming increasingly alloplastic and 4 becoming less so. Finally, remarks about paranoia as a defense were made in 3 instances with 2 people becoming increasingly paranoid and 1 becoming less so.* Finally, character defense was rated 3 times, counterphobia and pseudostupidity diminished, while in 1 instance counterphobia increased.

What Defenses Are Directed Against

Only 28 references were made to the "content" aspects of defensive patterns, namely, what defenses were used against. This may imply something of a predilection on the part of the research testers

*Speaking of paranoia as a defense, of course, raises a number of conceptual problems such as whether it can be considered a descriptive category without defensive purposes; that is, with projection as the defense and "paranoia" as the diagnostic label.

for formal aspects of test data, but it also suggests that specific content may be difficult to see as being linked directly with defensive patterning. A possible implication here is that defensive patterning with many patients achieves a kind of autonomy, and so can be described in its own terms and without reference to what generates it. Defenses were directed against the expression of aggression in eight instances, with more defenses having to be enlisted for this purpose by one person, with seven people having to use defenses against aggression less. Again, this may be to the good if the patient began with too tight controls over the expression of aggression. This was so with four of them, scaled 3 or 4 on the scale of tightness. Or it may reflect an unfortunate loosening of controls over aggression, as it did with two of these patients. Defenses were noted as being enlisted against depression seven times, with one person having become more defensive in this respect and six becoming less so. Seven persons were noted to have enlisted defenses against oral wishes with two persons having to use increased defenses of this kind and five using less. The lack of references to defenses being used against the anxiety generated by sexuality is surprising. Heterosexuality was noted only once in this regard, and homosexuality once.

Summary

1. Improvement in patterns of defense was judged with respect to the total personality and in the light of the assumed goals of the treatment. Defensive patterning showed a considerably greater incidence of improvement than did most of the variables, with 77% of the patients improving in this respect, although the improvements were often noted as being rather small and particularly noticeable in patients who were loosely organized to begin with.

2. Of patients who loosened in their defensive functioning about half as many worsened as improved, suggesting that the loosening of defenses can be a dangerous procedure.

3. In almost all instances tightening of defenses resulted in improvement. Contrasting this with the relative lack of conflict resolution reported previously suggests that changes for the better, by design or inadvertently, were, in significant respects, of a supportive nature.

4. The single most used defense was denial (77%).

5. Of the 14 patients who used avoidance, 12 of them also used denial, which supports the clinical notion that avoidance is an extreme of denial.

6. If one takes avoidance and denial together and adds repression and constriction—all being ways of blotting out ideas—this is the major cluster of defense patterns.

7. Obsessive-compulsive defenses—reaction formation, isolation, ruminative-ideation, and intellectualization—constituted the other major pattern of defense functioning (28%).

EGO STRENGTH

Introduction

Two rather different definitions of ego strength seem to have been used in making these evaluations. One, more lenient than the other with respect to being a criterion for improvement, corresponds to the standard Wallerstein and Robbins definition, namely, considering ego strength as an index of adequacy of coping with external and internal stresses. The implication of this conception is the rather circular one that improved overall adaptive behavior is a function of improved ego strength since, by definition, the ego is coping more adaptively with stresses. Yet, in other instances, patients were considered to have remained unchanged in ego strength despite their improved behavior. The implication of this latter, more stringent conception of ego strength, is that ego strength represents a more fundamental given, a sort of machinery which can, by putting oil on its clanking parts, be made to function better even though not structurally improved. One patient is perhaps the best example of this conception. His ego strength was scored as remaining the same despite the clear and considerable improvement in his behavior. (His improved behavior was judged to be a function of variation in character styles, and was considered to be tenuous. This is not to say that the variation necessarily responded to its intrinsic rhythm and was merely on the upswing at termination but rather to imply that psychotherapy had helped him bring forth the more efficient end of his range of adaptability.) Another patient's behavioral improvement was said to be based on borrowed ego strength rather than improved ego strength. On the other hand, another patient was judged to have developed "a slight rise" in ego strength, "using ego strength as a sort of a general index of current functioning. . . . While her present functional ego strength may be slightly greater than it was, there has been little or no basic change." On the basis of the latter comment, she was scored as not having an increase in ego strength. That conception of ego strength, as being separable from change in behavior, is the one adhered to most often in these write-ups. There is continued unclarity, however, as can be seen, for example, in the following write-up: "If by ego strength we mean to imply the ability more accurately and adaptively to appraise reality and its personal implications so as to be able to behave in ways more gratifying and advantageous, then there has been a clear increase in ego strength." The *if* at the beginning of the sentence concretizes the unclarity of the definition. With the liberal definition there should be no doubt about the increase in ego strength. If the stricter conception were applied, this patient would be considered not to have an increase in ego strength.*

Findings and Discussion

Ego strength is a variable which lends itself readily to evaluation on psychological tests, and so there is a comment about ego strength on each of the patients ($N = 34$). The following are the categories of comments and judgments made about ego strength and the quantitative findings with respect to these judgments.

Change in Ego Strength

Seventeen people showed an increase in ego strength. Six people showed a decline, and 11 people remained the same in this respect. On the face of it, it may seem rather discouraging that only slightly more than 50% of the patients showed a gain in ego strength. When one keeps in mind the two aspects of ego strength attended to, however, these figures are an underestimate (as a measure of coping and adaptation, and of fundamental intrapsychic functions). The 17 instances of improved ego strength, in a fundamental sense, can be taken as clear and unequivocal instances since it is difficult to think of improved ego strength in the fundamental sense which would *not*

---

*In one of the Project's other quantitative studies (Kernberg *et al.*, 1972) an attempt was made to define ego strength on the basis of the factor analytic study of the patient variables, not including psychological tests. In this definition, ego strength was considered a combination of (1) the degree of integration, stability, and flexibility of the intrapsychic structures (including variables such as patterning of defenses and anxiety tolerance, and, implicitly, the concepts of impulse control, thought organization, and sublimatory channeling capacity); (2) the degree to which relationships with others are adaptive, deep, and gratifying of normal instinctual needs (corresponding to the variable quality of interpersonal relationships); (3) the degree to which the malfunctioning of the intrapsychic structure is manifested directly by symptoms (corresponding to the variable severity of symptoms).

show itself in adaptive behavior. Several other patients, if judged more leniently on the basis of improved behavior alone, would probably have been scored as showing an increase in ego strength rather than as showing a decrease or as not having changed ego strength. The conceptual unclarity noted here gives rise to the next category.

Hypothesized Definitions of Ego Strength

In three instances the research tester, for some reason, specified a particular definition in the course of making his judgment of ego strength. This need to offer a definition, when a definition is already specified in the glossary, affirms the unclarity of this variable. The Project's difficulties in this regard reflect an unclarity in the clinical world at large.

Decompensation

The term *decompensation* is jargon for recent outbreaks of psychosis. More generally it means that one mode of adjustment has failed in its function and given way to another, and this other may or may not be psychotic. The general, inclusive meaning was used by the research testers. Four persons were considered to have reversed the decompensatory trend while two were considered either to have continued down the path of decompensation or to have begun such a path during the treatment.

Intrinsic Ego Defect

This refers to those instances, referred to specifically by the research testers, when persons have developed early, implicitly structural defects which have a strongly inhibiting effect on what they are able to accomplish through life in general, and in treatment specifically. Nine people had this comment made about them. In view of other Project test findings and clinical lore, namely, that severely ill people find it harder to improve in treatment than those less severely ill, one might expect that a preponderance of these people would have worsened or remained the same with respect to ego strength. On the other hand, people with severe difficulties have further to go, and on this basis might more easily show improvement. Two patients worsened, three remained the same, and four improved. So no clear trend emerges from this small sample.

Tenuousness of Change for the Better

The research tester commented that the observed changes for the better in 10 patients were tenuous ones. For 3 of them, tenuousness was on the basis of limits set by their fundamental ego defect. For 8 others, tenuousness was on the basis of the lack of impressive improvement in ego strength. (This was another example of the tester's thinking of ego strength as independent of improved behaviors.) In 4 patients behavior was considered to be improved primarily because of borrowed ego strength, and the research testers were leery of the ability of these patients to continue maintaining and using the introjected therapist in this way.

Controls

This refers to ego strength reflected in management of affects and impulses to action. Seven persons were judged to have improved ego strength in this respect, four were considered to have worsened in this respect, and three were judged to have remained the same.

Ideation and Reality Testing

In this category, ego strength is measured by ideational accuracy and reality testing in general. Six persons were judged to have improved in this respect, six were considered to have worsened in this respect, and three remained the same.

Defensiveness

This refers to changes in defenses which are considered to reflect changes in ego strength. Eight people were considered to have improved in their patterning or use of defenses, two people were considered to have worsened in this respect, and three people were considered to have remained the same.

On the 84 judgments on which ego strength was based, covering 10 categories, 50% were made on the basis of the 3 categories—controls, ideation, and defensiveness.

Adaptive Behavior

Here, the research tester specifically made judgments according to increased efficiency in coping with internal and external stresses as seen by adaptive behavior. Nine persons were judged to have improved in their adaptive behavior. Of these, five also showed increased ego strength. Three remained the same in ego strength despite more adaptive behavior, and one worsened in adaptive behavior while worsening in ego strength.

Borrowed Ego Strength

Here the patient was considered to have borrowed ego strength, a phenomenon described by the research tester as being based on introjection of the therapist. Four patients were so described. Of these, three were judged to have remained the same in ego strength despite their ability to "borrow," while one was considered not only to have borrowed but to have integrated so that his ego strength could be judged as having improved.

Symptoms as an Expression of Ego Strength

Here the increase or diminution of symptoms was taken as an indication of changes in ego strength. Two patients were considered to have improved in ego strength in that their symptoms had diminished, while one had worsened in this regard in that her symptoms had increased.

Ego Strength on the Basis of Change in Character

Two patients were considered to have shown improvements in their character, which was taken as a reflection of increased ego strength; one no longer devalued herself so badly, and another no longer was masochistically submissive, which had showed itself in impaired ego functions.

Summary

1. Slightly more than 50% of the patients showed a gain in ego strength.

2. Judgments of ego strength suffered from two conceptions or definitions of ego strength being used. At times ego strength seemed to refer simply to improved behavior. At other times ego strength was defined primarily with respect to intrapsychic functioning. While both of these are, in a sense, behaviors, the second more stringent conception of ego strength is based upon change in underlying ego functions, rather than simply improved or more adaptive end-products of

such functions. (Such discriminations can be made, among other ways, by inferring the process by which a response comes about as well as the response itself.) Since the most stringent conception of ego strength was most often used by the research testers, the 50% refers to unequivocal changes in ego strength, which would have been higher if based on the more lenient, less demanding conception of it.

3. Issues taken up with respect to ego strength include decompensation, intrinsic ego defect, tenuousness of change for the better, controls, ideation and reality testing, defensiveness, adaptive behavior, borrowed ego strength, symptoms as an expression of ego strength, change in character on the basis of ego strength, and brain damage.

ANXIETY TOLERANCE

Introduction

The Wallerstein and Robbins definition of *anxiety tolerance*, "the capacity to experience anxiety without having to act to discharge it (p. 245), is changed here to the one formulated by Siegal and Rosen (1962), "the ability to use anxiety as a signal rather than being overwhelmed by primary anxiety or being fearful of being overwhelmed by it." With this revised definition, it became possible to assess each individual with respect to anxiety tolerance, rather than limiting observations only to those people who act upon the environment, as required by the Wallerstein and Robbins definition.

In going through the data and picking out the categories of comments used to describe change in this variable, the following conceptual problem arose: Increase or decrease in anxiety tolerance was related in the research tester's write-ups to defense in general, to ideation, reality testing, impulse control, autoplasticity, and alloplasticity, with improvements in any or all of these going along with improved anxiety tolerance. What is unclear, however, is whether changes in these make possible a rise in anxiety tolerance, or a rise in anxiety tolerance makes possible such improved functioning; in short, whether these aspects of the person are *causes* or *effects* of increased anxiety tolerance. All of these characteristics, and anxiety tolerance as well, could be considered aspects of ego functioning. In that case there should be a high correlation between ego strength and these categories.*

* A factor analytic study (see Chapter 5) does in fact show that these structural variables are highly correlated.

Unlike many of the variables in which an increase or decrease, in and of itself, tells little of whether the change was for the better or worse, an increase in anxiety tolerance, as defined here, is beneficial.

Findings and Discussion

Change in Anxiety Tolerance ($N = 34$)

Anxiety tolerance changed more than most of the other variables, and such changes predominantly were for the better. Some change occurred in 27 of 33 patients, and 20 of the 27 (74%) showed improvement, i.e., an increased anxiety tolerance. One patient could not be judged one way or the other.

Changes in Anxiety Tolerance
+ = small increase; + + = moderate
increase; + + + = large increase;
− = small decrease; − − = moderate decrease

+ + + = 8; + + = 11; + = 1;
− = 5; − − = 2;
No change = 6

The Experience of Anxiety

Of the 34 patients, 11 experienced more anxiety and 7 experienced less anxiety. As one would expect on the basis of clinical observation, and as conceptualized by Siegal and Rosen (1962), it would not be expected nor was it found that an increase in anxiety tolerance is the same thing as an increase or a lessening in the experience of anxiety. Five patients showed both greater experience of anxiety and higher anxiety tolerance. Such people were considered to have achieved a sufficient tolerance of anxiety so as to allow anxiety into consciousness and to give up the maladaptive attempts at warding off anxiety. Four patients showed less experience of anxiety and greater anxiety tolerance. Such persons were able to reduce the anxiety already in consciousness to smaller, signal quantities. Four patients showed greater anxiety in consciousness, a flooding with primary anxiety, from which was inferred lowered anxiety tolerance.

Anxiety Used as a Signal

Anxiety was used as a signal in 10 instances with 8 of these showing increased use of anxiety as a signal and 2 showing anxiety being less used as a signal. By definition, in each of the 8 instances of increased use of anxiety as a signal there was increased anxiety tolerance; in both instances where anxiety was used less as a signal there was decreased anxiety tolerance.

Primary Anxiety

There were three instances of an increase in primary anxiety and seven instances of lessened primary anxiety. Again, by definition since primary anxiety is the panic that comes when controls are felt as lost, the three instances of increased primary anxiety are associated with decreased anxiety tolerance, and the seven instances of decreased primary anxiety are associated with increased anxiety tolerance.

Related Characteristics of Anxiety Tolerance

The following characteristics are related to changes in anxiety tolerance (whether such characteristics are causes or effects of changes).

Better Use of Defenses. Numerically most important characteristic related to change in anxiety tolerance: Twelve people showed better use of defenses, four people showed poorer use of defenses, and one person remained the same in this respect. Again, all four people showing poorer use of defenses showed decreased anxiety tolerance, and all showing better use of defenses showed an increased anxiety tolerance except for one who was judged to be the same in anxiety tolerance. The high positive relationship between anxiety tolerance and defenses is clear.

Alloplasticity-Autoplasticity. Notations of alloplasticity as being related to change in anxiety tolerance were made 9 times, and notations about autoplasticity in this connection were made 5 times for a total of 14. Of the 9 notations of alloplasticity, 6 were of greater alloplasticity and 3 were of less. Of the 6 who became more alloplastic, 3 showed an increase of anxiety tolerance. These three presumably became less anxious about acting, and so were judged to have developed greater anxiety tolerance. Two of the 6 showed lower anxiety tolerance. These people seemed driven toward alloplasticity as tension mounted which could not be "tolerated" or absorbed with the use of existing defenses. In the third instance the research testers could not decide whether anxiety tolerance had increased or lowered in connection with the increased alloplasticity. All 3 patients showing lessened alloplasticity showed at the same time increased anxiety tolerance; 2 of these showed increased autoplasticity, presumably having developed greater capacities to bind anxiety ideationally, which allowed them to give up previously used, maladaptive alloplastic behaviors. The third person showed diminished primary anxiety in connection with rearrangements of defense patterns. Corroborative of the impression that autoplasticity and alloplasticity are not simply extremes of a single dimension is the fact that not all patients were noted as being lower in one and higher in the other or vice versa.

Five persons were judged to have become more autoplastic and no patients were remarked upon as having become less autoplastic. Of those who became more autoplastic, four did so in connection with heightened anxiety tolerance and one remained the same in anxiety tolerance. This finding is corroborative of what might be expected clinically: Although there is not a perfect relationship between alloplasticity and autoplasticity, one would expect a general tendency for people to internalize conflicts during psychotherapy. People who become more autoplastic during treatment—that is, internalize their conflicts—develop, as a cause or a consequence of this, greater anxiety tolerance.

Better Reality Testing. Three people considered to have developed better reality testing showed at the same time greater anxiety tolerance. One person showed weakened reality testing and in conjunction with this showed less anxiety tolerance. Two persons remained the same with respect to reality testing, one showing a slight increase in anxiety tolerance and the other remaining the same in anxiety tolerance.

Ideation. Ideation was mentioned specifically in three cases. Two showed higher anxiety tolerance with increased ideation, and one showed less ideation with anxiety tolerance remaining the same. It is noteworthy that all three patients were not mentioned under autoplasticity, suggesting that the testers were making the fine distinction between autoplasticity and ideation.

Summary

1. Improvements with one or more of the following went along with improved anxiety tolerance: defense in general, ideation, reality testing, impulse control, autoplasticity, and alloplasticity. This gives rise to the conceptual difficulty of whether changes in these variables make possible a rise in anxiety tolerance, or if a rise in anxiety tolerance makes possible such improved ego functioning in general.

2. Anxiety tolerance changed more than most of the other variables (82%) and such change was usually for the better (74%).

3. An increase in anxiety tolerance did not invariably go along with a lessening of the experience of anxiety. Some people showed

both greater experience of anxiety and higher anxiety tolerance. Such people were considered to have achieved a sufficient tolerance of anxiety so as to allow anxiety into consciousness and to give up maladaptive attempts at warding it off. Other people showed less experience of anxiety and greater anxiety tolerance, evidently being able to reduce the anxiety already in consciousness to smaller, signal quantities. Still other patients showed increased anxiety in consciousness, even a flooding with primary anxiety, from which was inferred lowered anxiety tolerance.

ALLOPLASTICITY*

Introduction

The research testers found the original definition of the variable *alloplasticity*—"What is the nature and extent of the expression of the illness on the environment and what are the *deleterious* consequences to the environment?" (Wallerstein & Robbins, 1956, p. 243)—unsuitable for their purposes because "effect on the environment" cannot be seen through psychological tests. Later on in the Project a committee working on a glossary of terms made formal the following definition of alloplasticity which is the one the testers used: "By alloplasticity, we mean an individual's characteristic tendency to attempt to dispel or ward off consciousness of an affect (particularly anxiety) and its associated ideas through motor action (whether this leads to adaptive or maladaptive consequences). The individual may be entirely unaware of the connection between the threatening affects and his behavior."

The opposite of this propensity would seem to be "an individual's characteristic tendency to attempt to dispel or ward off consciousness of an affect (particularly anxiety) and its associated ideas through perceptual and cognitive means alone. This generally implies the function of one or more of the classically described mechanisms of defense." And there we have just defined the term *autoplasticity*.

The notion of there being a continuum between allo- and autoplastic behavior is supported by the finding in an analysis of variance ($p < .01$) that those who changed most in the direction of autoplasticity became less alloplastic. However, it is not *always* true that alloplasticity and autoplasticity are in reciprocal relationship. Many people became more of both or less of both. For such people alloplasticity and autoplasticity are not polar opposites. Each characteristic

*Original draft and analysis of data by Dr. Siegal.

had a range of its own. The findings were analyzed to help with this question.

Findings and Discussion

Quantitative estimates were made of the degree to which *an individual* decreased in alloplasticity (a slight reduction, a major reduction, or no change) and, on the other end of the scale, the degree to which he increased in alloplasticity (a slight increase or a major increase). Under the category "no change," we placed those people who demonstrated no quantitative change in alloplasticity, with more to begin with from those who showed no change in the amount they had to begin with.

Change in Alloplasticity ($N = 34$)

$- = $ less; $+ = $ more

$- = 4$; $-- = 7$;

No change $= 10$;

No change and none to begin with $= 3$;

$+ = 10$

While the research tester did not weigh autoplasticity separately, many comments were made on autoplasticity from which some estimate of the degree of its presence or absence or change could be extrapolated. We collated these in a similar way to the variable alloplasticity, though the findings may not be comparable to those made up of direct judgments of an explicitly stated variable.

Change in Autoplasticity

$+ = 6$ $++ = 6$;

No change $= 16$; No change and none to begin with $= 3$;

$- = 3$

With respect to alloplasticity, the largest single category was of those persons who changed quantitatively. This does not imply, however, that there had been no qualitative changes in this variable for these people. For example, about one patient it was noted, even though she seemed unchanged in the degree of her alloplasticity, that her ego seemed "more active in securing gratification for itself." Another patient, a very alloplastically oriented individual, showed a minor increase in autoplasticity but no change in alloplasticity. The change that was noted from the beginning of therapy until after therapy was that he developed a streak of paranoia, an autoplastic development, but this outlet did not take any of the pressure off his alloplastic rage outbursts and impulsive acts.

Unfortunately, for our purposes, most patients show no quantitative change in either of these variables. There are, however, eight cases in which decreased alloplasticity goes along with increased autoplasticity, and one case in which decreased autoplasticity goes along with increased alloplasticity. Thus, nine cases support the hypothesis that there is only one variable involved here, and that if one becomes more alloplastic he is likely to become at the same time less autoplastic. On the other hand, instances where it is clear that a patient has become both more alloplastic and more autoplastic at the same time tend to negate this. One sees such negation, clinically, in patients whose delusions (an autoplastic phenomenon) coincide with unrestrained impulsive action.

These data should alert the reader not to make the stereotyped assumption that an increase in autoplasticity necessarily leads to a decrease in alloplasticity or vice versa. This assumption is often tacitly made when we assume, for example, that if we stop the patient's acting-out, he will become not only anxious but more ideational and more willing to reveal himself. While it is quite clear that this does happen sometimes, perhaps even a majority of the time, it is also clear, in theory as well as in practice, that there is no reason to believe that it will happen all the time.

Drawing conclusions about alloplasticity is hampered by the problem (as with symptoms) of trying to extrapolate from intrapsychic material to behavior in the outside world, a risky and difficult procedure. Most of the test write-ups on alloplasticity do not contain any statement as to what the activity may actually be except in a few instances where it is clear that drinking or drug addiction is present. Other activities that were specified include impulsive uncontrollable behavior, breakthroughs of affect including rage attacks, low frustration tolerance leading to a need for immediate gratification and of the bad consequences if such gratification is not forthcoming.

Not surprising, on the basis of theoretical considerations, is the frequent mention of orality in connection with alloplasticity. Much of the alloplastic behavior represented in this population sample is drinking or some other kind of activity usually understood as being primarily oral.

Summary

1. If by alloplasticity we mean the attempt to ward off consciousness of an affect and its associated ideas through motor action, then the approximate opposite would be to attempt to ward off conscious-

ness of an affect and its associated ideas through perceptual and cognitive means, which would be one way to define autoplasticity. To a statistically significant degree those who changed most in the direction of autoplasticity became less alloplastic, suggesting that these two are on a continuum.

2. Despite the statistical finding of there being a continuum between alloplasticity and autoplasticity, there are patients who do not conform to this scheme, for example, those patients whose delusions, an autoplastic phenomenon, may coincide with unrestrained impulsive action. Thus, the stereotyped assumption that if we stop a patient's "acting-out," he will become more anxious and ideational will often be borne out, but there is no reason to believe that it will happen all the time or should be attempted without closer diagnostic understanding than the rule of thumb allows.

EXTERNALIZATION*

Introduction

The Wallerstein and Robbins (1956) definition of *externalization*—the extent [to which] the patient ascribes his "illness (or his difficulties) to forces beyond his control rather than accepting responsibility for his behavior and seeing the need to effect changes in himself" (p. 245)—was essentially the definition used by the research testers. Four aspects of externalization were discernible in the write-ups: (1) The initial presence of externalization; (2) the direction and magnitude of change in externalization seen at termination; (3) defensive patterns on which the externalization rested, and realignments in defensive functioning accompanying changes in externalization; and (4) changes in other aspects of functioning concomitant with externalization.

Findings and Discussion

In assessing the extent of externalization at initial, we rated the patients on a 3-point scale: 0= a minimal or insignificant degree of externalization; 1= the use of externalization to a moderate degree; and 2= externalization was a marked or prominent aspect of the patient's functioning. We were able to make a rating before treatment in 33 of the 34 cases. One case could not be assessed because of sparsity of data.

* Original draft and analysis of data by Dr. Rosen.

In only five cases was externalization rated initially as minimal or insignificant; in eight cases externalization was "moderate," and the largest group of patients ($N = 20$) showed marked or prominent externalizing tendencies.

This finding is, on the face of it, surprising. For here are 33 people who present themselves for psychotherapy feeling, to a moderate or marked degree, that the locus of their difficulties is external to themselves. However, before commenting further on some of the implications of this finding, we shall turn to the next aspect of externalization to be considered—its change in the course of psychotherapy.

In assessing the direction and extent of changes in externalization, we used a 5-point rating scale: $--$ equals a major decrease in externalization; $-$ equals a slight decrease; 0 equals for no change; $+$ a slight increase; and $++$ a major increase in externalization. The results are as follows:

Initial Group 0 ($N = 5$)
$-- = 1$; $- = 0$; $0 = 2$;
$+ = 2$; $++ = 0$

Initial Group 1 ($N = 8$)
$-- = 0$; $- = 5$; $0 = 0$;
$+ = 1$; $++ = 2$

Initial Group 2 ($N = 20$)
$-- = 7$; $- = 7$; $0 = 5$
$+ = 0$; $++ = 0$; $?* = 1$

Twenty of the total group of 33 patients for whom change in this variable was assessed (60%) showed, after treatment, a decrease in the extent to which it was utilized, and in Group 2 (those patients in whom externalization was most marked initially), 14 of 20 (70%) showed such a decrease (7 showing a marked decrease and 7 a moderate one). Analysis of variance reveals a significant difference between the amount of change occurring in the group most using externalization before treatment as compared to those using less of it ($p < .05$).

This finding might be considered moderately encouraging. In a more expressive, insight-oriented population, less externalization would be expected to begin with, and more patients would decrease in its use after treatment. In our patient population, especially among those who externalized a good deal, a substantial number took the first step of recognizing the internal nature of their difficulties.

In 21 of the 33 patients, the utilization of externalization was specifically linked to the functioning of one or more defenses (projection, denial, displacement, intellectualization, and rationalization) or to alloplasticity. Projection, which seemed to be the major defensive bulwark of externalization, was specified (either alone or in combination with other defenses and character style) in 13 patients, none of whom were in Initial Group 2, and 4 of whom were in Initial Group 1. In 8 of the 14 patients, projection appeared in prominent conjunction with other defenses, in 5 cases with denial, in 4 with alloplasticity—3 were of course overlapping—in 1 with displacement and 1 with intellectualization.

As externalization changed, one should expect to see alterations in the functioning of those defenses associated with its maintenance, and this is what occurred. In the nine cases in Initial Group 2, where projection was specifically noted, the strength and pervasiveness of projection diminished at termination in eight patients in conjunction with a decrease in externalization.

In the four Initial Group 1 cases where projection was specifically noted, the use of projection diminished in two and increased in two. Again, there is perfect correspondence between the diminution in the use of projection and a decrease in externalization. It may well be that we are dealing with a circularity here, that where a decrease in projection is noted on the tests, an automatic inference about diminished externalization was made. But the question still is whether there is any hint of a relationship between the nature of the defenses upon which the externalization rests, and its alteration in treatment (note Table 3).

Where the externalization rested more or less clearly on projection as a major defensive activity, changes in externalization were for the most part moderate and in the direction of decreasing magnitude. But when other defenses made significant contributions to the maintenance of the externalization, the changes in externalization were of greater magnitude in the directions of both increase and decrease. Such changes are, therefore, less predictable.

A number of qualitative intrapsychic changes were specifically described in relationship to changes in externalization. Such changes, specifically mentioned in seven of the eight patients, showing a marked decrease in externalization, include behavioral change, defensive realignment, affective changes, altered patterns of interpersonal relationships, and (in the cases involving phobias) symptomatic improvement. Increased anxiety and depression occurred in three patients when externalization diminished.

In one of the seven instances in which the tests detected little or no change in externalization, a "continuing need for support and narcissistic gratification from the environment" was noted. In two other

Table 3

Externalization resting principally on projection $(N = 6)$	Changes in externalization following treatment
Patient	−
"	−
"	0
"	−
"	− −

Externalization resting on projection with other defenses $(N = 8)$		Changes in externalization following treatment
Patient	Denial	−
"	Denial, Alloplasticity	− −
"	Denial, Intellectualization	±
"	Denial, Alloplasticity	− −
"	Denial	−
"	Alloplasticity	− −
"	Alloplasticity	+ +
"	Displacement	+

cases similar processes of partial internalization of the therapist's values and instructions were described. This internalization seemed to be of so archaic, unstable, and tenuous a nature as scarcely to warrant describing any genuine giving up of externalization by the patient; for in each of these two cases the aforementioned values of the therapist remained, so to speak, incompletely integrated into the self-concept of the patients. This is more true of these two patients than it is of another patient where a somewhat similar transference-based internalization of the therapist's attitudes seems to have occurred. In that instance, however, there seems to have been a process of at least partial acquisition of insight, the increased self-awareness being more stably incorporated into the self-concept, thus a more genuine internalization.

Finally, of the six cases in which externalization increased, two of the patients were in the 0 Group initially (showing minimal or insignificant use of externalization at the start of treatment). With one of them, initially given to withdrawal into fantasy as a retreat from painful aspects of reality, the increased externalization was accompanied by a slight increase in alloplasticity and a somewhat heightened freedom to enter spontaneously into interpersonal relationships. In the other patient a similar shift involving externalization occurred: Initially a ruminative, depressed, self-recriminating woman, she ascribed to herself in a highly unrealistic manner the entire blame for an unfortunate life situation. At the end of treatment, however, she was able to see the nature of her interaction with the environment (particularly her former husband) and some of the external difficulties inherent in that relationship. This seems to suggest that for some patients at least (like those who have developed a character-neurotic self-recriminatory approach to life) a shift toward externalization may be considered beneficial. But here we encounter a conceptual difficulty, for externalization as we have defined it involves "the extent to which the patient ascribes his illness or his difficulties to forces beyond his control, rather than accepting responsibility for his behavior and seeing the need to effect changes in himself." In this definition, externalization is at least implicitly seen as a deterrent to change or defense against the acquisition of insight. In many instances, as our results suggest, this is true and the relinquishing of an externalizing stance is concomitant with increasing self-awareness. But we must also ask whether patients (particularly those in whom masochism or depression is prominent) cannot feel too strongly or irrationally that they bear full, sole (and sometimes cherished) responsibility for their suffering, and can such a position not also stand in the way of the acquisition of insight?

The key question in assessing externalization seems to be "external to what?" The Wallerstein and Robbins definition implies that the answer is "external to the whole self"—outside the skin, so to speak, of the individual. But this is not always the case, for we know that symptoms, feelings, or behavior patterns may indeed be perceived as part of the *self*, yet not internalized. Can we say, for example, that the "Popeye" view of one's difficulties (I am what I am and that's all that I am) is an internalized one? Or is the patient who recognizes the inner nature of his difficulties but divorces them from considerations of control (either present or future) not also externalizing? The way out of this dilemma (hinted by Robbins and Wallerstein when they use the phrase "forces beyond his [the patient's] control" in their definition of externalization) is to regard "external" as meaning "external to the ego."

Such a formulation would then include those patients who lavishly ascribe responsibility to themselves for their difficulties, but who speak under the tyranny of an archaic or overpowering superego. It would also force us to include in our assessment of externalization the appropriateness of reality-congruence of the patient's feelings of responsibility for his difficulties.

The idea that externalization has the ego as its point of reference was especially applicable in two cases: In each of these cases we noted after treatment an increased and oscillating blame and recrimination against both the environment and the self. Blame is different from responsibility. In both instances, they believed nothing could be done about it. Difficulties were apart from the ego and beyond its control—external, so to speak, to themselves.

In two other cases, however, increased externalization following treatment seemed to occur in a fashion more in keeping with the original definition of externalization. That is, the external environment was increasingly seen by each of these people as the source of difficulty. In one case the shift rested on an increasing use of denial; in the other, on a more extensive and pervasive use of projection. These data, then, suggest the usefulness of broadening the concept of externalization to include placing the locus of one's difficulty both in the external environment and beyond the scope or control of the ego.

Summary

1. Twenty-eight of the 33 people, although presenting themselves for psychotherapy, tended to feel that the source of their difficulties was external to themselves.

2. Sixty percent of the patients showed, after treatment, a decrease in externalization. Of those in whom externalization was most marked before treatment, 70% showed a decrease.

3. Where externalization rested on projection, which occurred in 21 of 33 cases, changes tended to be moderate and in the direction of less externalization.

4. Where externalization rested upon other defenses, the changes in externalization were of greater magnitude in the directions of both increase and decrease.

5. In order to account for those instances where patients benefit from greater externalization, it seems useful to understand externalization as meaning external to the ego but within the self, rather than simply ascribing blame and responsibility to the external environment.

TRANSFERENCE PARADIGMS AT TERMINATION

Introduction

The definition of *transference paradigms* used in this study is relationship dispositions of which the patient at the beginning of the treatment is primarily unconscious, though he may have some glimmerings, versions, or part recognitions of them in consciousness. Transference paradigms would, in loyalty to theory, require separation from such conscious attitudes toward the therapist as that attributed to one patient: "She has experienced a relationship with her therapist as a helpful one." This may or may not have been modeled on a transference paradigm, but the tone of the research tester's write-up suggests that it is an attitude toward the real aspects of the therapist. This raises questions such as: To what degree is the therapist real and to what degree is he a transference figure and to what degree are "rich" perceptions and experiences free of the past idiosyncratic "transference phenomena" or "parataxic distortion"? Whether a patient is judged as manifesting a transference as against a "real" interpersonal response should, in principle, be determined in the light of the answers to such questions. For the most part, in the research tester's write-ups, these distinctions were not explicitly attended to, perhaps reflecting some unclarity about these issues. When there was an explicit reference to the patient's having used the "real relationship," this was noted under a special category to that effect. The assumption is that all other categories refer to unconscious or primarily unconscious transference paradigms modeled not on the real person of the analyst but rather on past figures in the patient's life.

Another issue which may have been slighted in the Project, including the test portion, is that of sex differences in analysts. This parallels the tendency within psychoanalysis to act, uneasily, as if the differences do not make much of a difference. When attending to transference paradigms, however, one is every now and again reminded that the sex of the analyst may facilitate the development of one particular transference paradigm or inhibit another, or lend a particular stamp to one or another. For example, submission to what is perceived as an authoritarian analyst may be different in a male patient with a male analyst, from a female patient with a female analyst, from a female patient with a male analyst, and from a male patient with a female analyst.

Findings and Discussion

This variable did not lend itself to the analysis of change in the same way most others did. The research testers primarily noted anticipated transference paradigms before treatment, but there were not many comments as to how these changed after treatment. Therefore, it is difficult on the basis of tests to ascertain a change in transference paradigms, perhaps in part because one is comparing a proclivity with an actuality rather than, as with most variables, comparing two actualities. Furthermore, by the time of termination transference proclivities in many of the treatments should have been resolved, at least in theory. This analysis of data yields more of an inventory of transference paradigms than of a quantitative assessment of change.

Three patients were not written about with respect to transference paradigms.

Of the 31 patients for whom transference paradigms were noted, 6 were remarked upon as changing, with 3 increasing and 3 decreasing.

One or another variation of orality ($N = 15$) and one or another way of creating interpersonal distance ($N = 14$) were the major categories of transference paradigms noted. In the following, + refers to an increase of a transference tendency, − refers to a decrease in it. No such notation means the paradigm was specified but without a judgment as to increase or decrease. The research tester included the following subcategories under orality: (1) oral rage (6 no notation of change and 2 increasing); (2) oral demandingness (1 no notation of change, with 1 increasing, 1 decreasing); (3) oral dependence (2 no notation of change, with 1 decreasing); and (4) references to the therapist as omnipotent and idealized in what sounded like oral terms (2 no notation of change). Although oral demandingness and oral rage could have been condensed under oral aggression, we assume that the research testers using the different terms reflected a meaningful delineation.

Subcategories under means of maintaining distance in the relationship with the therapist were: (1) distrust (six no notation of change); (2) fear (three no notation of change, one decrease); (3) superficial (two no notation of change); and (4) alloplastic measures to avoid intensification of the relationship (two no notation of change). The patient's emphasis on the realistic aspects of the relationship for presumed defensive purposes was separated from another category where the relationship was also described as having strong elements of reality but where it was used primarily as a support for the patient rather than for defensive purposes. These people related to the therapist as "helping hands" (two decreasing, one increasing). That this aspect was particularly mentioned by the research tester suggests that patients' attitudes were less a function of unconscious transference than conscious recognitions. One gets into a nice theoretical issue, however, if one asks how it is that some people are able to use the therapist as a benevolent support. Are these patients able to do this because of having unconscious predispositions to experience the therapist as benevolent, or does it reflect solely reality testing? In short, what is the relationship between unconscious dispositions toward others and the reality of others as perceived in the here and now?

The remainder of the categories were descriptive of content—the kinds of transference paradigms which emerged. These were: (1) submission to a powerful male by a male (four); (2) relationships of female patients characterized by competitiveness and penis envy (six); and (3) transference paradigms modeled on aggressive, malignant views of mother (four). Although the rest of the categories occurred very few times, they are included here to indicate kinds of comments which can be made about transference paradigms on the basis of psychological tests: (1) submission by a female to a male (one); (2) references to the power of the therapist, as distinct from the orally overidealized references (one); (3) ambivalent, anal struggles (three); (4) sexuality (somewhat to our surprise there were relatively few comments about this)—comments about sexuality were divided into heterosexuality (three) and homosexuality (two); (5) attempting to stimulate guilt in the therapist (one); (6) being a "good girl" (one); (7) seeing the analyst as stuffily conventional (one); (8) disappointment in the therapist (three); (9) reproach toward the therapist (one); (10) hostility to the therapist (one); (11) feeling unloved by the therapist (one); (12) depressed quality to the relationship (one); (13) a feeling of vulnerability in the relationship (one); (14) sadomasochistic relationship (one).

Having completed this analysis, we have a vague sense of disappointment. It seems to us that the test findings about transference paradigms should somehow be more clear or impressive than they seem to be. We are reminded of Mayman's belief (personal communication) that the standard test battery insufficiently allows for the emergence of transference paradigms (as well as other subjective, identity information). If not via supplemental tests, perhaps such information could be better exploited with the standard tests than was done here. It may be that a proposed new form for reporting test results (S. Appelbaum, 1972) explicitly requiring this kind of information will help determine whether such limitations as reported here are inherent in the test materials or due to the way the tests and findings are used and reported.

Summary

1. The tests seem to have been less powerful in ascertaining transference paradigms than in assessing many other variables, whether this was because of limitations of testing in general with

regard to this concept, limitations of these tests and the way they were used in particular, or the nature of the concept and data.

2. Transference paradigms need to be conceptually and practically discriminated from the "real" relationship, aspects of which may be unconscious. This raises the question of how some people are able to recognize and use the realistic aspects of relationships while others are not able to do so. Is it because of unconscious malevolent or benevolent transference dispositions?

3. Major categories of transference paradigms noted were one or another variation of orality (15) and one or another way of creating interpersonal distance (14).

INTERPERSONAL RELATIONS

Introduction

In a larger number of instances than usual, the research tester specifically remarked that he was being speculative. The inferences drawn from this data, therefore, are tempered by the possibility that this is a variable that does not lend itself well to scrutiny by way of psychological tests. It may share some of the same difficulties as noted with respect to the other object relations, person-centered variable, transference paradigms.

Findings and Discussion

The conclusions that *interpersonal relations* often change during treatment, almost always for the better though usually only to a limited extent, is based on ratings recorded on a 5-point scale of change, with 0 meaning the patient remained the same in this respect, + and ++ reflecting two grades of change for the better, − and −− reflecting change for the worse, and ? referring to unclarity as to whether change was for the better or for the worse. These data are tabulated below.

Change in Qualities of Interpersonal Relationships
++ = 8; + = 18
No change = 3
− = 3
? = 2

In one of the two instances of change of indeterminate quality, the patient changed from being the masochistic object in relationships to projecting anger and attacking those who angered her. But, in view of the fact that she was considered close to being psychotic at termination while she had not been so regarded before treatment, it is difficult to tell whether this change is for the better. It may turn out to be so, and the whole present situation may be a way station on the way to better functioning. Presumably these difficulties were there, hidden, so to speak, by the masochistic position. Is she more or less comfortable this way than she was before? Are those around her more or less comfortable with her? Do her interpersonal relationships "pay off" in better or worse ways at present than they did before treatment? A similar psychological situation obtained with another patient although without the issue of psychosis, in that she worked harder at her original defensive stance of being "proper," but that spurts of irritability and unsatisfactory control had increased. For example, what was belittling in a relationship with men took the form of more explicit "anger and fear toward men." It is difficult to say whether in the long run this will turn out to be a change for the better or for the worse.

Thirty-nine scaled units of change occurred on this variable, or an average of 1.1 over the N of 34.

We separated the patients into three groups of increasing severity of difficulty in interpersonal relations (Table 4). There were 17 patients in Group 1, 10 in Group 2, and 7 in Group 3.

The groups with the greatest difficulties show the least change for the better. Analysis of variance demonstrates that Group 3 showed significantly less change for the better than Group 1 ($p < .05$). Thus,

Table 4

	Sum of people change (directional)	Sum of people change (nondirectional)	Sum of units change (directional)
Group 1 $N = 17$	16+ 0− 0S 1?	17	22+
Group 2 $N = 10$	8+ 1− 1S 1?	10	10+ 1− 1?
Group 3 $N = 7$	2+ 2− 3S	4	2+ 2−

those with better interpersonal relations seem to have been better able to improve upon them than those who had poor ones to begin with.

In the following delineated analyses of qualities, remarks are made about changes for the worse or for the better which seem to contradict change for the better or worse as recorded above. This is because the judgments are molar ones standing, on balance, for change in the whole person, while the judgments which follow are molecular, based on change in the single variable.

Qualities of Change

The test statements yielded the following dimensions:

Inhibited–Freer. This is probably a continuum, though data were tallied separately. "Inhibited" refers to such descriptive remarks as "immobilized," "shy." "Freer" is based on such adjectives as "spontaneous," "more direct," "more frank." This proved to be one of the most quantitatively emphasized dimensions. One would expect after a course of therapy that, with repressions lifted, people would be more spontaneous and free in their interpersonal relationships. As can be seen from Table 4, eight people were considered more spontaneous and free and one was, speculatively, considered so. (When opinion of change in this variable was qualified as being speculative, it was tallied separately as "?".) One patient was considered more inhibited after treatment than before.

Warmth–Cold. Warmth refers to such comments as "invests feelings in," "the importance of object relationships," "sympathy." Coldness includes such comments as "detached." Three people were considered warmer and about one of these the tester also remarked upon his being less cold. This way of describing the change in interpersonal relationships was not heavily relied upon quantitatively.

Closeness–Distance. This proved to be a major dimension, quantitatively. Exactly what it means, however, is somewhat difficult to specify. It probably is a fairly impressionistic rating, and if one got down to theoretical specifics it would be something of a quagmire. One would likely get into the issues of whether one *behaved* closer to people or *felt* closer to them. Behaving as if closer could be for increased defensive purposes, though it might be evidence of greater needfulness. Increased distance, in someone distant to begin with, would seem to be a disappointing finding; but increased distance in someone who never seemed to get along without the constant stimuli of other people might be an encouraging finding. Some of these issues may be responsible for the fact that the greatest number of remarks qualifying the judgments as being "speculative." Three patients were considered to be closer in their interpersonal relationships, with six others being considered so, but only speculatively. Three patients were considered as being more distant; all would be better off if they were closer to others than more distant. One person was remarked upon as being less distant, speculatively, and one was judged as being the same.

Graceful. Graceful refers to such designations as "smoother," "more appropriate," "more adaptive." Two persons were scored as being more graceful, and one speculatively so. One was considered more awkward.

Anxious. Anxious refers to interpersonal relationships described as being anxious ones, and there were three notations, all of them indicating that the person is less anxious with respect to his interpersonal relations.

Aggression to Women. Aggression to women by men was remarked upon three times, with one instance being described as having diminished and two remaining the same. Aggression to women by women gathered four notations, with one having diminished, one having increased, and two the same.

Aggression to Men. Only one notation was made about aggression to men by men, aggression having diminished. Aggression to men by women diminished three times. In one instance it increased. In two instances it remained the same.

Theoretically, the following three categories might have been expected to have yielded more references, but they did not.

Sexualized–Heterosexual. This dimension was broken down into heterosexual inhibition and heterosexual promiscuity. Only one reference was made to it, and this was to a diminished heterosexual inhibition.

Sexuality–Homosexual. Homosexual inhibitions of interpersonal relationships were remarked upon as diminishing with three patients.

Aggressivized. One person was speculatively considered to have had his interpersonal relationships more suffused with aggression, and two were judged to be the same in this respect.

The next four categories all refer to a quality of orality in interpersonal relationships. While one might think, theoretically, that "oral-dependent" and "oral-aggressive" would have been expectable and sufficient categories, the following more delineated categories seemed better ways of grouping the data:

Oral–Narcissistic–Exploitative. Only one patient was judged to have improved in this respect, having become less orally narcissistic and exploitative. The improvement was slight, and when one adds that five people did not change at all in this respect, the impression is that when people have interpersonal relationships of a narcissistic-exploitative kind, they are not likely to develop significantly better relationships in this respect.

Oral Rage. Two persons were considered to show less oral rage. Three persons were considered to be the same in this respect.

Oral-Demanding. Two persons were judged as being less oral-demanding, and two were judged to be the same.

Oral-Dependent. Six people were judged to have become less oral-dependent in their interpersonal relationships, one a bit less so, and there were six question mark scorings.

Sadomasochistic. Four people were judged to have interpersonal relations less characterized by sadomasochism, and three were judged to have remained the same.

Form More Than Substance. This dimension includes those people whose interpersonal relationships were distinguished by compliance and superficiality. One person was considered to have worsened along these lines, and four persons were judged to be the same in this respect.

Self-Assertiveness. Five people were judged to have become more self-assertive in their interpersonal relations, while one was judged to have become less self-assertive. Again, depending upon where the person started from in this respect, one cannot say from this datum alone whether the change was a desirable one or not.

Range of Interpersonal Relations. Three people were judged to have increased their range, and one person was judged to have remained the same in this respect.

Miscellaneous. The effect of weak ego functioning on interpersonal relations was noted with respect to one person, and that person was considered to have improved in basic ego functioning, with interpersonal relations having improved at least in part because of it. One person's interpersonal relations were considered to have been inhibited by poor self-concept, critical, self-abnegating feelings, and this inhibition was judged to have decreased. Interpersonal relations were discussed with reference to control over impulse in two patients, one becoming worse in this respect, and one judged to be the same. Only two people had interpersonal relations mentioned in connection with insight, and both of these developed more insight. One person was considered to have become more distrustful. One person was considered to have become less manipulative. One person was considered to have been able to tolerate ambivalence better.

Perhaps even more than some of the other variables, the variable interpersonal relations overlaps with many other variables. Likely, improvement or lack of improvement in the quality of interpersonal relations is closely tied to improvement or lack of improvement in self-concept, patterns of defenses, change in core conflicts, better control of anxiety, etc.*

Summary

1. As with transference paradigms (the other "object relations," person-centered variable) the data for qualities of interpersonal relations were considered less powerful than others of the variables.

2. Interpersonal relations often changed for the better during treatment, though usually only to a small extent.

3. Those with better interpersonal relations at the beginning of treatment seem to have been better able to improve upon them than those who had poor ones to begin with.

4. One major change was in the direction of patients becoming more free, less inhibited.

5. A second major change was along the dimension of closeness–distance, with 9 of 12 becoming "closer," the other 3 becoming more distant, to their detriment. This dimension raises such conceptual issues of whether this clinically often-used dimension refers to patients *behaving* closer to people or *feeling* closer to them, whether relationships might go in one or another direction for defensive purposes or out of increased needs, and whether "closeness," so often considered in the abstract a good thing, may not be good for some people.

6. Oral-narcissistic-exploitative relationships seem especially difficult to change for the better.

SYMPTOMS†

Introduction

In psychoanalysis, the narrowest, most technical use of the term *symptoms* would restrict it to a compromise between two unconscious motives, one of which tends to be expressed while the other tends to

---

*How interpersonal relations change in relation with other changes can be seen in Chapters 5 and 6, where profiles and patterns of change are offered.
†Original draft and analysis of data by Dr. Siegal.

be repressed. From this point of view, a phobia is generally considered to be a symptom, a neurotic symptom. So is an obsession, or a compulsion. We could even extend the term, and still be within the technical bounds of the psychoanalytic concept, by including inhibitions, which are in a sense the opposite of a symptom.

If we in the Project had restricted the meaning of symptoms to this narrow definition, we would have had few cases with "symptoms." There were few patients in our study who were sufficiently well integrated as to present crystallized symptoms. Many of them showed a variety of diffuse, severe disturbances, particularly behavioral difficulties. Thus, in this analysis we used the term *complaint* as synonymous with *symptom* to illustrate a broadening of the concept, to refer generally to those aspects of the patient thought by him or others as a reason for his seeking treatment. We recognize the many complexities of using this general term. Is it possible to expect change in a complaint which is made by others and not by the patient? That would be like saying that a person could change in psychotherapy without having a wish to change. On the other hand, we know that patients at the beginning of the treatment may not see particular aspects of themselves as symptoms, as something to complain about, but they do come to see them that way in the course of the treatment. Without specifying the patient's attitude toward his symptoms, we allow the issue of motivation for change to be uncontrolled, treating as the same things complaints which may appear at one time or another to trouble the patient a great deal or not at all.

While many of our variables overlap, symptoms are a particularly flagrant example of overlapping. A number of the symptomatic behaviors, or complaints, which people bring into treatment are included as separate variables, for example, alloplasticity (when defined as behavior objected to by the environment), guilt, depression, anxiety. These being sufficiently ubiquitous and discrete deserve separate assessment, but that leaves our description of symptoms somewhat arbitrary, a part of the complete story of symptom change.

The whole question of attempting to discern symptomatology through psychological tests must be raised. Surely, testers would agree that psychological tests are not the best way to discern symptoms. The best way is to ask the patient what bothers him (or to ask those in the patient's environment what about the patient bothers them). Having said this, one must note certain exceptions. Sometimes a patient withholds from his doctors certain troublesome complaints. A hint that the patient is withholding *some* information may appear in the psychological tests. From a clinical point of view such a hint might be followed up in whatever is considered the most helpful and tactful way. On the other hand, there are certain conditions of which the patient may make no secret at all but which simply do not leave easily discernible traces in the psychological tests. Male homosexuality is a classic example. While it is possible that there may be certain expert psychologists who specialize in this area and therefore can better recognize the existence of overt homosexuality from tests, I think most of us would feel little confidence—in the absence of the patient's clearly alluding to his homosexuality during the testing sessions—in being able to infer the existence of *practiced* homosexuality from psychological tests. (Difficulty establishing a masculine identification and conflict over sexual role, of course, are rather easy to discern from tests; but these may or may not be acted upon homosexually.)

With these provisos we examined 33 patients from the point of view of what the psychological tests did say about their symptoms before and after treatment.

Findings and Discussion

Our first step was simply to go through the material and list all of the symptoms, complaints, and anything else which could appear under the heading of symptoms to get an idea of their range. At the beginning of treatment, 33 patients were judged through the tests to have some 83 symptomatic expressions; at the end of the treatment these patients were judged to have some 87 symptomatic expressions.

We classified symptoms into six different types:

Category 1—Classical Neurotic Symptoms. This category consists almost exclusively of phobias, though in addition there are mentioned "fear of homosexuality," "sexual malfunctioning," and "sexual inhibitions." Before treatment the 33 patients manifested 16 symptoms in this category. These were distributed among 14 patients. Twelve of the 14 patients improved,* one got worse, and one remained the same.

Category 2—Attitudes Toward Self and Others. This category includes the following symptomatic expressions:† Dissatisfaction with relations with parents; martyred-masochistic; feeling of inadequacy, feelings of impotence, masochism, and worthlessness; feeling of sex-

---

* "Improved" is used here in a rather broad sense. This does not mean that the symptom disappeared or even, necessarily, that it was no longer a problem to the patient. It simply implies that there was some degree of improvement in the symptom, in its being less prominent, or less troublesome.

† In this and succeeding analyses the research testers' remarks about the symptoms are quoted verbatim.

ual inadequacy and inadequacy as a mother. In this category there were eight patients, with eight instances of symptoms in which six improved, one remained unchanged, and one worsened.

Category 3—Alloplastic Behavior. This category includes homosexuality, manipulative and demanding behavior, rage outbursts, alcohol or drug addiction, sexual promiscuity, impulsive behavior, irrational hysteroid activities, irresponsible impulsive acts, perversion. In this category there were 18 such symptoms, distributed among 16 patients. Eight patients improved, 4 were unchanged, and 4 were worse.

Category 4—Feelings, Affects, and Moods. In this category we included depression, anxiety, panic, high-mood, projection, suspiciousness, hidden disturbing feelings, surges of affect and anxiety, inhibition of all feelings, fearfulness, poor control over feelings. The 34 patients contributed 22 instances of this category, distributed among 22 patients. Fifteen patients improved, while 7 got worse. In addition, in 4 cases symptoms appeared which were not present or which were not visible when the patient was initially tested, bringing the total N of patients to 26 at termination.

Category 5—Somatization. (*Somatization* is a separate variable all by itself and will be dealt with more thoroughly under its own heading.) Somatization as seen through the tests includes diffuse somatic worries plus specific somatic symptoms. The 34 patients contributed only 4 instances of this, distributed among 4 patients, of which after treatment 1 got better, 2 got worse, and 1 remained unchanged.

Category 6—Ego Malfunctioning. In this category we included autistic thinking, paranoid trends, projective perception of reality, peculiar ideas, transient borderline peculiarities (probably due in part to brain damage), disturbed thinking, psychosis, depersonalization, estrangement states, borderline psychosis. Of 33 patients 14 instances of such ego malfunctioning were noted before treatment. Nine improved after treatment, 3 got worse after treatment, and 2 remained the same. In addition, 4 instances of symptomatic ego malfunctioning appeared in the after-treatment set of tests, bringing the total to 18.

These data thus far have been presented with respect to change in symptoms as scored independently across the group. To report change in symptoms as restricted to individuals we took an algebraic sum of increases in symptoms and decreases in symptoms for each person. For example, one patient had three symptoms improved and one remained the same, so her score was -3. Another patient had two symptoms remain the same and one worsened, so her score was $+1$. The scores were then changed to fit the scale as follows: -3 and $-4 = ++$, meaning considerable improvement in symptoms; -1 and

−2= +, meaning some improvement in symptoms; 0= no change in symptoms; +1 and +2= −, some worsening of symptoms; +3 and +4= − −, considerable worsening of symptoms. The patients were distributed on a 5-point scale as follows:

Improvement in Symptoms
+ + = 8; + = 15
No Change
0 = 1
Worsening in Symptoms
− = 8; − − = 2

Symptoms, then, proved fairly easy to change, with 68% of the patients being less troubled by symptoms.

These data confirm the widely held psychoanalytical notion that classical neurotic symptoms respond best to treatment. The category which perhaps responded worse to treatment was alloplastic behavior. This is another expected finding as addicts and perverts and people with other such overt behavioral difficulties are difficult to help. The category which responded perhaps second-best seems to be those symptoms involving feelings and affects most of which consisted of varieties of depressive and anxious feelings. The category of ego malfunctioning provides a pretty successful set of results. When 9 of 14 instances of ego malfunctioning improve that is impressive. On the other hand, it is also impressive—and probably should not be surprising—that 4 additional cases of ego malfunctioning turned up at termination either because they were not spotted in the initial psychological test record or because these patients decompensated to some extent during the treatment.

Summary

1. Rather than defining symptoms solely as a compromise between two unconscious motives, we have broadened the concept here to mean, in effect, "complaint," whether this be by the patient or the environment.

2. Psychological tests are probably not the best way to ascertain the existence of symptoms since symptoms are often a kind of external, behavioral event.

3. Classical neurotic symptoms, distributed among 14 patients, improved in 12 of them.

4. Attitudes toward self and others, distributed among eight patients, improved in six of them, with one unchanged, and one worsened.

5. Alloplastic behavior, distributed among 16 patients, improved in 8 patients, while 4 remained the same, and 4 got worse.

6. Feelings, affects, and moods, distributed among 22 patients, improved in 15 patients, with 7 getting worse and 4 developing or showing evidence on tests of symptoms not visible before treatment.

7. Somatization, distributed among only four patients, improved in one, remained the same in one, and got worse in two.

8. Ego malfunctioning, distributed among 14 patients, improved in 9 patients, got worse in 3, with 2 remaining the same. In addition, ego malfunctioning appeared in the after-treatment tests of 4 patients who did not manifest such malfunction in the before-treatment tests. Calculating algebraically, change of various symptoms within each patient resulted in 23 patients on the whole improving, 1 remaining the same, and 10 getting worse. Symptoms, then, proved fairly easy to change, with 68% of the patients being less troubled by them at termination.

9. Classical neurotic symptoms responded best to treatment. Varieties of depressive and anxious feelings responded second-best. Alloplastic behavior responded worst. Improvements in ego malfunctioning were, on the other hand, impressive, while at the same time it is sobering to note that four instances of ego malfunctioning turned up after treatment, either because they were not spotted in the test record before treatment or because the patients had decompensated in this respect during the treatment.

DEPRESSION

Introduction

Depression is a catchall term. One does not know from the word alone whether the patient feels depressed, or behaves in ways related to an imminent feeling of depression, whether the person is depressed because of guilt, because of loss, to what extent his depression is part of every person's "existential" depression or has reached a degree which most people would consider "symptomatic." In an attempt to make such distinctions the research testers' statements were categorized as follows: (1) The existence of feelings of depression: This category is based on the Robbins and Wallerstein description that implies strongly that the intended referent of the variable depression is consciously experienced depression. (2) The qualities of depressive feelings were classified into "oral" and "guilty." Under oral we included patients who were described as: anaclitic, not getting what he wants, pessimistic, hopeless, gloomy, disappointed, abandoned, lonely, apathetic, zestless, rootless, insatiable, hungry, lost opportunities, regretful, and frustrated. The "guilty" category refers to patients described as feeling guilty, self-depreciating, bad, and evil. We do not mean to imply that these categories are mutually exclusive, or that they are a full conceptualization of depression. They simply represent empirical clusterings of statements made. (3) Defenses against depression: In this category the testers included denial, avoidance, and character patterns. (4) Structural: This category included lability, tolerance for depression, and deleterious effects on formal ego functions. (5) Reactive: This category included reactive to the end of treatment as well as reactive to other events. The remaining categories were (6) suicide, (7) depression about the future, (8) depression over sexual inadequacy, and (9) resigned depression.

Findings and Discussion—Depression

Thirty-two of the 34 patients had feelings of depression. Since depression was not the major presenting complaint, this large number suggests that feelings of depression are part of the human condition or at least the condition of psychiatric patients such as these, either as concomitant with their other difficulties or as reactive to these difficulties. Only in one case was it said that the person did not have depressive feelings, neither at initial nor at termination, but this can hardly be taken as meaning that depressive feelings were not "there." Rather, her alloplastic defenses and capabilities for fantasy were suggested as being sufficiently available to prevent her experiencing depressive feelings. One has to keep in mind that the research testers were using the Project's narrow definition of depression, namely, *experienced* feelings, and so avoided the implication that patients who do not experience these feelings are free in all ways of the effects of depression. In addition to situations where the feelings are warded off by activities of a defensive sort, one may expect depressive equivalents, such as psychomotor retardation and various character traits and attitudes, all of which may be driven in some sense by the potentiality for depressive feelings although not experienced as such.

Of the 32 persons who had feelings of depression, 23 could be classified as having "oral" depressive feelings, and 7 as having "guilty" depressive feelings. (Three had both kinds of guilty feelings.)

Change in Depression
+ = increase; − = decrease
+ = 9; ++ = 6
− = 8; −− = 7
No change = 4

(The distribution of change was just about the same within the "oral" and "guilty" groups.) In the guilty depression group, three of seven had increased depression, four had decreased depression.

In the "oral" depression group, 9 of 23 had increased depression, 13 had decreased depression, and 1 remained the same.

That almost half of the patients have more depression than when they started is, of course, in one sense a startling finding. This "sense" is based on the simplistic expectation that depression *per se* is a pathological thing for people to have (rather than an aspect of the human condition, or at least the human "patient" condition) and that the increase of depression must *ipso facto* be bad in some way. But, for example, if someone has been living a chaotic and harmful life in an effort to ward off the feelings of depression, it makes clinical sense that, should he develop the strength and courage to organize his life better and to give up the self-destructive devices which he used to prevent the experience of depression, he would feel more depressed at the end of treatment. In other respects he may very well have improved his functioning. Two patients seem to fall into this category. One patient was depressed as part of his reaction to the end of treatment and as part of his regret for the wasted years before treatment. This, too, may signify a change for the better in that the capacity to survey and plan one's life, while it may involve regret, could be a means or a concomitant of changing life patterns for the better. Seven patients seem to have gotten more depressed as a part of a general picture of increased disturbance. With two of them, particular emphasis was put upon their having relaxed the use of denial and avoidant defenses.

Of the 16 patients for whom depression lessened, 4 showed also a lessening of the defense of denial. We assume from this that these people moved effectively into the therapeutic process, at least in this respect. Two patients showed a lessening of depression with greater ideation, which also might be a relatively healthy sign since one aspect of treatment for most people is to assert ideational control.* For 7 patients there was no notation about any greater defensiveness, and so the lessening of depression in them seems a helpful change. Three patients showed less depression, but in the context of increased use of denial; and 1 patient showed less depression but in the context of increased use of a variety of patterned defensive life-styles which we labeled "characterological." These last 4 were quite ill people for

---

*This implies correctly that a value for psychoanalytic workers is the right amount and use of ideational control. It applies even to those ruminating, intellectualizing, indecisive people, many of whom come to treatment with just this as a complaint. In our view, their overcontrol (often alternating with a subtle impulsivity) is not the assertion of adequate ideational control. The latter is just as much an objective in their treatment as it is with action-oriented, unreflective people.

whom the increased effectiveness of defenses could be considered an improvement.

Defenses against Depression

Denial-avoidance was the most frequently invoked defense against depression. There were 11 such instances: Five showed an increase of denial and 6 showed a decrease in denial. This 11 compares with 3 mentions of "characterological" defenses (1 increase, 1 decrease, 1 the same), 3 ideational defenses (3 increases), and 4 alloplastic defenses (2 increases, 2 decreases.) The denial people fall into the following categories: (1) Less denial and less depression, which we would assume would reflect a general improvement—4 cases. (2) More denial and less depression. Here, we would assume that the treatment included the strengthening of the defense of denial, advisedly or inadvertently, so that less depression was experienced—3 cases (in one instance, more denial was used, with depression judged as being the same). (3) Less denial and more depression. Here, the treatment by "weakening" the defenses may have made the experience of depression more prominent—2 cases. (4) More denial and more depression. Here, one might assume that things had gone from bad to worse, with the patient struggling even more to deny his depressed feelings, but unsuccessful at it—1 case. We were surprised to see only 3 mentions made of ideation enlisted against depression. Since psychotherapy is a verbal process which lifts repressions against verbal symbols, one might expect that the use of verbal symbols for purposes of decreasing unpleasant feelings would increase, at least in expressive treatments. Is this paucity of ideational defenses the obverse of the nonideational favored defense of denial? Or does it mean that this general run of patients did not include many with a penchant to use ideational defenses, at least at termination? Or it may be that depressive feelings are more subject to nonideational defenses than to ideational ones.

Suicide

Suicide was mentioned with respect to eight patients, with suicidal feelings having increased in three of them, decreased in five of them.

Structural

Relatively few statements were made about structures in the context of depression. "Affective lability" as a structural attribute garnered four notations. In two instances lability decreased, in one instance it increased and in one instance remained the same. "Tolerance for depressive feelings" (yielding to them less) garnered four notations. Two patients developed greater tolerance for depression while two kept the same low tolerance. One statement was made about "deleterious effects on ego functioning as a result of depression," and here it increased at termination.

Four patients showed depressive feelings which were reactive to the end of the treatment itself. Obviously, these cannot be scored as being greater or lesser, and simply mean presence. Only one patient contributed a statement about the depression being reactive to any other kind of event, and this was to the relatively recent loss of father.

Depression about the Future

Two patients were referred to as being depressed about the future. These indications came up in the context of reactions to the end of treatment, and it might be better to consider them under that rubric. Also, with respect to one other patient, the research tester remarked about a depressive-sounding regret over lost opportunities, and it may be that, too, is one reaction to the end of treatment. In other words, we wonder if at the end of treatment there is not a tendency to survey one's life, one's past and future, which may be depressively toned. The research problem is whether to include these under depression *at* the end of treatment or to keep the category specific *to* the end of treatment, which implies also depression about the loss of the therapist. This research problem is the same one therapists face regularly when assessing the advisability and timing of termination.

Sexual Adequacy

Two patients were considered to be depressed over their sexual inadequacy, and both showed an increase in such feelings.

Behavior Inducing Depression

We thought that this might be more prominent with this group of patients, a goodly number of whom seem to show disorders of behavior. We guessed that there would be a kind of secondary depression to what they were doing to themselves and others, but in fact only one patient was mentioned in this regard. He was described as experiencing more depression, as alloplasticity (alcoholism) "is increasingly enlisted to neutralize increasing feelings of oral depression, and then the patient feels guilty depressions secondary to the drinking itself."

Resigned Depression

The comment that the patients were feeling a kind of resigned or stoical depression was made about three patients, and in each instance these feelings increased at termination. Again, we have the impression that this category might well be included in a broadly defined category of reactions *to* the end of treatment. It may be that such resignations are the result of the previously mentioned tendency to survey past and future at the end of such a key life event as extended psychotherapy. This possible connection was, indeed, noted by one research tester with respect to one patient although he thought it was at least in part evidence of a pervasive masochism. In both of the other cases, the resigned feelings were connected with seeing themselves irrevocably as women, which in their view was a cause for depression.

Summary

1. Recognizing that depression is a catchall term, data were classified according to feelings of depression, whether of an oral or guilty kind, defenses against depression, structural issues, whether depression was reactive, depression about the future, depression over sexual inadequacy, resigned depression, and suicide.

2. Thirty-two patients had feelings of depression; 15 feelings increased and 15 decreased, with 4 remaining the same. Increase and decrease did not necessarily mean the same thing as better or worse.

3. Twenty-three were classified as having oral-depressive feelings, seven as having guilty depressive feelings, three with having both oral and guilty depressive feelings, with the distribution of change just about the same within the oral and guilty groups.

4. The most frequently invoked defense against depression was the pattern of denial-avoidance, with five patients increasing in the use of this pattern and six decreasing in its use.

5. Suicide was mentioned with respect to eight patients, such ideas or feelings having increased in three of them, decreased in five of them.

6. Relatively few statements were made about ego structure in the context of depression. Affect lability decreased with two patients, increased with one patient, and remained the same with one patient. Two patients developed greater tolerance for depression, while two

remained the same in this regard. One patient showed deleterious effects on ego functioning as a result of depression which increased at the end of treatment.

7. Four patients showed depressive feelings understood as being reactive to the end of the treatment itself.

8. Three patients were concerned in a depressive-sounding way about the future, which could well have been a reaction to the end of treatment itself, posing for the research the same problem that therapists sometimes face when assessing the advisability and timing of termination.

9. Two patients increased their depression over sexual inadequacy.

10. Only one patient showed depression secondary to his alloplastic behavior.

11. Three patients showed an increase in their feelings of resignation or stoicism, perhaps related to the end of treatment, perhaps related to idiosyncratic aspects of their personality.

CONSCIOUS GUILT

Introduction

Especially since *unconscious guilt* is a separate variable, *conscious guilt* can be taken to refer to feelings of guilt, as described in the Wallerstein and Robbins definitions. While many patient variables can be assessed on the tests by way of both formal functioning and content, conscious guilt is dependent upon content alone. As a consequence, it may well be that conscious guilt is elicited easier by psychiatric interviewing than by tests, especially with those patients for whom such guilt is a mild or subtle experience. On the other hand, it may appear by way of inferences from the tests, though not verbally acknowledged by the patient.

Findings and Discussion

The 34 patients were categorized into four groups on the basis of their tests before treatment. Groups 1, 2, and 3 correspond to mild, moderate, and severe degrees of guilt feelings. The fourth group, Group 0, includes people for whom feelings of guilt were not an issue that was apparent in the psychological tests. Again, this is an empirical rather than a theoretical distinction.

Sixteen people were in category 0, 11 in the mild category, 4 in the moderate category, and 4 in the severe category. The large number of patients in Group 0 is noteworthy, particularly in contrast to the ubiquity of feelings of depression in this sample. While it is possible that guilt is less a part of this patient population's human condition than depression, there are alternate explanations. One should consider the presumed difficulty in noting guilt by way of psychological tests, and also that the pathology which made patients of many of these people may have functioned to ward off the unpleasantness of guilt feelings. The latter was specifically noted with respect to several patients.

To assess the direction and extent of change in conscious guilt feelings, we used a 5-point scale: $0 =$ no change, $- =$ slightly less guilt feelings, $-- =$ considerably less guilt feelings, $+ =$ slightly more, and $++ =$ considerably more. Changes in each patient are indicated in Table 5.

After treatment, 11 patients remained the same with respect to conscious guilt feelings, 12 showed diminished guilt feelings, and 11 showed increased guilt feelings. Thus, conscious guilt feelings seem relatively resistant to change, with about one-third (32%) showing no change.

Of the 16 people in the 0 Group at initial, only 6 of them had changed (perforce in the direction of increased guilt) at termination. Of the 11 people in Group 1, 9 (81%) had changed at termination (3 having developed more guilt, 6 having developed less). Of the 8 people in Groups 2 and 3, 6 showed less guilt. An analysis of variance comparing change in Group 0 with Group 1 showed a difference of borderline significance ($p < .10$), while the comparison between the 0 Group and Groups 2 and 3 showed a significant difference ($p < .01$).

Table 5

Initial group 0 ($N = 16$)	Initial group 2 ($N = 4$)
$-- = 0$	$-- = 2$
$- = 0$	$- = 1$
$0 = 9$	$0 = 0$
$+ = 6$	$+ = 0$
$++ = 1$	$++ = 1$
Initial group 1 ($N = 11$)	Initial group 3 ($N = 4$)
$-- = 1$	$-- = 1$
$- = 5$	$- = 2$
$0 = 2$	$0 = 1$
$+ = 3$	$+ = 0$
$++ = 0$	$++ = 0$

Thus, those people who do not show guilt tend to be more resistant toward changing in this respect or have less to change than those who show moderate or severe guilt before treatment. At termination, 25 people showed evidence of guilt while 9 did not, as compared to 19 at initial who did and 15 who did not. So, again, as was noted with depression, contrary to any simplistic ideas that psychotherapy should necessarily result in patients having less disagreeable feelings, in this group approximately as many people developed more of the feeling of conscious guilt than had it diminish, and overall there was an increase in feelings of guilt.

Further data are tabulated in Table 6. Units of change refers to the + and − score, each one of these equaling one unit: + = increased guilt, − = decreased guilt.

A close look at individual cases offers plausible, internally consistent evidence for guilt increasing with psychotherapy. In two instances the patients' less employed behaviors may have been designed, at least in part, to ward off the experience of guilt. To put it another way, with less externalization and displacement being used, they began to experience guilt as a concomitant to a now internalized conflict. With one patient the behaviors were continued, but apparently with some increasing awareness of what he was doing to himself and others. This gives rise to the hypothesis that patients who do not improve according to their expectations may develop a conscious guilt around this issue in itself. This provides for an iatrogenic aspect of psychotherapy. Should demands on the part of the therapist

Table 6

	Sum of people who change (directional)	Sum of people who change (nondirectional)	Units of change (directional)	Units of change (nondirectional)
Group 1	3+	9	+3	10 ÷ 11 = .81
N = 11	6−		−7	
	2S			
Group 2	1+	4	2+	7 ÷ 4 = 1.7
N = 4	3−		5−	
	0S			
Group 3	1+	3	1+	5 ÷ 4 = 1
N = 4	2−		3−	
	1S			
Group 0	6+	6+	7+	7 ÷ 16 = .44
N = 16	9S			
N = 34				

or society be in excess of the patient's capacities, he now has something else with which to devalue himself.   ·

With two patients, guilt seems to have arisen through a relaxation of tightly knit defenses, particularly over the expression of hostility. One patient may have felt more guilty as the symptoms which had monopolized her attention were given up and she became more aware of the anger embedded in them. Two other patients may have become more guilty due to their greater recognition of their internal difficulties, which came about through a relaxation of avoidant defenses and as part of greater internalization. One patient seemed to have yielded some of her narcissistic aloofness and so was put in greater touch with her previously warded-off feelings. Again, this finding of greater discomfort at the end of psychotherapy raises questions about how one decides whether a patient has improved, gotten better, or benefited. Do you judge from the effects on the environment? Do you judge from the pleasantness or the discomfort of the patient's feelings and, if so, which feelings? Do you judge from his life-style and pattern of functioning in general? It could well be that some or all of these patients might report that they felt more uncomfortable with respect to anxiety, depression, and guilt, but more comfortable about themselves as spouses, workers, and citizens.

Categories of what patients were guilty about are: (1) general badness and self-depreciation, (2) being a bad parent, (3) guilt over hostility, (4) guilt over heterosexual–homosexual behavior. There were no indications in this data that one particular kind of guilt is any more or less amenable to change than any other.

$- =$ less; $+ =$ more
1. General sense of badness as shown by self-depreciation
    $- = 3$
    $+ = 2$
2. Guilt over being a bad parent
    $- = 2$
3. Guilt over hostility
    $- = 5$
    $+ = 3$
Same $= 1$
4. Guilt over sexual behavior
    $- = 2$
    $+ = 1$

People attempted to manage guilt through insight, denial, ideation, character defenses, freer expression, alloplasticity, projection, and internalization.

Insight   *Alloplasticity*
+ = 3   − = 1
Denial   + = 1
− = 1   *Projection*
+ = 2   − = 2
Ideation   + = 2
− = 1   *Internalization*
+ = 2   − = 0
Freer Expression   + = 4
− = 1
+ = 3

Of all of the above categories only "character defense" stands out with anything like a numerically impressive rating. We mean by character defense those personalities, particularly the infantile and coldly narcissistic ones, who are protected from the experience of guilt by their character styles. Seven patients who employed such character defenses against guilt were unchanged in this respect, and six of these showed no conscious feelings of guilt to begin with. It seems that patients who ward off guilt by way of these encompassing pervasive character defenses are among those that are refractory to change in this respect.

Of the patients who showed diminished guilt feelings, one showed additional ideational and denial defenses along with freer expression, a somewhat atypical combination. Another patient showed freer expression along with diminished guilt feelings—a desired combination at least in expressive treatments. One patient showed diminished guilt feelings along with diminished alloplasticity, with the guilt being related to the alloplastic activities and diminishing as these activities did. One patient's guilt diminished, apparently as he gained more control over his socially unacceptable behaviors. One patient showed diminished guilt feelings as she developed greater tolerance for her oral wishes and less concern about her behaviors being "discovered." One patient became less guilty through greater tolerance of herself in general, and specifically about her conflicts relative to being a parent. One patient became less guilty as he was able to use his therapist as a source of dependence rather than using other and less socially unacceptable addictions. One patient showed what might be considered the ideal pattern, at least with respect to the results of expressive treatment, in that along with diminished guilt feelings, she showed greater insight, less denial, greater capacity for ideation in general, and freer expression of feelings. One patient showed diminished guilt feelings along with the diminution of behaviors which induce guilt, and so her guilt apparently stemmed from these behaviors. One patient showed diminished guilt feelings along with increased denial, less free expression, and less tolerance for guilt feelings, suggesting that intensification of defenses enabled her to overcome disagreeable feelings. One patient showed less guilt feelings along with increased use of projection, a probably unhoped-for result.

It is noteworthy that there was only one mention of suicide (only once in the data on unconscious guilt as well). This raises some questions about the theoretical relationship between conscious and unconscious guilt feelings and suicide, our means of detecting such feelings by way of psychological tests, and whether the sampling was so atypical as to exclude people whose route to suicide is by way of guilt.

Summary

1. While many patient variables can be assessed on the tests by way of both formal functioning and content, inferences about feelings of conscious guilt are dependent upon content alone and thus may not be as apparent to the tester as they are to those who question patients directly about their complaints. In other instances conscious guilt may appear by way of inferences from the tests, though not acknowledged verbally by the patient.

2. Of 34 patients, categorized into groups of mild, moderate, severe, and "no" guilt feelings before treatment, almost half were judged as having no guilt feelings before treatment, meaning that guilt feelings were not a pertinent issue on the tests. This high number may reflect difficulty in noting guilt by way of psychological tests, or that the pathology of these patients may have functioned to ward off the unpleasantness of guilt feelings.

3. After treatment, 11 patients remained the same with respect to conscious guilt feelings, 12 showed diminished guilt feelings, and 11 showed increased guilt feelings. Thus, conscious guilt feelings seem relatively resistant to change for the better.

4. Those with no guilt feelings before treatment tended to change significantly less often than those who had guilt feelings before treatment, although change for many people was in the direction of increased guilt.

5. A qualitative look at those patients who showed increased guilt made such an increase understandable with respect to changes in their total functioning.

6. Categories of what patients were guilty about included general sense of badness, being a bad parent, guilt over hostility, guilt over

heterosexual–homosexual behavior. There was no indication that one particular kind of guilt was any more or less amenable to change than any other.

7. Categories of ways in which people attempted to manage guilt included insight, denial, ideation, character defenses, alloplasticity, projection, and internalization, with character defense being the most prominent of these and also as being refractory to change with respect to guilt feelings.

UNCONSCIOUS GUILT

Introduction

In previous analyses, depression was inferred on the basis of content and formal indices. Conscious guilt, inferred on the basis of content only, was assumed to be somewhat more difficult to ascertain from tests. *Unconscious guilt* was remarked upon by the research testers as an extremely difficult inference to make on the basis of tests. Rather than having particular test data from which to make such an inference directly, the research testers had to rely on the theoretical abstraction of unconscious guilt in order to string together a plausible, internally consistent, logical chain between theory and the data they did have. Inferences about unconscious guilt, therefore, are more speculative than those about many of the other variables. Indeed, in 10 instances the research testers made particular reference to the amount of speculation they were forced to use in order to make any statement at all about unconscious guilt. And in 4 cases, after calling attention to the difficulties in making the inference of unconscious guilt, the examiner in effect refused to make it. So on this variable the N is reduced from 34 to 30. The research tester's reasoning, as applied to one case, is trenchant: "Applying our *theoretical* knowledge to this particular case, one might say that with the intrapsychic pain of the anxiety, the recurrent depression, the self-defeating aspects of her symptomatology—there *must* be a high degree of unconscious guilt kept in check and warded off by these aspects of her functioning. Not necessarily. This is a plausible inference but not the only one possible, or to my mind most probable. The anxiety seemed principally to stem from deep-seated separation problems, the depression related much more to conflicts around oral (and later genital) deprivation and emptiness, and the self-defeating aspects of her symptomatology seems to me to say little more than the fact that any neurotic behavior is in a measure self-defeating. If it wasn't somewhat self-defeating, it

wouldn't be a symptom. Therefore, I should say that while unconscious guilt may be inferred on a theoretical basis, its clinical significance in this case is not apparent on the tests." Another way of saying
this might be that the inference of unconscious guilt is often made on
the basis of relatively global overt behaviors, and changes in such behavior can be brought about by the influence and interaction of a
number of variables, the most difficult of which to specify on the basis
of test data being unconscious guilt.

Just as the research testers were forced to be unduly speculative,
so was the research psychologist in making judgments. Although we
have nonetheless carried through the same analyses, we think that the
safest way of evaluating these data is by attending to general and
gross trends and minimizing small differences as probably having
little validity.

Findings and Discussion

We grouped the patients as to the severity of unconscious guilt at .
initial. Twenty patients were judged as being in Group 2, "moderate,"
with only five being in Group 1, "mild," and five in Group 3, "severe." Thus, there is a pronounced general tendency to consider unconscious guilt in these patients as being midway between the extremes of excessive and minimal.

With respect to change in this variable, we set up a scale similar
to that used with other variables, one plus, two pluses, three pluses,
referring to increases, with decreases being reflected by minus, two
minuses, three minuses. As it turned out we used only the minus,
double minus, single plus, and zero categories.

Unconscious Guilt

$+ = 4$

$0 = 10$

$- = 9$

$-- = 7$

The four instances of increased unconscious guilt raise a theoretical issue. How can unconscious guilt be increased? With respect to
one patient the research psychologist asked, "How can we conceivably
talk of an increase in unconscious guilt—in view of our implicit assumption that unconscious guilt stems from infantile forces and infantile rage?" Later, the research testers reformulated the variable by
judging it according to the degree to which postulated unconscious
guilt affects behavior. Or, from another point of view, what is being
measured might be the ego's reactions to its forbidden impulses.

The same difficult theoretical issue arises, it seems to us, with respect to a decrease in unconscious guilt. Such a decrease could come about if, in successful expressive treatments, hitherto unconscious conflicts were resolved to the extent that the unconscious guilt associated with these diminished. Yet, as can be seen from other data reported (particularly the conflict resolution results), this is not the situation which obtained in most patients who nonetheless were considered to have had a decrease in unconscious guilt feelings. The likelihood is that the research testers made this judgment more on theoretical grounds than empirical grounds, basing their inferences of change of unconscious guilt on observable other changes.

We grouped the data into the following categories:

1. Manifestations of Unconscious Guilt
    + = increase; − = decrease
    Self Destructive Behavior
        − = 4
        + = 3
    Same = 2
    Depression
        − = 4
        + = 3
    Feeling of Badness and Self-Denigration
        − = 5
        + = 1
    Same = 1
    Avoidance of Pleasure
        − = 4
    Self-Punishing Behaviors
        − = 1

2. Content of Unconscious Guilt
    Aggression to Parents
        − = 3
    Same = 1
    Oral Aggression
        − = 2
        + = 1
    Same = 1
    Aggression in General
        − = 5
    Same = 1
    Over Sexuality
        − = 1
    Over Phallic-Oedipal Issues
        − = 3
    Same = 1

3. How Unconscious Guilt Dealt With
   Denial
           + = 2
   Reaction Formation
           + = 1
   Ideation
           + = 1
   Insight with Conflict Resolution
           + = 3
   Alloplastic Behavior
           − = 2
           + = 1
   Projection-Externalization
           − = 1
           + = 2
        Same = 1
   Freer Expression of Feelings in General
           + = 2
   Constriction
           − = 2
   Punishment by External or Extrapsychological Life Events
           − = 1
   Internalization
           + = 1

4. Miscellaneous
   Suicide
           − = 1
   Masochism
           − = 6
           + = 2
        Same = 2

We should like to remind the reader again that these categories were not selected on an *a priori* basis but rather were derived empirically by going through the research testers' statements. None of the categories is mutually exclusive of any other. Nor, because there may not be a specific reference by the research tester, can we assume that a particular issue played no part. We are simply assuming that the research tester selected the most salient issues for his brief statement about each variable.

Unconscious guilt (see Table 7) may be assumed to play a part in a wide variety of behaviors disadvantageous to the patient, and this may explain its being noted as occurring in 30 of 34 cases despite the theoretical and practical difficulties noted. On theoretical grounds it is difficult to conceive of anyone not having some unconscious guilt. The

Table 7. Change in Unconscious Guilt

	Sum of people change (directional)	Sum of people change (nondirectional)	Percent people change	Sum of units change (directional)	Sum of units change (nondirectional)	Average change per person
All 3	9S			4+[a]	29	.97
groups	17−[b]	21	70%	25−		
	4+					
Group 1	3−	5	100	3−	7	.14
	2+			4+		
N = 5						
Group 2	12−	14	70	19−	19	1.3
	2+			0+		
	6S					
Group 3	2−	2	40	3−	3	1.5
	3S			0+		
N = 5						

[a] + = increase
[b] − = decrease

numbers are too small to be conclusive, but there is a nonsignificant tendency for greater change to occur when unconscious guilt is *less* prominent to begin with. This is just opposite to what we found with conscious guilt. While the people in the group with more conscious guilt may have further to go, this may not be as determining as the likelihood that a lot of unconscious guilt is inimical to change. The group of highest initial unconscious guilt even contributes one-half of the four who, atypically for this population, developed more unconscious guilt. This supports the clinical impression that considerable unconscious guilt is a marked handicap for psychotherapy.

Around one-half of the patients showed a decrease in depression, one-half showed a decrease in conscious guilt, and now only slightly more (56%) of these patients (17 out of 30) showed a decrease in unconscious guilt. Why all three of these unpleasant affects should decrease in approximately the same number of patients is hard to know except for the possibility that they may all occur with the same patients. But they did not all occur in the same patients. Only 9 of the 15 showing a lessening of unconscious guilt also had lessened conscious guilt, and only 6 of the 15 had lessened feelings of depression. Evidently, the approximately 50% figure is a coincidence.

There is little heavy clustering throughout the results of any characteristics associated with unconscious guilt except for masochism which was noted 12 times, as against its only being noted once with respect to conscious guilt. Thus, masochistic behaviors seem related to guilt which is unconscious much more often than guilt which is consciously experienced.

Summary

1. It is easy to consider theoretically that much pathological behavior is self-defeating, and to assume that it is brought about by unconscious guilt. Such an inference might best be invoked only after corroboration with clinical data.

2. Unconscious guilt requires a good deal of extrapolation and longer chains in inferences than do other variables. For conceptual and practical reasons inferences about unconscious guilt are highly speculative.

3. The speculativeness of inferences about unconscious guilt may be the reason that 20 patients were judged as having a moderate degree of unconscious guilt before treatment, as compared to only 5 judged as having a mild degree and 5 as having a severe degree. In contrast to our findings with respect to conscious guilt those with a high degree of unconscious guilt to begin with tend to change less than those with a low degree suggesting that unconscious guilt is a marked handicap for psychotherapy.

4. A little more than half of the patients (17 out of 30) showed a decrease in unconscious guilt while 4 showed an increase and 9 remained the same.

5. The four instances of increased conscious guilt raise the thorny issue as to how unconscious guilt can increase, in view of the implicit assumption that it stems from infantile patterns. It may be that what is being measured is not so much a quantity of unconscious guilt, but the ego's reactions to the emergence of guilt-inducing impulses. This would appear as an increase of unconscious guilt in those instances where the ego has become less sufficient in the face of the emergence of such impulses.

6. Data are reported as to manifestations of unconscious guilt, content of unconscious guilt, how unconscious guilt is dealt with, and miscellaneous relationships to it.

SOMATIZATION

Introduction

As with symptoms in general, psychological tests are probably not the best means of assessing the mere question of presence or absence of *somatization*. A simpler way would be to ask the patient, exceptions being those patients who may withhold such complaints or those who exaggerate them. But if somatization is understood, as it is here, as referring less to a concrete complaint than to an intrapsychic disposition, it is possibly better assessed on the tests than are other symptoms.

In addition to this test-specific problem, the conceptual status of this variable is cloudy and somewhat arbitrary. The human body is the capsule for all psychological functions, and even casual observation indicates how the "mind affects the body" (blushing) and how "body affects mind" (depressions reactive to somatic illness). So when we speak of somatization we are probably speaking of an exaggeration of a universal disposition. In their write-ups, the research testers adhered to a more or less classical understanding of somatization—an attempt to bind anxiety.

One problem raised by this strict definition, however, comes up around one patient who had rheumatoid arthritis. The research testers described her attitude toward her illness, but did not specify the arthritis as a somatization, i.e., an attempt to bind anxiety. A case can be made for its being so, however. The classical psychological explanation for arthritis as an expression of inhibited aggression (and this seems to fit the general understanding of this patient) can also be looked at from the defense point of view, with arthritis being a means of binding the anxiety that the patient otherwise anticipates in connection with the expression of aggression. That is, the id definition (an impulse is transformed into a bodily symptom) can be viewed from the standpoint of the ego—the impulse can be judged as dangerous, anxiety aroused as a signal, the body "chosen" as a defense. In this sense, the arthritis *is* a somatization. Since the theoretical formulation just described was used by the research testers to describe this patient, we feel confident in including the arthritis as a somatization even though it was not named as such by them.

Findings and Discussion

One patient was not written about in this connection apparently through inadvertence. Only 13 patients used somatization. Nine used it prominently and 4 used it to a minimal degree.

Of the 13 patients who used somatization, 8 showed a decrease in its use at termination. Six of the 8 had used it prominently at initial and 2 had used it minimally. Five patients showed an increase in somatization or had begun to use it during treatment. At initial, 2 of these used somatization prominently, 1 used it minimally, and 2 did not use it at all. Thus, in every instance where somatization was relied upon as a defense, it changed in the course of treatment. In 7 of the 8 patients showing a decrease in somatization this was a favorable sign in that ideation and reflectiveness "replaced" bodily symptoms as a means of expression, a goal for each of them. With the eighth patient, the decrease in use of somatization was probably at least a temporarily unfavorable development since he evidently failed to develop other anxiety-binding measures of a more adaptive sort, and was presumably left even more vulnerable than before (he committed suicide after termination). Four of the patients showing an increase in somatization did so as an apparent alternative to alloplastic behavior, a favorable development since diminution of alloplastic behavior was a prime goal for them. Somatization could have been a first step toward replacing symbolic action with verbal symbols. With another patient increased somatization seems an indication of her continued flailing attempts to find some comfort, and can be considered in itself neither a favorable nor an unfavorable development, though the general picture of shifting defenses in a continued context of distress appears unfavorable.

Summary

1. If by somatization one means the patient's complaints, as with symptoms in general, then tests are probably less useful than interviews, except in those instances where patients may withhold or exaggerate complaints. But if somatization is understood, as it is here, as referring to an intrapsychic disposition to develop somatic symptoms as a means of binding anxiety, then it is probably better assessable on tests than are other symptoms.

2. Only 13 of 33 patients used somatization, with 9 using it prominently and 4 using it to a minimal degree. Somatization changed in all 13 patients, with 8 patients showing a decrease in its use, and 5 patients showing an increase or beginning use of it during treatment. With 7 of 8 patients the decrease in somatization was considered a favorable sign that ideation and reflectiveness were "replacing" bodily symptoms. Three of the 5 patients showing an increase in somatization did so as an apparent alternative to alloplastic behavior, for them a favorable development.

ANXIETY*

Introduction

The Wallerstein and Robbins (1956) definition of *anxiety* is "as a subjective experience, an inferred experience, and an observable manifestation" (p. 241). The definition used by the research testers both observes and departs from this definition. Obvious manifestations of

---

*Original draft and analysis of data by Dr. Siegal.

anxiety play a more important role in the nontest judgment of anxiety than it played in the research testers' judgment. One reason is that a good number of the test judgments were made without the research testers' seeing the patient and, thereby, having any opportunity to note trembling, stuttering, swallowing, perspiration, or other manifest behaviors considered to be indicative of consciously experienced anxiety. Another reason is that the tests provide a standardized, systematic range of opportunities for patient behaviors from which anxiety can be inferred. This is not different, in principle, from inferences of anxiety made by interviewers, but it is different in the tests having greater standardization than interviews and in the greater indirectness of test stimuli, e.g., inferring anxiety from a person's attending to achromatic shadings in inkblots.

This distinction between manifest and inferred anxiety should not be taken as implying a belief in so-called unconscious anxiety as a construct. The closest the research testers come to using anxiety as a construct is when they talked about so-called bound anxiety. When this was used by them, they were talking about a potential for feeling which is, for the moment, kept from consciousness or at least sharply reduced in experience by defenses. Thus, bound anxiety is not a construct but rather a potential or tendency toward some feeling which would be experienced more fully and directly if it were not defended against as efficiently as it is. These feelings may not be permanent, they may not be strong, they may not be long-lasting, perhaps only brief premonitory flashes (as in signal anxiety). Yet such anxiety has a great influence on behavior, as, for example, when it touches off a whole set of defense mechanisms or behaviors characteristic of the person designed to ward off any greater experience of anxiety. This discussion yields the hypothesis that psychological testers and clinical interviewers, while using the same term and sometimes even the same definition of anxiety, may nonetheless be observing and rating different phenomena. If the term *anxiety* is used in different ways by different people, as with any word carrying surplus meanings, it may be as dangerous as it is helpful. To the extent that testers use it one way, and those who treat the patient use it another, useful communications of test findings are handicapped.

Findings and Discussion

Increase or Decrease of Anxiety

The degree to which anxiety had increased, decreased, or stayed the same was judged on a 5-point scale, with ++ standing for consid-

erable increase, + standing for increase, S standing for the same level
of anxiety, − standing for less anxiety, − − standing for considerably
less anxiety.

All patients in this group (N = 34) were judged with respect to the
vicissitudes of anxiety rather than whether they had anxiety or not.
For many psychological traditions, especially a psychoanalytic one, it
is a truism that all people have anxiety. Yet there are those who conceive of anxiety as necessarily pathological. In this study it is considered as a universal, and in that respect normal, phenomenon which
may be at any given moment, for any given person, adaptive or maladaptive, too intense or too mild, centered around substitute objects
rather than the originally feared ones, an aspect of existential uncertainty or "neurotic" conviction.

Four patients were judged to have shown a considerable increase
in anxiety; 14 patients were judged to have shown a lesser increase in
anxiety. No patients were judged to have remained the same in the
degree of their anxiety. Fifteen patients were judged to have become
less anxious; 1 patient was considered to have become considerably
less anxious. Thus, 18 people showed more anxiety at termination
than they showed at initial, and 16 people showed less anxiety at termination than they had shown at initial.

This simple compilation of increases and decreases in anxiety
does not include a judgment as to whether such an increase or a decrease is favorable or unfavorable. In a clinical context, of course, such
a judgment is centrally important. It is made according to different criteria for different people, and it can involve a number of points of
view: efficiency of intrapsychic agencies as seen in structural, eco-
nomic, and dynamic terms; the mores of society; the opinion of those
central to the patient's environment; the therapist's objectives or the
patient's objectives. But we had no conception of these criteria for improvement, and tests are not particularly relevant to learning about
many aspects of such questions. Instead, we used as a criterion for the
"better" or "worse" question *the efficiency of intrapsychic functioning*
with respect to anxiety. These intrapsychic workings were (not)
judged as to (how well they process emotions and ideas in the abstract, but) whether they produced in the right way at the right time
what was required from them, according to a complex of assumptions
about particular objectives for a particular person.

Of the 18 cases with increased anxiety, 13 were judged to have
changed in this respect for the better. Of the 16 cases with decreased
anxiety, 14 were judged to have changed in this respect for the better.
Thus, 27 of the 34 patients were considered to have changed for the

better with respect to their management of anxiety, although just about half as many of the patients had an increase in anxiety as had a decrease in anxiety. Of the 7 patients who changed for the worse, 5 showed increased anxiety and 2 showed decreased anxiety.

In summary, about half of the sample had more anxiety after treatment and half had less. Seventy percent of those who showed an increase in anxiety were judged as improved with respect to the place of anxiety in their total intrapsychic situation. Eighty-seven percent of those who showed decreased anxiety were seen as improving in this respect.

How one reacts to such findings depends upon what one's theoretical and clinical expectations are. The lay view of psychiatric treatment, derived from other models of medical treatment, is that a patient should have little or no anxiety after treatment, since, after all, anxiety is an unpleasant experience. A sizable number of psychotherapists, outside the psychoanalytic and perhaps existential traditions, believe similarly. This can be seen, for example, in the "discomfort-relief quotients" and many other researches which take diminution of anxiety as a criterion of change for the better. Anxiety is a symptom which commonly brings people to physicians for treatment.

A different ideology from this familiar and traditional one is necessary to change the expectation that success will be measured by removal of the originally offending symptom. Our shorthand clinical knowledge often fosters the simplistic view of anxiety, as when we describe patients as less anxious (meaning "better") when what we actually have in mind is less a judgment of absolute quantity than a recognition that the patient manages anxiety more adaptively than he did before. He may or may not experience anxiety more or less. Or he may experience it in a qualitatively different way. In short, once past the belief that after treatment a patient should have less anxiety than he started with, one has to know what kind of patient has what kind of anxiety used for what purposes before being able to judge whether the change is for the better or for the worse.

Three coherent clinical patterns emerge from these data. Group A includes those patients who can be described on the whole as "healthier" and more "neurotic" than the other patients. Over the course of treatment they seemed to have increased in anxiety tolerance, with the use of anxiety as a signal, along with increases in such other variables as ego strength, patterning of defenses, and organization of thought and affect, as reported in other chapters. All these categories of observation go along with a picture of stronger, more flexible, ego functioning. Fifteen patients are included in Group A. Of these, 12 showed increased anxiety. This finding leads to the hypothesis that a major pattern of beneficial change is for patients to be able to experience increased anxiety and still behave more adaptively.

Three patients in Group A conformed to the general pattern but different in a particular way. They overcame primary anxiety*—anxiety that is too strong to be used adaptively, such as for a signal. This occurred to one patient through presumed organic impairment and to two patients through functional decompensation of basic ego functions who then went on to diminished anxiety through even better ego functioning. Except for these three patients, this group started from a somewhat higher level of ego functioning than the other groups. As will be seen below, closer analysis of these group discriminations and the terms used to define them reveals obscurities, discontinuities, and exceptions which disprove the rules. Nevertheless, we think the clinically informed reader will respond empathically to the general picture of this group being made up of more or less neurotic patients who became more anxious in the course of psychotherapy and learned how to deal more adaptively with this.

The second major grouping of change in anxiety, Group B, includes those four patients who experienced an increase in anxiety, but primary anxiety rather than signal anxiety. They became increasingly unable to tolerate instinctual pressures, were more fearful of being inundated, and so had a justified fear of loss of control. In short, they showed less effective ego functioning than patients in Group A.

The third major grouping (Group C) includes patients who seem to have been at the beginning of treatment in the throes of a decompensatory process, whose experience of anxiety after treatment diminished through the arresting or reversal of the decompensatory process. Of the seven patients in Group C, three persons showing diminished anxiety through overcoming decompensatory processes went on to develop the ego functioning and use of anxiety as a signal; two showed increased anxiety but now of a different kind and used differently; and one showed a diminution even of this source, kind, and use of anxiety.

While these groupings may be recognizable clinically, we ought not pass over the many theoretical issues embedded in these gross distinctions. Recall that of the healthier group (Group A) all but two showed increased anxiety. One may speculate that the two who showed decreased anxiety not only developed greater ability to im-

---

*See below, and Siegal and Rosen (1962) for a fuller explanation of this concept.

prove in an overall way in the management of anxiety, to allow it into consciousness and to allow more of the experience of it, but may have then mastered it through an additional step which allowed its diminution. This is suggestive of the paradigmatic process of expressive psychotherapy where ideas coming to consciousness are often associated with greater anxiety, but when "worked through" they remain in consciousness but without as much anxiety attached to them. Could it be, then, at least insofar as anxiety is concerned, that the great majority of the patients in our population who improved, nonetheless, terminated treatment at a point short of the kind of "working through" which would have permitted a decrease in anxiety? An alternate possibility is that the anxiety stemmed from the termination itself. Still another possibility, rooted as much in philosophy as in psychology, is that improvement in neurotic conditions is a function of the person's ability to confront existential uncertainty, to allow himself to experience and live with (without being forced to maladaptive consequences) anxiety inherent in life which must be marked with a series of losses before the ultimate one. One is reminded of Freud's (1955) comment that the purpose of analysis is to turn hysterical misery into common unhappiness.

A question that arose during the write-up of the variable ego strength is relevant here with respect to the use of ego strength as a criterion for grouping patients according to one or another pattern. Is it possible to describe the greater effectiveness of defenses which leads to a more constricted picture of ego functioning as a gain in ego strength? Or is ego strength to be defined in such a way that a greater tolerance for instinctual derivatives is to be the only kind of ego strength worthy of the name? In short, is there more than one kind of ego strength? Indeed, there must be, or else we would be working with an implicit belief that there is only one allowable pattern of "normal" or "healthy" ego structure, which is something we do not accept. We asked the same kind of question about anxiety tolerance. Does one tolerate anxiety better if he can allow himself to feel it, thus "being more anxious," or should anxiety tolerance be used to describe those persons whose defenses have become strengthened, who no longer need maladaptive behaviors with which to deal with anxiety and for whom anxiety has apparently diminished?

Another dimension according to which patients can be categorized as to kinds of change in anxiety, discussed in greater detail by Siegal and Rosen (1962), is the dimension of primary anxiety and signal anxiety. These are polar in the sense of extent or intensity with primary anxiety being overwhelming to ego functions and being experienced as panic, while signal anxiety institutes ego functions which, if successful, may lead to adaptive behaviors and to the minimization of anxiety. As rated above, and explicated below, some people change from struggling with primary anxiety to using anxiety as a signal.

A look at the nine cases which are not classifiable according to the major groupings gives us the opportunity to see other patterns of change in anxiety. Two patients were described as having less anxiety because they borrowed in a relatively direct fashion the strength of the therapist. The implication here is that the support from the therapist is more responsible for the diminution of anxiety than a wide range of intrapsychic strengthenings which would have allowed these patients to be included in Group A. One patient showed a diminution of anxiety through constriction of ideation, and she employed the ultimate avoidance by leaving treatment. One patient showed a mild diminution of anxiety through an increase in denial and alloplasticity as well as, possibly, direct support from the therapist. One patient showed greater anxiety due to a lessening of her need to defend herself against it with overideational and projective thinking, and an increase in obsessional-phobic ideation. Another patient experienced more anxiety, though the anxiety was less disruptive of her functioning. One other patient experienced a diminution of anxiety based on an increase in the use and effectiveness of denial, greater ideational constriction, and less awareness of conflicts, along with increased alloplasticity. She, too, left treatment.

Fear of loss of control was remarked upon with respect to nine patients. But this single phrase turns out to have referred to two quite different situations. If one takes the fear of loss of control to be a reference to the fear of primary anxiety with its consequences of defenses being overwhelmed, leaving the person open to the experience of panic, then the "fear" was justified in four instances. In one of these, the primary anxiety was of the catastrophic nature associated with brain damage; this fear diminished through the course of treatment. With the other three patients, the fear increased along with the emergence of primary anxiety, so that by the end of treatment it might better be described as a fear-laden recognition of loss of control. With five patients, again taking the fear to be of an emergence of primary anxiety, the fear was groundless. At least as far as these tests were concerned, the emergence of primary anxiety, with the associated implications of defects of basic ego functions, was not an issue with any of these patients. Not mentioned, however, by the research tester is the possibility that fear of loss of control might better be understood with these last patients as a fear of change, which may be dynamically connected in their minds with various consequences. That is, all people can be thought of as having developed certain defensive attributes, triggered by signal anxiety, a signal based on various unconscious fantasies of feared situations. Thus, these patients could have feared these situations rather than fearing primary anxiety, and the fear of loss of control would be justified in that sense. Of the five patients, four of them showed diminished fear after treatment, while one showed increased anxiety. The last is an example of someone who, without primary anxieties being an issue, had considerable fear of what may lie in wait should she relax, rearrange, or alter her defensive stance; indeed, she did develop some insight into what these fears might be, which frightened her enough so that she left treatment.

In short, fear of loss of control is justified for all patients, though what they may be afraid of may be different in those people categorized as having defects in basic ego functionings as against those without such defects. Crudely, this is a distinction between borderline psychotic people and neurotic people. Gross as this distinction is, we ought to recognize and admit that it plays a large part in the everyday therapeutic work of most of us. We often say, for example, that one is as "expressive" as one can be in a psychotherapy. But the factors which limit the degree to which one can be expressive are of two major kinds. On one hand, there are some patients one cannot work with very expressively until a great deal of work on the defenses has "opened up" the patient and made him receptive to the kind of connections, interpretations, etc., which expressive work implies. On the other hand, there is another type of patient for whom it is not the strength of defenses which limits the degree to which one can be expressive, but rather the weakness of defenses. One cannot be too expressive with these patients because one expects that any comment or therapeutic intervention that goes "a little too far" will produce disorganizing, regressive, or disruptive responses. Our groupings here pick up the extremes of this diagnostic scheme. It is just such extremes that have led to the generally held distinction between "supportive" and "expressive" psychotherapy, one which does not stand up well to subtle examination but which does allow for a distinction which we are better off making than not making. In short, by dealing with extremes, we sound as if we intend two discrete categories while, in fact, signal anxiety and primary anxiety are at opposite ends of a single dimension or regulatory process (Menninger, 1954).

The line of reasoning about the distinctions subsumed under the phrase "loss of control" applies equally to the concept of "decompensation." The latter is usually used to refer to a state of affairs in which the person is "decompensating" into a degree of disorganization called "borderline" or "psychotic"; that is, these people are overusing defenses with decreasing effectiveness, experiencing more anxiety and becoming less realistic as they retreat along their own lines of defense, more prone to distortion in reality and to the experience of primary anxiety. But the term can, theoretically, be used just as well to describe decompensation of character defenses and defense mechanisms which, without its overtones of psychosis, also results in a disorganization of the equilibrium.

Summary

1. Anxiety may be manifest or inferred (without invoking the construct "unconscious anxiety"), bound or unbound, signal or catastrophic. It is thus a term which requires much specification if people are to rate and communicate about the same phenomena.

2. Eighteen people showed more anxiety at termination than they showed at initial, and 17 people showed less anxiety at termination than they had shown at initial. Eschewing any prior notion that an increase of anxiety is always bad and a decrease is always good, and using the criterion of efficiency of intrapsychic functioning, 13 of the 18 cases of increased anxiety were judged to have changed for the better. Fourteen of 16 cases with decreased anxiety were judged to have changed for the better. Thus, 27 of the 34 patients were considered to have changed for the better with respect to their management of anxiety, although just about half as many had an increase as had a decrease in anxiety. Of those having shown an increase in anxiety, 70% were for the better. Of those having shown a decrease, 87% were for the better.

3. Fifteen patients, of whom 12 showed increased anxiety, were considered to have improved with respect to anxiety being used as a signal, along with their improvements in a number of other aspects of ego strength. Thus, a major pattern of beneficial change is for patients to be able to experience increased anxiety and behave more adaptively.

4. A second pattern was for anxiety to increase to the point of becoming primary rather than functioning as a signal, and this pattern was associated with decreased effectiveness of ego functioning.

5. A third pattern of change with respect to anxiety, exhibited by seven patients, was to have begun treatment in the throes of a decompensatory process and have arrested or reversed this process with diminished anxiety.

6. Exceptions and additions to these major patterns suggest a va-

riety of vicissitudes of change in anxiety. Included among these is the relationship to anxiety tolerance, lowering anxiety through borrowing the strength of the therapist, and fear of loss of control as related to anxiety.

SECONDARY GAIN

Introduction

The distinction between primary gain, as the compromise outcome of intrapsychic conflict, and secondary gain, as lateral effects of symptoms or illness which are felt to the patient to be beneficial, was carefully attended to by the research testers.

Findings and Discussion

This variable was commented on for 32 patients. Two patients were missed apparently through oversight.

Incidence

Increase. Seven patients showed an increase in secondary gain. As with so many of the variables, whether a change is for the better or for the worse depends on who has the change. Three of these patients were considered by the research testers to have improved a good deal, yet secondary gain was judged to have increased. Two of the three overcame their borderline psychotic difficulties through establishing particular kinds of Bohemian, arty, somewhat pretentious identities from which they extracted secondary gains. The third, who was judged to have become more uncomfortable in a number of ways as he overcame some of his symptoms and behavioral difficulties, gained increased solicitousness from the environment through this discomfort. Thus, one can think of secondary gain with these three patients as providing a kind of pleasurable reinforcement to solutions of primary difficulties, and thus presumably helping to maintain these solutions. Secondary gain, then, often used as jargon to mean malingering or something else "bad," may play a beneficial role in the total personality configuration.

Decrease. Twelve patients showed a decrease in secondary gain. With 10 of these patients, decrease came about through insight into how the primary difficulties were being used to elicit benefits from the environment. But with 2 patients rather different means of achieving the decrease were specified: With 1 patient a secondary gain from invalidism, previously brought about through her depressive symptoms, was, as the depressive symptoms lifted, brought about through worsening of arthritis. It seems, then, that she may have achieved insight into the primary difficulty leading to the depressive symptoms (aggression), but insufficient insight into her oral needs led to her affinity for one or another kind of sickness. Another possibility, of course, is that the developing arthritis simply made it unnecessary for her to achieve primary gains from depressive symptoms, e.g., punishment, absorption of aggression; the more circumscribed, even "acceptable" physical symptom, can now be employed for the same purposes. In any case, with a situation such as this, one cannot say that the decrease in secondary gain is necessarily representative of psychological change for the better. The other patient seems to have exchanged the dependent gratifications heretofore gained from his symptoms for those inherent for him in his positive relationship toward his therapist. Thus, one might say that the patient has exchanged one symptom for another rather than that the secondary gain has gone down. That the research testers did not choose to view it this way is hardly special to them. While a transference may be considered technically a symptom, under some circumstances it is one of the best kinds of symptoms to have. Ideally, when it occurs during the treatment, it aids further change, and the patient then rids himself of the transference. In this particular instance, however, the testers make the following point: "Nor does this positive transference appear to have been completely dissolved. . . ." Thus, with this patient, the decrease in secondary gain refers to a decrease in secondary gain that he brought to treatment, with a coincident increase in another kind of symptom developed during the treatment, considered overall as beneficial to him.

Same. Six patients were judged to have maintained their secondary gains at about the same level as when they started treatment.

No Secondary Gain. Only four patients were judged not to have shown evidence of significant secondary gain either at initial or at termination.

Judgment Could Not Be Made. In three instances the testers felt they simply did not have sufficient information to make a judgment on this variable.

Kinds of Secondary Gain

Oral. This category refers to the patient's gaining, from his difficulties, solicitude, nurturance, and varieties of passive, infantile, and other oral gratifications. This was the most frequent kind of gratification from secondary gain, and perhaps suggests one reason why secondary gain sometimes is described in terms suggestive of childish malingering. Of the 12 patients in this category (some patients showed this along with other kinds of secondary gains), 3 patients showed increased secondary gain of this kind, 6 patients showed a decrease, and 3 patients remained the same in this respect.

Means of Expressing Hostility. Almost as common as oral secondary gain was using emotional difficulties as a covert means of expressing hostility. Thus, the patient may not, as with alloplasticity, act upon the environment more or less directly, but nonetheless he may injure others, and this provides gratification to him. Three patients showed an increase in this means of expressing hostility, five patients showed a decrease, and three remained the same in this respect. Thus, the number of increases, decreases, and not changing is about the same in the two most frequent categories—oral, and expression of hostility.

Masochistic Gratification. Six patients were considered to have gained masochistic gratification as secondary gain: One showed an increase in this respect, three showed diminished gratification of this kind, and two remained the same.

Manipulating, Controlling. Surely, there are hostile elements in the gratifications from manipulating and controlling, and these cases might have been included under the category "Means of expressing hostility." But specific comments of this particular kind were made in three cases thus implicitly recognizing that there may be other motives than hostility for this behavior. One person increased in this way, one decreased, and one remained the same.

Narcissistic Gains. Narcissistic gain as related to secondary gain refers to fantasies that one is superior or special. As indicated previously, an increase in the development of such a special or pretentious identity is for some people a hoped-for and perhaps beneficial development, and this seems to be true of both instances where this kind of gain increased. Both of these patients overcame semidisorganized functioning, at least partly through the establishment of pretentious, arty, Bohemian identities, which among other things led to an increase in their self-esteem. One patient decreased in her narcissistic gains, apparently through the gaining of insight into them, and through the diminution of her symptoms. Two patients remained the same in this regard.

To Be Likeable. One patient derived from his inhibitions of hostility the liking of others for him because he was such a nice person. This secondary gain decreased during treatment.

Absolution of Responsibility. One patient was considered to have had as a secondary gain an avoidance of responsibility. This gain decreased during the course of treatment.

It should be noted that the small number of people in many of these categories is due to the strict adherence to the distinction between primary and secondary gain in this analysis of data. Patients' gains, generated by their primary dynamic conflicts, were considered "primary gains" and so were not included here.

Summary

1. Secondary gain is often used as jargon to mean malingering or something else "bad." With three patients an increase in secondary gain was judged to be beneficial. Seven patients in all showed an increase in secondary gain.

2. Twelve patients showed a decrease in secondary gain; with 10 of these, decreases came about through insight into how the primary difficulties were being used. Six patients were judged to have remained the same with respect to secondary gain, and 4 patients were judged not to have shown evidence of significant secondary gain either at initial or at termination.

3. Solicitude, nurturance, varieties of passive, infantile, and other oral gratifications were the most common kinds of secondary gain. Other kinds of secondary gain included: means of expressing hostility, masochistic gratification, controlling of others, narcissistic gains, to be likeable, and to absolve one of responsibility.

HONESTY

Introduction

No patient (or person) is completely honest in an ideal sense. The "truth," as with any other percept, is influenced by the observer's needs, fears, preconceptions, prejudices. For example, someone who might be described as an out-and-out liar may nevertheless be true to his own set of beliefs and loyalties. Yet clinicians know, in a general way, the differences between an honest and a dishonest patient, and the special difficulties posed by dishonest patients in psychotherapy are familiar to any experienced therapist. In this write-up, abstract ideals of honesty are eschewed in favor of honesty in an operational sense, with respect to what could be expected and what occurred in psychotherapy.

Findings and Discussion

Thirty-one patients were commented on in regard to the variable *honesty*. Statements about honesty were missing from the write-ups of three patients, apparently through oversight.

Statements about Honesty

Degree of Honesty. At initial, five patients constituted a group that was considered unusually frank and candid. None of these became less honest, three remained the same in this respect, and two of them even improved over their initial high level of honesty as their defensiveness lessened. A second group ($N = 10$) was described at initial as not having honesty as a potential problem for them in treatment; they were considered honest but not unusually so. Not one became less honest, five remained the same in this respect, while five improved. Taking these two groups as one ($N = 15$), about one-half of the patients were considered to be "honest" in the sense of being direct, candid, truthful. About half (eight) remained the same in this respect, while seven became even more honest.

This analysis does not imply that all the rest of the people were dishonest. What it does mean is that for these 15 people there were test data of sufficient clarity to stir the research tester to make particular note of this quality. By the same token it does not mean that even among these 15 patients honesty was always easy for them or that there was nothing that could be called by some stretch of the word *dishonesty*. Twelve of them, in fact, garnered comments about difficulties they had to overcome in order to be honest. Five of these experienced such difficulties because of their defensiveness, and all but one improved in this regard. One of them was considered as deceiving himself even though he was honest with the therapist to the best of his ability, and he remained the same in this regard. One had limits set to his ability to be honest by a lack of psychological-mindedness, and he improved in this regard. One had limits set to his honesty by his tendency to distort matters, and he became worse in this regard. One became more direct, even though not necessarily more honest in any other way. Two people were considered to be honest for pathological reasons—narcissism and masochism. Both remained the same in this regard. So, honesty is not a unitary trait. It can be helpful, it can be "normal," it can be pathological. One can have it although hampered by difficulties which set limits to its expression, and so presumably it is more available or manifest under some conditions and less so under others, e.g., at times when the person is most defensive and when distortions are less necessary. That there were only 15 of 33 people whose test protocols were impressive enough of honesty to encourage a comment to that effect may be a rather foreboding finding from the point of view of the Wallerstein and Robbins description of this variable: "It is felt that it is necessary for patients to be 'honest' in the sense of being frank or sincere in respect to treatment. If this exists, then psychotherapy can proceed." It is possible to make at least a rough test of this proposition by seeing whether these 15 patients are the ones who did in fact make the best use of their psychotherapy.

The Project's Prediction Study (A. Appelbaum and L. Horwitz, 1968) included a 5-point scale of patients according to global change. The 15 most honest patients (according to the tests) are listed below with their scaled rankings on the extra test, outside criterion ("5" reflects the greatest amount of change for the better).

−4	−4	−1
−4	−4	−5
−4	−3	−4
−3	−4	−3
−3	−2	−5

Testing the frequencies of 1 or 2 (same or worse) and 3, 4, or 5 (improved) global change ratings for these 15 patients against expected frequencies based on the proportion of ratings given to the total sample yielded a chi square of 4.564 with 1 df which was significant at <.05 level. Testing them against equal expected frequencies yielded a chi square with 1 df of 8.066, significant at <.005 level. Thus, there is a positive relationship between honesty and the amount of change for the better.

Reasons for Honesty. Reasons specified for being honest included exhibitionism, with one person remaining the same and one person improving in this regard. Honesty in connection with narcissism was noted two times, and both patients remained the same. Masochism was cited as the reason for honesty in three instances with one improving, one remaining the same, and one getting worse.

Dishonesty

Kinds of Dishonesty. Again, that someone was noted under the category of dishonesty does not mean that he was always dishonest any more than it means that someone noted under the honesty category was always honest. The following data are included because of the test findings which suggested, strongly enough to stimulate the research tester to note it, that these were instances of people being dishonest in one way or the other with respect to treatment. Conscious dishonesty, such as breaking rules and promises or consciously withholding information, was noted in three patients, with two of them remaining the same and one getting worse. Another kind of dishonesty was self-deception. In the words of one of the testers, "They believed the lie." One might argue, of course, that people who are dishonest as a result of defensiveness also believe their lie and this is probably true. But again, the point was specifically made with respect to five people that their dishonesty had the quality of self-deception, and so we assume that it was a more prominent issue with these people. Two patients remained the same in this regard, and three changed for the better.

Reasons for Dishonesty. Twelve people were considered to be dishonest as a result of their defensiveness. Eight of these were considered to have improved in this respect, two were considered to have remained the same, and two were considered to have gotten worse in this respect. The preponderance of improvement here is consistent with what one hopes for and expects in psychological treatment, namely, a lowering of defensiveness which makes greater honesty possible. Dishonesty as a result of distortion was remarked upon five times, with two people remaining the same in this respect, and three people getting worse. One person was considered to be dishonest out of fear, and he remained the same. Two people were considered to be dishonest out of the need to put up a good front, and both improved in this respect.

Change

Patients were ranked on a 4-point scale (+ + standing for substantial change for the better; + standing for some change for the better; 0 standing for no change; − standing for change for the worse).

Change in Honesty
($N = 31$)
$+ + = 1; + = 14;$
$0 = 12; - = 4$

Of the 15 who changed for the better, only 6 were from the group which was considered to be quite honest to begin with. This is not surprising since the people in this initially honest group did not have much room for improvement. All 6 were considered to be essentially honest but were hampered in various ways in their honesty. Thus, the treatment evidently made it possible for them to overcome these difficulties and to exploit their basically honest orientation. The 4 people who changed for the worse were among the sickest of the group. Three of them did poorly in treatment. Among the 12 people who remained the same, 8 were considered quite honest to begin with; no attention was called to issues which restricted their honesty, and so it is hardly surprising that they remained the same. The other 4 patients who remained the same and the 4 who got worse were from the group not conspicuously honest to begin with. Since one would hope and expect that people would become more honest during the course of treatment, the fact that 8 persons or almost 26% of the sample did not improve in this respect is a rather gloomy finding. While one can understand and appropriately take comfort from the finding that many people become more guilty, anxious, and depressed after treatment, one is hard put to find comfort in so many patients not being able to overcome noteworthy limitations on their honesty.

Two people are considered to have become more direct after treatment although not necessarily any more honest in other ways than they were before. One person expressed himself honestly although he had to do it in various kinds of action, and he improved in this regard, i.e., he used this mode of communication even more honestly at the end of treatment than before. One person was considered to be hyperhonest—honest out of a sense of scrupulosity. He improved in this regard, which meant in this context that his honesty was less spurred by this motive. Four people tended toward dishonesty through their lack of psychological-mindedness: Three improved in this regard, one person remained the same. This strains somewhat the concept of honesty, but the point made here is that the lack of psychological-mindedness puts limits to the degree to which the people could be honest, and these limits were extended in those people who improved in this respect. This seems a variation of the self-deception category, but again was kept separate because the research testers specifically implicated psychological-mindedness.

Summary

1. The "truth," as with any percept, is influenced by the observer's needs, fears, preconceptions, prejudices, and so honesty cannot be discussed in an abstract, ideal sense. The honesty rated here refers to the usual serviceable understandings that clinicians employ in considering whether the patients are "honest."

2. Of 5 patients constituting a group at initial considered to be

unusually frank and candid, not one became less honest. Three remained the same, and 2 improved over their initial high level of honesty. Of 10 patients described at initial as being neither unusually honest nor having honesty as a potential problem in treatment, 5 remained the same in this respect while 5 improved. About one-half of the patients, then, were considered not to have honesty as a special difficulty for psychotherapy at initial. Not one of these became less honest than originally thought, with half remaining the same in this respect and about another half becoming even more honest.

3. A significant positive relationship was found between honesty and the amount of change for the better.

4. A wide variety of characteristics facilitated and inhibited honesty.

5. Kinds of dishonesty included conscious dishonesty, such as breaking rules and promises or withholding information, with two patients remaining the same in this respect and one getting worse; and self-deception, with two patients remaining the same and three changing for the better.

6. The major reason for dishonesty was defensiveness, eight patients having improved in this respect, two having remained the same, and two having gotten worse. Such a finding is consistent with what one hopes for and expects in psychological treatment, a lowering of defensiveness which makes possible greater honesty. Other reasons for dishonesty included dishonesty as a result of distortion, being dishonest out of fear, and being dishonest out of the need to put up a good front.

7. Of 15 patients who changed for the better in honesty, only 6 were from the group which was considered to be quite honest to begin with, a not surprising finding since such people did not have much room for improvement. Four people who changed for the worse with respect to honesty were among the sickest of the patients, 3 of them doing poorly in treatment in general. The 4 people who remained the same and the 4 people who got worse, from the group not conspicuously honest to begin with, add up to 8 persons, or almost 26% of the population, who did not improve in this respect. While one can understand and appropriately take comfort from the finding that many people become more guilty, anxious, and depressed after treatment, one is hard put to find comfort in this many people not being able to overcome noteworthy limitations on their honesty.

8. Other kinds of changes included having to use action as a means of expressing themselves honestly, hyperhonesty, and shifts in honesty through shifts in psychological-mindedness.

SELF-CONCEPT

Introduction

The Wallerstein and Robbins (1956) definition of *self-concept* is built on Erikson's ideas of "ego identity"—"a way of describing the trait configurations that make up one's image of oneself as a person" (p. 244). On the basis of this idiographic conception, one might expect that the remarks made about patients with respect to self-concept would be more idiosyncratic or individualized than remarks made about some of the other variables. This seems to have been true since we came up with long lists of comments, with relatively little general groupings of patients around each one.

As the reader will notice, the kinds of comments included under self-concept include those which may be experienced by the patient as well as those which seem to represent the viewpoint of somebody else, e.g., "The patient is egocentric." The formal Project description of self-concept as a patient variable does not specify that the patient consciously feels this aspect of himself, and in fact notes that self-concept is ". . . not just a conscious percept, but a more basic unconsciously determined (and not necessarily consciously perceived) constellation of attitudes about one's self and about the role one plays." An intriguing question then arises, whether one can have attitudes about one's self, as a *percept*, without *feeling* this aspect of the self? Certainly if one *does* feel one of these attitudes or self-concepts then it is likely to be a percept. If one does not feel it, the feeling may be unconscious, and that would still be considered part of the self-concept, as defined in the Project. But some of the words which are used by the research tester to describe the person raise a question whether the patient ever could feel or be aware of himself in this respect. We have in mind such words as *moralistic, Pollyannaish, struggling toward goodness, shallow object ties, danger of identity dissolution.* Such words as *competitive, devouring beast* may represent feelings or self-percepts which are, or could be, perceived or experienced by the patient. Or they, too, may represent an abstraction on the part of the research tester which may be felt by the patient or perceived by the patient in ways different from what is represented by these words. For example, the patient described as being "competitive" may notice that he becomes ill at ease when someone has more than he does or seems to be doing better than he, etc. This feeling may be related to his self-concept as an inveterate failure beneath which is another self-concept as one who deserves to be the best. Words connotative of either of these identities would more surely reflect the patient's feeling experience or self-perceptual experience than would such a word as *competitive*. We mention this as something that might be borne in mind whenever psychologists address themselves to variables of at least an implicitly subjective sort. For many testers, as with the research testers, major attention is paid to concepts rather than patient experience. Each would seem to have its uses, and should be decided upon advisedly. Separating kinds of statements made in test reports, in this and other ways, is one purpose of an offered outline (S. Appelbaum, 1972a).

Findings and Discussion

Change in Self-Concept

Twenty-eight of the 34 cases were judged to have changed in self-concept. In the other 6 instances, the self-concept was judged as remaining the same. We scaled the degree of change on a 6-point scale with zero meaning the same, with plus, double plus, and three pluses referring to increasing change for the better, and with minus, double minus, and triple minus referring to worsening self-concept. The 28 people who had changed contributed a total of 44 units of change regardless of direction (the mean change for each of these people was 1.57). Thirty-four units of change were for the better, only 2 units of change were for the worse. With respect to people rather than units of change, of the 28 people who did change in self-concept, 22 did so for the better, and only 2 for the worse, each of the latter by one scale unit. Four people could not be scored as to whether the change was for the better or for the worse. Thus, people change in self-concept more than they do on the other variables, and this change tends to be for the better. A speculative hypothesis might be that the very act of being in psychotherapy, having someone of professional stature take seriously one's problems, may contribute to a better feeling about one's self. If this is true, it may be that these patients when they are no longer in treatment would show a diminished self-concept. And yet, perhaps this suggestion may continue and even be instrumental in better living.

In an attempt to see whether beginning severity of difficulty with self-concept was related to change, we separated the groups into "mildly self-critical" ($N = 28$), and "severely self-critical" ($N = 8$). The "severe" group accounted for the two changes for the worse and for the six who remained the same. All the people in the "mild" group changed for the better. An analysis of variance showed significantly less change for the better in this group ($p < .001$). Thus, the rich get richer and the poor get poorer, with those people who think most severely toward themselves not changing for the better, or even changing for the worse.

Of the changes for the better, 11 were one-scale unit; 10 were two-scale units, and 1 was three-scale units. In 4 instances, changes of one-scale unit took place, but it was indeterminate to us as to whether this change could be categorized as being for the better or for the worse. The reason for this difficulty seem instructive. One of these was considered to have a somewhat better self-concept, but not only was this thought to be tenuously held but it was based on a euphoric pseudo-fulfillment seemingly entirely dependent upon a "little-boy" relationship with the therapist. This could be an improvement, especially since the patient at the time of initial study was in danger of losing control over eruptive aggressive impulses. Yet, at termination, according to the research tester, he "has become less troubled by reality limitations . . . in which [he] feels not only irresponsible to superego strictures, but to reality consequences as well." Two questions are implicit in this issue. One is whether the therapist achieved his objective—what he thought was feasible to expect for this patient. The second is whether, from the point of view of his functioning or some other criteria for improvement, the present state can be considered an improvement over the previous state. To investigate these questions we turned to the A. Appelbaum and Horwitz Prediction Study write-ups (1968)—overviews of the whole course of treatment based on all sources of information—for the purpose of tracing the fate of explicit predictions. In these write-ups, one patient was described as having decompensated, on the verge of psychosis, and in her self-concept moving from "the role of the accepting, resigned, 'good-natured' conforming person" to regarding the "environment as more harshly demanding, more severely persecuting, more constantly critical of her, and so much less ready to accept her previous passively resigned 'martyred' role." Since this change represents less well-organized ego functioning, it seems to be a change for the worse. Yet as she is less downtrodden, she may feel better, while the environment suffers more from her. Further, this concept of herself may be an overreaction to the previous one, which can be expected to simmer down as she makes further use of what she may have learned in the treatment. In another instance, the patient is described at termination as much less thinking of herself as "cool, detached, self-sufficient, superior and masculine," showing "much less arrogance and coolness, much more passive dependence." At termination she is hospitalized, and it is unclear from the write-up whether in other respects the change has been for the better or for the worse. That she is now hospitalized, while during psychotherapy she was an outpatient, might suggest that change has been for the worse. Yet the other material fails to support unequivocally this inference, and one might consider it necessary that the characteristic attitudes of coolness, detachedness, self-sufficiency would have to be dropped before substantial beneficial change might be possible. With another patient there was practically no change in her self-concept, and yet the report does say that closer to consciousness is the feeling that she "has been deprived and along with this she seems to remind herself, as it were, more frequently that she is a grown-up individual who need not experience deprivation as a child would." That such a recognition of herself may be closer to consciousness may or may not be an advantage to the patient. Since hers was intended to be an expressive treatment—psychoanalysis—one might assume that bringing the element closer to consciousness is at least on the way to a change for the better; but with this being the only aspect of her self-concept considered to have changed, it remains speculative whether bringing this element closer to consciousness can be considered an improvement. (The patient left treatment precipitously.)

Kinds of Change

Negative Self-Feeling. This refers to those attitudes the patient has toward himself which are presumably troublesome. Plus is scored when the negative self-concept changed for the better; when these changes are considered tentative or especially weak in intensity, the scoring is "tendency to +"; minus is used to denote that change of some kind occurs but not for the better; a question mark refers to those instances where it was unclear whether or in what way the self-concept had changed; and "S" refers to the same. The defining words are quoted from the research testers' remarks.

Oral Passive—helpless, yearning for succorance, dependent, passive (N = 10):

$$+ = 6 \qquad - = 2$$
$$\text{tendency to} + = 1 \qquad ? = 1$$
$$70\% \text{ improvement}$$

Oral Aggressive—rapacious, parasitic, greedy, grasping, pouncing, and devouring (N = 3):

$$+ = 1 \qquad S = 1$$
$$? = 1$$
$$33\% \text{ improvement}$$

Self-Depreciating—slovenly, wasteful, ugly, drudge, inept, oddball, fraudulent, self-loathing, cast aside, awkward ($N = 7$):

$$+ = 4 \qquad - = 1$$
tendency to $+ = 2$
86% improvement

Castrated (Male)—impotent, feminine, a little boy ($N = 6$):

$$+ = 4 \qquad - = 1$$
tendency to $+ = 1$
82% improvement

Masochistic—sufferer, subjected to trials for a just purpose, poor me, martyr ($N = 5$):

$$+ = 3 \qquad - = 2$$
60% improvement

Sexual Identity (Female)—degraded, weak and little-girlish, castrated, unworthy ($N = 8$):

$$+ = 5 \qquad ? = 1$$
tendency to $+ = 2$
87% improvement

Narcissistic—arrogant little princess, the pretentious intellectual, "special" ($N = 3$):

$$+ = 1 \qquad - = 1$$
$$S = 1$$
33% improvement

Limited, of course, by the small Ns, these data suggest that troublesome sexual identity conceptions of the self are highly amenable to change in both sexes. So are self-depreciating feelings in general—six of the seven dimensions of self-concept change for the better in half or more of the cases.

Benevolent Self-Feeling. This represents a judgment from the research testers' point of view as to feelings about one's self which for a particular patient seem conducive to better experience and, by implication, functioning. One would assume that if statements were made about benevolent self-concept they would refer to desirable change and so most of them would be expected to be scored with a plus. In only one instance was this kind of self-esteem mentioned as having been lowered.

Tolerance of the Self: $+ = 7$; tendency to $+ = 2$
Increasing Self-Esteem: $+ = 3$; $- = 1$; $? = 1$

Feeling One's Self More in Control: + = 1
Feeling One's Self More Capable: + = 8
Feeling One's Self More Masculine (Male): + = 2
Feeling One's Self More Feminine (Female): + = 5

Defensive Self-Concept. This refers to those concepts of the self which according to the research tester are enlisted for defensive purposes. For most psychotherapies one would assume that a defensive self-concept would have to change in the course of a successful treatment process. However, with some patients one could have as his objective the strengthening or developing of a defensive stand, as seemed to occur with three patients. Thus, plus indicates change, whether it represents yielding of the stance (as it usually does) or whether it represents a strengthening of the stance. Minus indicates that there has been no change in the stance. Theoretically, it would be possible for a defensive stance to become strengthened despite efforts to the contrary. We could imagine, for example, a rigid character formation which became more rigid in the face of anxiety aroused by the treatment. No such instances were found in this group, so the minus can represent simply no change in the defensive character stance.

Proper—a rather gross category including such comments as neat, precise, hardworking, orderly, prim (N = 6):

$$+ = 4 \qquad - = 1$$
$$? = 1$$

Superior—another gross category including arty, pretentiously intellectual and cultured, authoritarian (N = 6):

$$+ = 3 \qquad ? = 2$$
$$\text{tendency to} + = 1$$

*Overly Compliant**—good natured, amiable, martyred (N = 4):

$$+ = 2 \qquad - = 2$$

Overly Assertive—(N = 1)

$$- = 1$$

Changeable. This is a description of a structural characteristic rather than a content one, and includes such remarks as "ingrained" and "in flux" (+ = 1; S = 2).

---

* "Overly" represents an opinion as to the defensively driven quality to the behavior rather than an arbitrary social or personal preference.

Summary

1. People change in self-concept more than they do on the other variables, and this change tends to be for the better. Perhaps the very act of being in psychotherapy, having someone of professional stature take seriously one's problems, may contribute to a better feeling about one's self.

2. Patients who were only mildly self-critical at initial changed for the better in their self-concept significantly more often than patients who were severely self-critical at initial.

3. Kinds of negative self-feeling included oral-passive (70% improvement); oral-aggressive (33% improvement); self-depreciating (86% improvement); castrated, male (82% improvement); masochistic-sufferer (60% improvement); sexual identity, female (87% improvement); narcissistic (33% improvement).

4. Kinds of benevolent self-feeling included tolerance of the self, increased self-esteem, feeling one's self more in control, feeling one's self more capable, feeling one's self more masculine, feeling one's self more feminine. Almost by definition, notations by the research tester of benevolent self-feeling denoted change for the better.

5. Defensive self-concepts included being proper, superior, overly compliant, and overly assertive.

6. Words used to describe the patient's self-concept could be construed as representing how the patient feels about himself, as well as denoting concepts which could not be felt in such terms by the patient but rather were expressions from the observer's point of view. These differences of language illustrate some of the conceptual complications of the term *self-concept*. A person may consciously feel or experience himself in various ways, be unconscious of how he feels or perceives himself, be described by himself or others with terms which may or may not reflect self-experience.

SUBLIMATION

Introduction

The conceptual difficulties surrounding *sublimation* are well-known by all people who work with it, not just testers: the obscurities about the change in object, aim, and source of energy; the id emphasis in the original formulation of sublimation; and the issues of ego autonomy and independence of drive which can be taken to complement the original formulation. Psychological testers have special difficulties judging sublimation since such a judgment depends in part on extra-test knowledge of the patients' activities. What the psychologist does do with respect to this variable is to make inferences about intrapsychic changes which logically could be expected to lead to sublimated activities, and to judge test references to activities which frequently lend themselves to sublimation. Intrapsychic changes are probably necessary accompaniments or causes of newly developed sublimations, though probably insufficient conditions in and of themselves.

Findings and Discussion

Judgments of sublimation are difficult to make, requiring greater than usual inferential leaps. From this point of view, it is no surprise that a statement about sublimation was made in only 16 cases. Of these, only 10 showed the presence of sublimations, the remaining 6 being comments on why particular behaviors should not be considered as sublimations. While it is doubtless true that the assessment of a variable that depends upon extratest knowledge is difficult to make from tests alone, it is also expectable that in this sample of severely disturbed people there should be relatively few instances of sublimation.

Incidence

Three people were judged to have increased in the development of sublimations; two of these showed small and equivocal change. Seven people were judged to have increased their capacity or potential for the development of sublimations. Six people were considered not to have had nor to have developed sublimatory activities during treatment. If one can separate out the difficulty of making this inference from the apparent difficulty in developing sublimations, it appears that sublimations did not develop often or to a great degree in this group. That few of these patients changed in an across-the-board and impressive fashion is not surprising since sublimations are more or less recognized as the crowning point of substantial and encompassing change.

With those patients in whom no sublimations were observed at initial, none developed during treatment. Of the six people who neither had sublimations before treatment nor developed them in treatment, several changed in other respects. Thus, it seems that when the research testers did note developed sublimations they were not being persuaded by "halo" effects from other beneficial changes. In summary, sublimations did not develop or improve impressively, at least as judged by way of the tests.

Bases for Increase

One person was considered to have increased her capacity for sublimation through increased ideational capacities; two people were considered to have increased their potential for the development of sublimations through conflict resolution; and one was considered to have fully developed sublimatory activities through conflict resolution. One person was considered to have increased his capacity for sublimation through improved general ego functioning, and one through being less rigid in his defensive operations in general and in his relying on a less sterile use of fantasy in particular.

Bases for the Lack of Sublimatory Activities

Two people were considered to be unable to develop sublimations because of their energies being tied up simply in maintaining equilibrium. Two people were considered to be handicapped with respect to sublimations because of their energies being bound by conflict. Two people were considered to be handicapped with respect to sublimations by the poorly modulated quickness and directness of their affect expression.

Summary

1. Sublimation is an especially unclear concept, and judgments of it are especially difficult to make on the basis of tests. It is expectable that in this sample of severely disturbed people there would be relatively few instances of sublimation. Therefore, it is not surprising that presence of sublimation was noted in only about one-third of the patients.

2. Over the course of treatment, sublimations did not develop often or to a marked degree.

3. Bases for increased sublimation included increased ideational capacities, conflict resolution, improved ego functioning in general, and less rigidity in defensive operations. Bases for the lack of sublimatory activities included being tied up simply in maintaining equilibrium, having energies bound by conflict, and poorly modulated affect expression.

EXTENT OF DESIRED CHANGE

Introduction

The Wallerstein and Robbins definition of the variable *extent of desired change*—"This is a question both of what the patient conceives his therapeutic need to be and the role he expects to play in the therapeutic process" (p. 248)—is described solely from the standpoint of assessment at initial and seems to imply that change no longer should be desired at termination or follow-up, just as a patient no longer wants to take more medicine once his symptoms have cleared.

But suppose one thinks of the psychotherapy not as something done to the patient in order to bring about an *a priori* condition but as providing the patient with an opportunity to view himself in successively different ways. Then psychotherapy would set in motion a series of desires for change (A. Appelbaum, 1972). Just as one may not know where he wants to go until he climbs a hill and sees the many places to go—each horizon begetting more horizons—the patient may develop new interests, feelings, wishes as he becomes aware that these may be available to him. The treatment may equip him with the tools to continue change, whether by self-analysis or by the demands for change posed by the new experiences that the psychotherapy has helped to make available, or by the inevitability of new experiences and opportunities just through changes intrinsic in living. Rather than termination of psychotherapy marking the end of change, it may set in motion a widening trajectory of change which continues to widen throughout life. If this line of reasoning is correct, there are limitations to assessing psychotherapy at termination. Rather than psychotherapy being "over" at termination, one may think of the patient as having achieved through formal psychotherapy an opportunity to begin "psychotherapy" in the sense of a self-conscious attempt to change under motivational, structural, and cognitive conditions different from the ones he had when he began his formal treatment. The data were examined for support for any of these conceptions of psychotherapy.

Findings and Discussion

Only 13 of 34 patients were described with respect to this variable, which suggests that the testers did not estimate tests as especially good instruments for the assessment of this variable. Indeed, of the 13 cases, 5 write-ups included reference to the lack of convincing test evidence, and the tone of several other write-ups was also speculative. This is not surprising. Extent of desired change is, in a number of respects, a different order of variable from most of the others. Most of the other variables require an examination of test performance, such as objective measures of efficiency (IQ) or first-order inferences from test data, e.g., "depression" from seeing much blackness in the ink-blots. By contrast, extent of desired change is an opinion, or point of view, about the patient which requires that an assessment be a long chain of inferences departing successively from the test data proper.

Decrease in Desire for Change

One way change might no longer be desired would be if the patient had gotten everything he wanted and was satisfied with himself at the end of treatment. This ideal, or perhaps idealistic, situation apparently did not occur among these patients. Another way additional change might not be desired would be if the patient had become so disappointed at the lack of realization of his wishes for himself that he gave up on the possibilities of change. Three patients did show a decrease in extent of desired change through an attitude of resignation, as if there was no point desiring more change as they had gotten all they could expect to get. One patient was considered too disturbed to integrate a desire for change into his thinking. One patient did not acknowledge herself as needing change.

Extent of Desired Change Remains the Same

The wish for change could remain the same in instances where motivation for change was high to begin with and continued high through the treatment. There were no such instances among these patients. Three patients showed low motivation for change to begin with, and their desire for change, or for a different kind of change, never developed during the treatment. Two of these recognized at the beginning a wish to relieve themselves of unpleasant feelings; one was mentioned as having insufficient ego strength to convert this to a useful desire for change; and one had pleasure-seeking attitudes, along with poor ego strength, which prevented his developing a drive to change other than to gain momentary relief. The third patient did not see herself as a person needing help, even symptomatic relief, and this remained the same at termination.

Increase in Desire for Change

Three people who came to treatment with a desire simply to overcome symptoms were able to see many more aspects of life as troublesome and to desire more far-reaching changes. As noted above, one showed at the same time a decrease in desire for change through an attitude of resignation. Two persons were remarked upon as having become sufficiently less defensive so as to allow either a new recognition or a more open acknowledgment of a wish for better things in their lives. It was remarked of one of them that he had gotten a taste of what he liked and wanted more of it, recognizing that this required further change in himself. Thus, there were five instances of increased desire for change, three of these being through moving from complaints about symptoms to complaints about life, with two others coming about through decreased defensiveness which allowed the emergence of the desire for more change.

Three people were considered to be skeptical about their change for the better. One was seen as intent on continuing the process of change toward more change. One was seen as interested in maintaining the change that she had accomplished, which considering her starting point was a slight increase in desired change. The question of stability of change for the better was raised in two instances.

The five people who by termination developed an increase in desire for change support the idea that psychotherapy sets in motion a liberating process whose ultimate results may be more properly assessed at a time later than termination. That no person was found to have lost his desire for change through having achieved his original goals may reflect failures in treatment or it may reflect the "open-endedness" of people—the more people change, the more possibilities for change appear. But no support is adduced, in these data, for the idea that at termination psychotherapy results in cessation of desires for change.

Summary

1. Extent of desired change was originally conceived by the Project solely from the standpoint of assessment at initial, how the patient thinks of the forthcoming treatment in this respect. But one can conceive of psychotherapy as setting in motion a series of desires for change, which logically could continue after the treatment itself is over.

2. A decrease in desire for change, in the sense of having gotten everything that was wanted, did not occur. A decrease in desire for change through an attitude of resigning one's self to having gotten all that could be expected occurred in three patients. No instances were reported of having gotten all one wanted with the result that there was no need for further change. Three instances were reported of low mo-

tivation for change, which remained the same throughout the treatment. Three people came to see more aspects of their life as troublesome and to desire more far-reaching changes than simply to overcome the symptoms they had come with. Three people were considered to be skeptical about their change for the better, but intent on continuing or maintaining what they had accomplished.

3. These data adduce no support for the idea that at termination psychotherapy results in cessation of desires for change. They do offer support for the idea that for some people psychotherapy sets in motion a liberating process toward new and different changes from those originally anticipated.

IQ

CHANGE IN IQ DURING AND AFTER LONG-TERM PSYCHOTHERAPY*

A number of studies have examined change in IQ with advancing age and before and after various kinds of psychotherapies. However, no systematic analysis of change in IQ has been done after long-term psychotherapy and 2 years after that. Do IQs change in adults over periods of 5 to 10 years? Are such changes different for men and women, for long-term psychotherapy or psychoanalysis? Are they due to other systematic influences such as effects of practice, or are they random fluctuations? This study is an attempt to answer these and related questions.

Method

The mean length of time between the I [Initial] and T [Termination] testing was 57.4 months and between the T and FU [Follow-Up] testing 26.2 months. Although equivalent forms of the Wechsler-Bellevue would have guarded against practice efforts, Form 1 was used for each of the testings. The research project was conceived as a naturalistic study, changing as few of the standard clinical practices as necessary, and Form 1 is used routinely in clinical evaluations. Thus, the psychologists could employ in the research their subjective clinical norms based on extensive experience with this form of the test. This

* Excerpts of this article by Stephen A. Appelbaum, Lolafaye Coyne, and Richard Siegal are reprinted here with permission from the *Journal of Projective Techniques & Personality Assessment*, 1969, *33*, 3, 290–297.

was particularly important for the nonquantitative assessments of the rest of the variables, since these were dependent upon comparisons based on the same test stimuli. The research design called for each patient to be his own control rather than for the use of a control group, which could also have clarified the effects of practice. . . .

These data made possible a quantitative analysis based on Verbal, Performance, and Full-Scale IQ, and a quantitative treatment of a qualitative analysis based on the psychologists' judgments as to meaningfulness of change in IQ. Finally, correlations are reported between change in IQ and a test rating and a nontest rating of overall change in the patient. Both kinds of IQ judgments were obtained by one author (Appelbaum) going through the psychologists' statements based solely on the tests. The judgments as to whether quantitative changes in IQ should be considered meaningful or due to random fluctuations or effects of practice were ordinal ones, each patient being compared with himself on a + (increase), 0 (no change), − (decrease) scale. The criteria for these judgments, using the clinician as the measuring instrument in the tradition adhered to elsewhere in the Project, included the assessment of such objective and subjective elements as the S's quantitative starting point, his motivation and approach to the tests, the place of intelligence in a dynamic understanding of his personality, and the extent and quality of personality changes logically related to change in IQ.

Subjects

Thirty-seven subjects were given the WB at I, 35 at T, and 33 at FU, but not always the same Ss in each group. Through death, and other reasons for unavailability, only 26 of the 42 Ss took the WB at all three points. Therefore, questions requiring a comparison of these three temporal points will be based on an N of 26 (12 males, 14 females). Comparisons of I to T will be based on an N of 31 (14 males and 17 females). Comparisons between T and FU will be based on an N of 30 (13 males and 17 females). The mean FS IQ before treatment of all three overlapping groups was the same, 124. Mean age of the patients at the beginning of treatment was 30, SD 8.6.

Results

Quantitative Findings

In order to test the significance of differences among mean IQs at the various points in time, these IQ scores were subjected to repeated measures analyses of variance. Six such analyses were done; all analyses included a Time factor with three or two levels and factors of Sex and Treatment Modality. Three analyses also include a Verbal versus Performance factor. Following significant main effects, individual mean comparisons were performed using the Neumann-Keuls test. Following significant interactions, simple effects tests were run. . . . [With] 26 cases, the I to T comparison was significant at less than the .001 level ($\chi^2 = 18.539$) and the T to FU comparison was significant at less than the .05 level ($\chi^2 = 6.221$). With 31 cases, the I to T comparison was significant at less than the .001 level ($\chi^2 = 18.420$) while that of T to FU with 30 cases was significant at less than the .01 level ($\chi^2 = 9.733$). Since the clinician's judgments were made on the basis of an overall change in IQ and not specifically for V, P, or FS IQ changes, no such comparisons were possible. In summary, then, the qualitative judgments of IQ changes parallel the quantitative ones—both report a rise in IQ at T and FU.

Turning now to a comparison between changes in IQ from I to T ($N = 31$) and T to FU ($N = 30$), one sees that more Ss gained in IQ from I to T than from T to FU, 52% as against 43%. This result lies in the expected direction. The longer period of time gives anything productive of change (other than practice effect) more time to become effective. Thirty-two percent showed no change from I to T, 47% showed no change from T to FU. Ten percent showed a significant loss from I to T, 7% from T to FU. Six percent showed a change of pattern from I to T, 3% from T to FU.

Using the 26 Ss tested at all three points, it is possible to trace the fate of individual patients' IQ from I to T and from T to FU. . . . There is not only a tendency for IQ to rise during the time of treatment, but there is a strong tendency for these gains to be maintained or improved upon after treatment. Further, among those who failed to gain, or lost in IQ during treatment, more than half do gain by the time of FU. *The general hypothesis given rise to by these data, then, is that psychotherapy encourages a rise in IQ, though with some people one has to wait for some time after T for it to show itself.*

A good deal has been written about the existence of practice effects in IQ . . . and there is experimental evidence that all three IQ means, Verbal, Performance, and Full-Scale, increase significantly from test to retest for intervals up to 6 months. Experimental evidence also suggests that such practice effects are usually about twice as large for the Performance IQ score as for the Verbal IQ score. These results based on such short intervals between testings are of dubious comparability to ours, which are based on much longer intervals. Two other studies using the WAIS report little appreciable IQ change over 10 years and 3 years, respectively. . . . To our knowledge there are no test–retest IQ studies of adults with the WB at anything like comparable time intervals between testings. If practice effects are involved to some extent, then (1) the increases from T to FU ought to be greater than those from I to T since the mean time interval from T to FU is less than half that for I to T, and since FU was the third testing, and (2) the increases should be greater for P IQ than for V IQ. The analyses of variance of the IQ scores indicates that this is only somewhat true. In two analyses P IQ increases are more significant than those for V IQ. However, the I to T difference is more significant than the T to FU difference in all analyses where they can be compared.

Changes in personality variables, presumably unaffected by practice, which parallel IQ changes make for the presumption that IQ changes result from general personality change rather than practice effects. One author (Appelbaum) judged whether or not there were parallel changes at T in other variables along with change in IQ. This judgment was based on test assessments of all patient variables. (Here the frequency data are available for only 24 Ss, since the question of parallel change was unanswerable for 2 Ss.) Assuming a fifty-fifty chance of parallel change, the resulting χ^2 of 6.000 was significant at less than the .02 level. There is a possible "halo effect" in the judges of other patient variables knowing IQ changes as well. We, therefore, correlated the tester's judgment of overall change with a nontest judgment of overall change, made by other clinicians of the Project (based on interviews with the patient, his family, and therapist, etc.). This correlation was .71 (<.001). These data support the idea of IQ change going along with general personality change rather than being an isolated effect of practice.

Discussion

While the probable existence of some practice effects beclouds the specific extent of demonstrated upward change in IQ, that IQ does change to some significant extent during psychotherapy and sometime after psychotherapy seems tenable. This is especially so considering that Ss were in the superior range of intelligence to begin with, with consequent small room for improvement, and that the WB has a curtailed upper range. Conceivably, one might argue that the rise in IQ was due to a more encouraging, benevolent atmosphere at T—the treatment was over, and the patients knew that the testing was for research purposes rather than clinical–diagnostic purposes. Further, they had taken the tests already, and were familiar with them and the testing situation. But being a research S, for many people, carries its own anxieties, and T is often a time of turmoil—Ss may be preoccupied with what the examination will show, how justified their investment of time, money, and energy was. The influence of situational effects cannot be assumed categorically one way or another, and there seems no *a priori* reason to believe that they were instrumental in bringing about the demonstrated rises in IQ.

How general these findings are remains to be demonstrated with a different sample, especially a larger one and a less bright one. Conceivably, the changes demonstrated here may be restricted to bright people since these people may be the only ones able to benefit from individual psychotherapy, as is often assumed in the selection of patients for psychotherapy.

Another plausible restriction on the generality of these findings is that they may only come about by way of treatments which are judged to be successful. But this sample is not distinguished by impressive therapeutic success. This finding is not surprising since the population from which these cases were drawn is among the most difficult in the range of Ss to whom individual psychotherapy is usually offered. Ss who come to the Menninger Clinic usually have had previous, unsuccessful tries at treatment. Most of those relatively healthy Ss who present themselves for the first time for treatment at The Menninger Foundation are members of the psychiatric community, and these patients were excluded from this experimental sample for reasons of confidentiality. Rather than IQs changing for the better only in successfully treated cases, *a more reasonable hypothesis is that there is a tendency for IQs to change for the better during psychotherapy even though the Ss may not have had particularly successful results.*

The lack of differences between men and women in change in IQ scores is not surprising. We can think of no theoretical or clinical reason why one should expect such a difference. The same cannot be said for the finding of no difference between Ss who receive psychoanalysis and those who receive psychotherapy. One might expect that those receiving psychoanalysis would show greater rises in IQ through the lifting of repressions which inhibit ideas. On the other hand, a rise in IQ also might be expected in severely disturbed Ss, for whom psychoanalysis is usually not recommended, as such Ss become better organized. Probably one should not put too much credence in this finding of no difference in IQ change between those treated with psychoanalysis and psychotherapy since, for this particular analysis of data, the subsample sizes are quite small, the analytic group comprising only 15 Ss, the psychotherapy group only 11.

That IQ gains from T to FU are maintained or improved suggests that the effects of the psychotherapy noted at T are not transitory ones, at least they do not disappear 2 years after. In fact, for the FS and P IQs, an additional gain occurs between the end of treatment and the FU point. It is not too likely that the additional 2 years in age is responsible for this change by way of aberrant influence on the WB age norms. Rather, this finding raises some fundamental issues for conceptions of psychological treatment. These issues are further underlined by the finding that 6 Ss who did not change in IQ at T did so by the time of FU, 1 S who showed a significant loss at T showed a significant gain at FU, 3 Ss who showed a significant gain at T showed another significant gain at FU. Thus, 10 of 26, or 38%, showed a rise in IQ from T to FU. That people continue to change after the "treatment is over," and that those who have not changed up to that point do so after, implies for research in psychotherapy that T is an arbitrary point, and in many cases an inaccurate one, at which to assess the effects of psychotherapy. An implication for clinical practice is that one criterion for deciding to terminate treatment is the judgment as to whether gains are achieved, but not yet expressed, or are truly not yet achieved. For conceptions of psychotherapy, these findings suggest that psychotherapy puts a process in motion which may have a gradually increasing effectiveness, as gains are reinforced by environmental rewards which in turn reinforce gains. It is as if at the time of psychotherapy an ascending line is begun whose extent of rise may be quite small toward the beginning, but throughout life achieves increasing height. That the P IQ, but not the V one, rises significantly between T and FU suggests the hypothesis that during the time of treatment *per se* the V IQ was raised as repressions were relieved and ideation encouraged by way of the verbal procedures of psychotherapy. The P IQ, however, in part reflects the practical application of intelligence to the solving of problems. This ability may be more meaningfully put into practice and exercised when the person has left the somewhat artificial state of introspection, encouraged during the treatment, for the more workaday application of his new learnings to environmental problems. Another possibility is that the process of T has a temporarily inhibiting effect. If this is so, then the time of treatment does bring about the fundamental changes, reflected in part in a rise in IQ, and these are simply obscured by the emotional turbulence inherent in T. That the quantitative IQ changes and the subjective judgments of IQ changes are so similar is not surprising and suggests that despite some special instances a rise in IQ is held in general by clinicians to be better than a loss in IQ, and that the more points the IQ rises, the more likely that the change is meaningful.

ROUTES TO CHANGE IN IQ DURING AND AFTER
LONG-TERM PSYCHOTHERAPY*

We have shown that IQs tend to go upward during psychotherapy and in the 2 years after psychotherapy, and that these changes are positively related to overall change in the patient's well-being. How can we understand such changes? IQ is assumed by most clinicians to be an innate capacity influenced by motives (e.g., need to be right, need to fail) and by feelings (e.g., anxiety about being examined). Thus, the reporting of IQ is often amplified with statements about how well it represents the patient's expectable or potential functioning, apart from these influences. Since psychotherapy would not be expected to alter innate capacity, examination of the correlates of IQ change in psychotherapy may shed light on other variables that are determinants of IQ, and on the malleability of such characteristics in psychological treatment. We are able to offer some at least hypothetical answers to these questions. . . .

Method†

A statement was written about each of the patient variables on the basis of the tests alone for each of the three testings. . . . The statement about intelligence included the IQ, as taken from the Wechsler-Bellevue, and qualitative remarks about intelligence gleaned from the rest of the test battery (The Rorschach Test, Word Association Test, Story Recall, BRL Object Sorting Test, and Thematic Apperception Test). [These statements were made on the usual Project research forms.] At T and FU these test-based statements included an assessment of how change in IQ could be understood with reference to changes in other single variables and to shifts in the personality configuration. . . .

Results

Quantitative Findings (I to T)

Five of the changes for the better in patient variables correlated with IQ change at less than the 1% level of significance; self-concept

*Excerpts of this article by Stephen A. Appelbaum, Lolafaye Coyne, and Richard Siegal are reprinted here with permission from *The Journal of Nervous and Mental Disease*, 1970, *151*, 5, 310–315. Copyright 1970 by The Williams & Wilkins Co.
†For complete Method and explanation of Subjects, see those sections from the reprinted article, "Change in IQ During and After Long-Term Psychotherapy."

($r = .58$, $N = 26$), ego strength ($r = .47$, $N = 29$), patterning of defenses ($r = .49$, $N = 29$), thought organization ($r = .51$, $N = 25$), and overall change ($r = .57$, $N = 29$). (The number of cases varied from correlation to correlation because the psychologists made ratings of change only if there was sufficient information to warrant making a judgment.) Five of the changes for the better in patient variables correlated with IQ change at less than the 5% level of significance: affect organization ($r = .43$, $N = 25$), anxiety tolerance ($r = .44$, $N = 28$), and anxiety ($r = .45$, $N = 29$). (Three patient variables changed for the better independent of IQ change: conscious guilt, psychological-mindedness, and symptoms.) Of the 23 variables left after excluding intelligence, then, 10 are significantly related to change in IQ. Clearly, IQ change is not independent of personality change, as noted with respect to developmental changes in IQ by Moriarty (1966). . . . These findings strongly support the belief that IQ is a function not only of innate capacity but of other aspects of the person. What aspects are these?

Of the 23 patient variables, 5 are clearly structural, i.e., enduring characteristics of formal ego functioning. And changes in all 5 of these are positively correlated with IQ change, 3 at less than the 1% level of confidence (ego strength, patterning of defenses, thought organization) and 2 at less than the 5% level of confidence (affect organization and anxiety tolerance). Honesty, self-concept, and secondary gain could provide alternate, or additional, motivational explanations. This collection of positively correlated variables, structural and motivational, is a grouping one might expect to have change in generally supportive–strengthening treatments. This expectation does, in fact, jibe with the results of the treatment of these patients.

Qualitative Findings (I to T)

The correlations reported above represent group trends. But from the idiographic, clinical point of view there can be in principle as many routes to IQ change as there are Ss. Further, any one S may have gained (or lost) in IQ in a way opposite from group trends, e.g., with most Ss lessened alloplasticity was associated with higher IQ, but with one constricted S, IQ went up concomitant with increased alloplasticity. Following are some inferences made by the research psychologists about what specific change in each subject was most likely to explain the change in his IQ. We attempted to condense those inferences that seemed to be saying the same things with different words, and to eliminate the highly speculative ones, but even so 13 categories of explanatory statements emerged. It seems that many different kinds of intrapsychic change are associated with IQ change. The greatest number of Ss in any one category was 5; the least was 1. Numbers of subjects in each category are noted in parentheses. Those characteristics which *increased along with increased IQ* were use of secondary process (3 Ss), stylistically better organized work habits (4 Ss), ideation (1 S), the ability to take an objective approach to the task (1 S), alloplasticity (1 S), and attention and concentration abilities (1 S). Those characteristics which *increased with decreased IQ* included alloplasticity (1 S), constriction-avoidance (1 S), anxiety (1 S), and pseudostupidity (1 S). A characteristic which *decreased with increased IQ* was anxiety (1 S). With some patients, autoplasticity (2 Ss) and increased use of ideation (1 S) were associated with increased verbal IQs and lower performance IQs. As can be seen in the instances of alloplasticity, concentration, anxiety, and constriction avoidance, which are related positively with both raising and lowering of IQs, there is no *a priori* way of telling whether changes in these in one or another direction lead to changes in IQ for better or for worse. It depends upon the use to which these particular characteristics are put in a particular personality configuration. Mirroring the quantitative findings, most of these explanations were varieties of structural considerations.

Qualitative Findings (T to FU) and Discussion

At FU, also, a wide range of hypothetical explanations for IQ changes was noted. The closest to a massing of instances occurs on anxiety, where six Ss were considered to have improved in their IQ performance by virtue of being less anxious. Those changes just described as occurring from I to T occurred at FU also. But rather than repeating the same explanations we should like here to offer another way of generalizing about the changes noted. We were impressed (as we were in assessing several other patient variables reported elsewhere) with the general dimension of "loosening" and "tightening" as an explantory principle for change. Characteristics of "looseness" include greater availability of ideas to consciousness; more experience of affects including anxiety, depression, guilt; and greater inclinations to action or alloplasticity. By "tightening" is meant more constriction and tighter controls over action, affects, and ideas. To judge the effects on any one person, however, these general dimensions require a knowledge of the use to which these changes are put and the position from which S starts. For example, if ideas become more available to the consciousness of a precariously adjusted S, they may result in a lowered IQ through his being unable to concentrate on tasks, through intrusiveness and preoccupation with ideas rather than tasks. If ideas become more available to a constricted S, they may enable him to think more efficiently.

Some examples of patterns of change categorized according to loosening and tightening follow.

At T one S seemed to have loosened (given freer rein to) his masculine assertiveness though his IQ remained the same. His assertiveness at that time was described as being overcompensatory. At FU, when his IQ did finally raise, overcompensatory aspects of his assertiveness had subsided, allowing greater play for his genuine abilities.

Loosening occurred with one S who shifted from a rigid reliance upon an externalizing-projective stance to greater internalization and freedom of expression of thought and feelings, but with consequent increased anxiety and depression. Coincident with these changes, he lost IQ points. In a world previously seen as malevolent, he had spurred himself to use his superior intelligence to the utmost for defensive purposes, and he no longer needed to do this when his experience of danger diminished.

Other Ss became more ideational as part of a general tightening of their personality. Here ideation seemed to have been used to establish controls over alloplasticity and anxiety. One such S achieved a higher IQ at FU through overcoming a flagrant psychosis noted at T, which at that time had resulted in a significantly lowered IQ. He not only had made up that loss at FU, but had even increased his IQ by 5 points.

Instances which run counter to the general trend reveal some further possible linkages between personality change and IQ. One S, who had shown an increase in IQ at T and another increase at FU, showed increased distress at FU and came back into psychotherapy. The change at T was seen as a result of her becoming less alloplastic, more "neurotic," more involved in the conflicts which she had previously defended herself against through her behavior, and hence she was now more anxious. The increased IQ at follow-up was related to her continued involvement with the need to master conflicts internally, employing ideas for this purpose. Another patient's increased IQ at T was attributed largely to her greater social attunement, and she maintained this change at FU, although some of the difficulties that had led her to seek treatment had meanwhile recurred. *These instances give rise to the hypothesis that there may be a specificity to abilities whose improvement leads to a raise in IQ, and that these abilities may be retained despite other difficulties.*

One S whose IQ had not increased at T did show significant increase in her IQ at FU as part of a general continued increase in her ability to do the job, to be efficient, and to exert better concentration and control over impulsive actions. The explanation offered for her not showing an increase in IQ at T was that she responded regressively even to slight object losses, and she felt the end of treatment as a rejection.

Two Ss of very superior IQ simply maintained their IQ from I through FU despite extensive other changes. One of them moved from an acute decompensation of ego functioning to outright psychosis at T and to a settling down of the psychosis at FU. The other S, also with a very superior IQ, made extensive changes for the better from I to T and maintained these from T to FU with IQ remaining the same throughout. *This gives rise to the possibility that with some people IQs, perhaps especially those over 130, may reflect ego structures which are relatively autonomous of the effects of conflict and changes in other ego functions.*

CONCLUSIONS FROM ANALYSES OF SINGLE VARIABLES

Introduction

The project was organized largely around the idea of analyzing separate variables, whether these be environmental variables, treatment variables, or patient variables. With respect to the patient variables, this research strategy reflects the belief that people are, to an extent, composed of parts; that these parts can be isolated through diagnostic instruments, particularly psychological tests; that they may vary to a degree independently; and that their variation has clinically plausible and meaningful consequences. In recent years, this point of view has decreased in popularity. Nowadays people tend to be thought of, in some quarters, as political and social units, or simply as humans. An atomistic approach to people is criticized as relating one's self to people as if they were mechanical objects; as a source of cognitive satisfaction to the observer without benefit to others; as an intellectualization which diverts the mind from a true, feelingful, and meaningful engagement between people; and as a pigeonholing device perpetrated by an authority upon a passive victim.

Many of these objections are reasonable in that some diagnostic practitioners do indeed conceive of people in the ways criticized, and often fail to make beneficial use of the possibilities inherent in the diagnostic enterprise. Yet to our mind there is an irresponsible eliding of facts in these criticisms. Diagnostic categorization does reflect reasonably high correlations between intrapsychic variables which are, to a greater or lesser extent, measurable. Variables do vary independently; but a recognition of them leads to the recommendation of differentiated treatment procedures and is an aid in the execution of treatment procedures.

We had our own discomfiture which stemmed from sources other than these common criticisms. We knew that some variables would be easier to measure by way of psychological tests than would others. We were aware of the intercorrelations reflecting substantive relationships between the variables which made for a perhaps damaging artificiality in analyzing them separately. How useful, except for heuristic purposes, would it be to separate, for example, depression, conscious guilt, and unconscious guilt? Could it even be done, we wondered. Although research testers worked independent of a knowledge of the whole, each analysis of single variables if remembered could influence forthcoming analyses. As it always does in clinical thinking, the parts tended to merge into familiar clinical personality configurations.

Against the background of these issues, we analyzed and summarized, as a group, the data from the analyses of single variables.

Findings and Discussion

The patient variables are not equally ascertainable by way of tests, nor are they equal in conceptual clarity. We categorized the variables according to how well suited they were to analysis by way of the tests, making our judgments on the basis of the research testers' comments. (In the following lists, rank order is not intended.)

Variables Considered Most Suitable to Test Analysis

Depression	Core neurotic conflict
Conscious guilt	Anxiety
Patterning of defenses	Self-concept
Affect organization	Ego strength
Thought organization	IQ

Variables Considered of Moderate Suitability for Test Analysis

Externalization	Honesty
Psychological-mindedness	Secondary gain
Insight	

Variables Considered Least Suitable for Test Analysis

Alloplasticity	Somatization
Anxiety tolerance	Symptoms
Extent of desired change	Quality of interpersonal
Transference paradigms	relations
Sublimation	Unconscious guilt

Variables were more or less clear conceptually. They were also categorized according to their level of difficulty, and judgments were based mostly on the comments of the research testers but also on the judgments of the research psychologists. (In the following lists, rank order is not intended.)

Variables Considered as Presenting the Least Conceptual Difficulties for the Testers

Quality of interpersonal relations	Patterning of defenses
Conscious guilt	Core neurotic conflict
Anxiety tolerance	Transference paradigms
IQ	Self-concept

Variables Considered as Presenting Moderately Difficult Conceptual Problems for the Testers

Depression
Affect organization
Thought organization

Variables Considered as Presenting the Greatest Conceptual Difficulty for Testers

Symptoms	Extent of desired change
Externalization	Anxiety
Somatization	Honesty
Psychological-mindedness	Sublimation
Insight	Secondary gain
Unconscious guilt	Ego strength
Alloplasticity	

It might be well to keep in mind that these variables, in and of themselves or for other testers, may not present similar conceptual difficulties. Some of these difficulties, as noted in the single variable analyses, were due to the way the Project had defined them. Working by themselves, and able to define the variables with specific reference to testing dimensions, the research testers may have had less difficulties with some variables, and conceivably more difficulties with others.

One might wonder whether the difficulties in ascertaining data about variables from tests were due solely to conceptual difficulties with the variables. Of the 9 variables judged most difficult to ascertain on the tests, 6 also appeared in the group of greatest conceptual difficulty. Only 5 of the 10 variables judged easiest to ascertain from the tests appeared in the list judged most conceptually clear. Thus, it appears that conceptual unclarity makes a substantial contribution to difficulty ascertaining data from tests, but there are other reasons as well.

All other things being equal, the following variables which are both hardest to ascertain from tests and conceptually least clear are likely to provide the shakiest data base for generalizations:

Symptoms	Extent of desired change
Unconscious guilt	Sublimation
Alloplasticity	Somatization

Variables which are easiest to ascertain from tests and present the least conceptual difficulties are likely to provide the strongest data base for generalizations:

Conscious guilt	Self-concept
Patterning of defenses	IQ
Core neurotic conflict	

We turn now to the question of how often patients changed on each variable regardless of whether such changes were for the better or for the worse. Listed in Table 8 are the percentage of patients who changed with respect to each of the variables (percentages are used because of the varying numbers of patients on which each variable was judged). It would be well to keep in mind that these percentages refer to numbers of patients rather than to degree of change over the group as a whole. It is conceivable that each patient could have changed with respect to a variable but the change would be small; thus it would be erroneous to assume that the variable, despite its high percentage, was subject as a general rule to great change. The percentage on insight can also be misleading. Almost by definition it

Table 8

Variable	Percent	Variable	Percent
Insight	100	Anxiety tolerance	81
Patterning of defenses	100	Core neurotic conflict	78
Thought organization	100	Externalization	78
Anxiety	100	Conscious guilt	68
Somatization	100	Ego strength	68
Symptoms	97	Unconscious guilt	66
Depression	94	Extent of desired change	62
Affect organization	89	Alloplasticity	62
IQ	88	Honesty	61
Secondary gain	87	Psychological-mindedness	59
Quality of interpersonal		Sublimation	55
relations	86	Transference paradigms (Could not be judged
Self-concept	82	as to change)

would have to be rated 100%, for it is hardly likely that a person can be in psychotherapy and not develop at least some insight.

The first 11 of the 23 variables, from the midpoint up, include patterning of defenses, thought organization, and affect organization (anxiety tolerance is only 2 down from this cutoff point). All of these can be considered as variables which primarily measure structure. Ego strength, another structural variable, is not included; the conceptual unclarity previously noted seems to have been responsible.) So much structural change occurred.

Of the variables most directly referring to feeling—depression, anxiety, and conscious guilt—more change occurs in anxiety (100%) and depression (94%) than in conscious guilt (68%).

Many patients change greatly in somatization and symptoms.

Few patients change on those five variables judged as being hardest to ascertain from tests and most difficult to deal with conceptually (unconscious guilt, alloplasticity, extent of desired change, sublimation, somatization), which implies that when the testers were in doubt they were more inclined to judge patients as not changing than as changing on these variables. If this is so, the findings of change are more likely to be valid than findings of no change.

The 78% change in core neurotic conflict (60% for the better, as noted below) seems somewhat low and implies that a good portion of the treatments might not have been highly expressive.

In conformity with long-established clinical agreement, and as supported elsewhere in this Project, the resolving of neurotic conflicts brings about structural change. Indeed, many clinicians say that structural change can only come about through the resolution of neurotic conflict. In another report of the project, however, Horwitz (1974) points out that considerable structural change occurs in relatively nonexpressive, supportive treatments, for which he offers a rationale in object relations terms.

Data which bear on this question are reported in Tables 9 through 12. "Structural change" (referring to change in patterning of defenses, thought organization, affect organization, anxiety tolerance, and ego strength) is categorized in the tables as follows: plus (+) stands for five, four, or three variables changing for the better with no more than one remaining the same or changing for the worse; plus and question mark (+?) refers to three variables changing for the better and two remaining the same; minus (−) refers to fewer than three changes for the better. "Conflict resolution" refers to those patients judged as showing conflict resolution through classical expressive means; "miscellaneous means" refers to those people who changed in neurotic conflicts by various means other than conflict resolution; "no change" refers to those people who showed no change in management of conflict. One patient having two changes for the better, two remaining the same, and one changing for the worse were considered not classifiable.

Table 9

	+	+?	−	Total	
Conflict resolution	10		1	11	$\chi^2 = 12.07$
Miscellaneous means	6	2	1	9	$df = 4$
No change	1	2	4	7	$p < .025$
	17	4	6	27	

Table 9 shows a clear positive relationship between conflict resolution and structural change—the more conflict resolution, the more structural change. This relationship is statistically significant ($p < .025$), yet there are exceptions. Seven of 17 patients without conflict resolution did show structural change. Thus, both points of view, that structural change is associated with resolution of conflict and that structural change can come about in the absence of conflict resolution, receive support from this analysis.

Table 10

	+	+?	−	Total	
Conflict resolution	10		1	11	
Miscellaneous means	6	2	1	9	$\chi^2 = 13.33$
No change	1	2	4	7	$df = 6$
Increased awareness					$p < .05$
In consciousness	3		2	5	
	20	4	8	32	

Table 10 reflects a similar analysis with the addition of "increased awareness in consciousness." These patients showed what one might consider a necessary, though perhaps insufficient, step toward conflict resolution (one would have to become aware of a conflict before being able to solve it). The addition of this category continues the statistically significant relationship between conflict resolution (now more broadly defined) and structural change ($p < .05$).

Table 11

	+	+?	−	Total	
Conflict resolution	10		1	11	$\chi^2 = 2.83$
Miscellaneous means	6	2	1	9	$df = 2$
	16	2	2	20	n.s.

Table 11 reflects a comparison between conflict resolution and miscellaneous means of change with respect to structural change. As can be seen, despite the demonstrated relationship between conflict resolution and structural change, when these two groups are compared there is not a statistically significant difference. This is another piece of evidence suggesting that conflict resolution cannot be considered essential to structural change and may be independent of it in some instances.

Table 12

	+	+?	−	Total	
Conflict resolution and miscellaneous means	16	2	2	20	$\chi^2 = 9.95$
					$df = 2$
No change	1	2	4	7	$p < .01$

In Table 12, conflict resolution and miscellaneous means of change were combined and then compared on structural change with those patients who showed no change in means of solving conflicts. Data indicate that regardless of the route by which change occurs in neurotic conflicts, there is a statistically significant difference in structural change between those with change in neurotic conflict ascertainable on tests and those who offer no indications of change in neurotic conflict. In effect, the no change group serves as a control. Structural change rarely happens without the patient's showing on tests some plausible explanation for it. Tests seem sensitive to the causes of structural change, and structural change is not arbitrary or accidental.

These data provide support to clinicians who attempt to effect fundamental change through expressive means. The more conflicts are resolved, the more structural change is liable to come about. These data also provide support to those clinicians who, one hopes on the basis of diagnostic assessment, design their strategy to help patients in a variety of ways other than, or along with, the resolution of conflict, e.g., therapists using themselves as an alternative object of addiction, or as lending ego strength. This finding lends dignity to their efforts, which are sometimes cavalierly labeled as "just supportive." It may be that at least for some patients the feeling of being understood is more important than insight into neurotic conflict. This theme is amplified and delineated by Strupp (1975), who posits the interpersonal relationship as one among three essential conditions for change in psychotherapy. These data also reassure those who believe that talking on a regular basis with a psychotherapist is a good thing despite a gloomy initial diagnostic picture. Such findings imply that a wide range of patients are amenable to fundamental change through psychotherapy.

In evaluating and applying these conclusions, one should take into consideration qualities of structural change (and possibly qualities of conflict resolution, too), as well as quantitative change. The patients who showed little conflict resolution and developed little insight yet showed structural change were among the most sick of our patients. They usually were disorganized in basic ego functioning. Therefore, they had the greatest room for improvement. They were also the people for whom the nutrients of an interpersonal relationship were most lacking, and most needed. By contrast, those who received and benefited from expressive treatments were less sick, and needed less in the way of nutriment from a relationship than to undo faulty behavior patterns fixed in place by repression and other defenses. Structural change, for them, might well have to come about through analysis of defenses, this being in a sense harder to achieve and certainly less measurable than is flagrant malfunctioning of basic ego functions. Structural change, then, in the comparative analysis reported above may well not have reflected a comparison of equal scale units.

In addition to such research considerations, practical clinical consequences stem from this point of view. Clinicians may be dealing with (to overstate and bifurcate excessively to make the point) two kinds of patients, two kinds of egos, and can expect different kinds and amounts of change through different means of intervention for each. This point of view puts a heavy burden on the diagnostic process so that patients can be correctly identified as to kinds of expectations and interventions. Clinicians who take this task seriously would do well to find and use psychologists who can make these discriminations (see Chapter 7).

The number of patients changing is not necessarily the same as saying that these patients improved or worsened with respect to the variable. For that one would have to know the functions that the behavior served in the total personality configuration. Such an encompassing and differentiated understanding for each patient was not available to the research psychologists when making their judgments of change since (as noted in Chapter 1) the task was to analyze patient variables in their own right. With a number of variables, increase or decrease could be assumed as corresponding to change for the better or worse. Depression, for example, was described by the research testers simply as increasing or decreasing. A plausible clinical case can be made for either possibility—an increase in depression can be for the good or for the bad just as a decrease can. Nonetheless, all other things being equal, a decrease in depression is more likely a change for the better than is an increase in depression.

Table 13

Change for the better	Percent
Insight	100 (increase)
Symptoms	68 (decrease)
Somatization	61 (decrease)
Core neurotic conflict	60 ("resolved")
Externalization	60 (decrease)
Psychological-mindedness	59 (increase)
IQ	54 (increase)
Unconscious guilt	53 (decrease)
Secondary gain	49 (decrease)
Depression	47 (decrease)
Anxiety	47 (decrease)
Conscious guilt	36 (decrease)
Alloplasticity	30 (decrease)
Change for the worse	
Anxiety	53 (increase)
Depression	47 (increase)
Psychological-mindedness	41 (remain same)
Somatization	39 (increase)
Conscious guilt	32 (increase)
Alloplasticity	32 (increase)
Symptoms	29 (increase)
Secondary gain	29 (increase)
Core neurotic conflict	26 (no change)
Externalization	18 (increase)
Unconscious guilt	13 (increase)
IQ	11 (decrease)
Insight	0 (none developed)

Listed in Table 13 are the percentage of patients judged as improving on each variable, or getting worse on each variable, all other things being equal. For 10 of these 13 variables, the percentage of patients who changed for the better was greater than the percentage who changed for the worse. By the sign test this is significant at < .05 level. A *t* test of the difference between the mean percentage of patients changing for the better (56%) and the mean percentage changing for the worse (29%) on all 13 variables was significant at < .005 level.

In contrast to these variables whose change for the better or worse required judgments by the research psychologists, on an all other things being equal basis, there were variables whose change for the better or worse was made directly by the research testers. An example is sublimation, which was rated directly as having changed for the better or having changed for the worse. With some other variables, though not rated directly as a change one way or the other, the meaning of the change was clear from the context. Quality of interpersonal relations is an example. When writing that a patient was, for instance, less inhibited in interpersonal relations, the research tester used such words as *spontaneous, more direct, more frank*.

The percentages of patients who were judged directly as changing for the better and for the worse on each variable are listed in Table 14.

Table 14

Change for the better	Percent
Thought organization	80
Self-concept	79
Patterning of defenses	77
Quality of interpersonal relations	77
Affect organization	62
Anxiety tolerance	60
Sublimation	55
Ego strength	50
Honesty	48
Change for the worse	
Affect organization	27
Patterning of defenses	23
Thought organization	20
Anxiety tolerance	21
Ego strength	18
Honesty	13
Quality of interpersonal relations	9
Self-concept	7

(Change for better or worse on each variable does not add up to 100% because some patients remained the same.)

Since the data for extent of desired change were skimpy and of questionable meaning, this variable could not be rated in ways that lent themselves to a categorization of better or worse.

The mean percent changed for the better (65%) was significantly larger ($p < .05$) than the mean percent changed for the worse (19%). Thus, there is clear evidence that, with respect to intrapsychic variables, patients changed often, and that this change was significantly more often for the better.

A more direct test of questions pertaining to change in the variables is the Binomial Test, which ascertains whether the probability of improving is significantly greater than the probability of getting worse. The results of this analysis, done for each variable one at a time, are given in Table 15. As in previous analyses, the first 12 variables* are based on a judgment of better or worse, all other things being equal. Below the double line are 9 variables which were judged *directly* as having changed for the better or worse.

While the previous analysis showed that 10 variables changed for the better, it can be seen that on this test only 5 variables on the "all other things being equal" kind of judgment changed for the better significantly. As will be recalled, insight does not tell us more than that patients in psychotherapy develop at least some insight. Symptoms and unconscious guilt were considered the hardest to ascertain from the tests and least clear conceptually. IQ is the only one of the 5 which was considered easiest to ascertain from the tests and most clear conceptually, and is therefore the only one of the 5 about which one can be confident in drawing generalizations of change for the better on this test. Thus, this is an unimpressive demonstration of variables changing for the better.

In sharp contrast, all of those variables *directly* judged with respect to better or worse, except for sublimation, showed significant change for the better, a most impressive demonstration of variables changing for the better. Why the difference? It could be that the difference noted merely recognizes actual differences in change for better or worse among the variables of the two groups. A more plausible explanation lies in the differing criterion for judgment. We do have theory, practice, and findings in this study to show that all things are

---

* Core conflict cannot be analyzed because it is based, not on independent subjects but on a mixture of repeated observations on each subject and independent subjects, and this did not fit a suitable statistical model.

Table 15

Variable	p
Insight	.00001
Symptoms	.0175
Somatization	n.s.
Externalization	.0020
Psychological-mindedness	n.s.
IQ	.0064
Unconscious guilt	.0059
Secondary gain	n.s.
Depression	n.s.
Anxiety	n.s.
Conscious guilt	n.s.
Alloplasticity	n.s.
Self-concept	.00002
Patterning of defenses	.0015
Quality of interpersonal relations	.000008
Thought organization	.0007
Affect organization	.0214
Anxiety tolerance	.0096
Sublimation	n.s.
Ego strength	.0173
Honesty	.0096

not equal, that change for the better cannot be validly judged in the abstract. Rather, such change requires a judgment as to its functioning in the individual, or can be judged directly as having a better or worse direction, as was done in the second group of nine variables. As we have seen, most variables judged directly as better or worse did change for the better.

Summary

1. Those variables which were both hardest to ascertain from tests and conceptually least clear provided the shakiest data base for generalizations. Those variables easiest to ascertain from tests and presenting the least conceptual difficulties provided the strongest data base for generalizations.

2. Percentage of patients changing with respect to each of the variables ran from 100% to 55%. Variables reflecting structural change ranked high on percentage of patients changing on them. As to vari-

ables directly referring to feeling, anxiety and depression changed in a very high percentage of patients while conscious guilt changed in only a moderately high percentage. Variables reflecting crystallized and specific symptoms changed in a high percentage of patients.

3. The more that conflicts are resolved through expressive means, the more structural change is liable to come about. Yet a substantial number of patients showed structural change even in the absence of resolution of conflict through expressive means. This suggests that fundamental changes can be brought about in people even though they are unable to develop much insight. This is, therefore, an encouragement to supportive treatment. A similar conclusion was drawn from a separate analysis of test and all other data (Horwitz, 1974). At the same time, structural change is probably of a somewhat different order, and easier to bring about in people who show a disorganization of basic ego functioning to begin with. The implication from this dichotomy is that different goals and different means of interventions may be maximally useful for different kinds of patients. This underlines the need for careful initial diagnostic assessment.

4. Disregarding the place and function of a particular variable in the context of a particular patient's personality ("all things being equal"), the mean percentage of patients changing for the better and the mean percentage changing for the worse on all variables so judged was significant. On variables directly judged as having changed for the better or worse, the mean percentage changing for the better was significantly greater than the mean percentage changing for the worse. Thus, there is clear evidence that with respect to intrapsychic variables patients changed often, and this change was more often for the better.

5. In a more direct test of change in variables for the better or worse (the Binomial Test), only five variables of the "all other things being equal" kind changed significantly for the better, while all of the variables judged directly with respect to better or worse changed for the better. This may reflect actual differences in changeability of the variables. A more plausible explanation lies in the recognition that all things are *not* equal, that change for the better often cannot be validly judged in the abstract. Rather, whether a change is for the better or the worse often requires that its function in the context of individual personality has to be assessed in order to know the value of the change.

CHAPTER 4

Overall Assessment of Change for Better or Worse

INTRODUCTION

The degree to which patients get better or worse was studied by way of psychological testing at termination. Ideally such a study should have provided an answer to the question of how well psychotherapy works. But, as discussed in Chapter 1, we found that our data provided a very limited answer to such a question. The results merely told us the fate of a small population of patients, who were among the most difficult for whom psychotherapy was recommended.

These patients had been treated under the environmental conditions of being in Topeka. Most of them were away from home, family, and occupation, and had been treated by psychotherapists with varying degrees of skill and experience. Because of these limitations little can be learned from these data about the effectiveness or lack of effectiveness of psychotherapy in general in other settings with different psychotherapists, and with different patients. Even with a larger and more representative sample of patients, therapists, and other treatment conditions, outcome data are of limited use with respect to deciding for or against psychotherapy for any one patient. But, through such studies as ours, one would hope to shed light on what is likely to change and the routes to these changes. This kind of information should help determine whether a particular person should have psychotherapy, with whom, and under what environmental conditions. It is not a simple question, and there is no simple answer. (For one delineation of the complexity of evaluating psychotherapy, see S. Appelbaum, 1976.)

In this report, we presume on our use of clinician-to-clinician discourse. We are well aware of the surplus meanings and unclarities in the use of such terms as *better or worse, healthy or sick,* but for our purposes at this moment it is not necessary to solve these semantic and conceptual problems. Rather, we will do here what any therapist does when he turns over in his mind the various ways his patient is changing or has changed, with feelings of satisfaction or dissatisfaction with what has been achieved. He would, as we do here, compare the patient as he is now with how he was before treatment, and assess to what extent the goals thought realizable at the beginning had been achieved at the end. Thus, we are not reporting here absolute judgments of "health" or "sickness" (as is done elsewhere in the Project, for example, by way of the Health-Sickness Rating Scale [Luborsky, 1975]), for, in principle, someone who changed the most (according to judgments based on the tests) could still be the sickest patient in the group, and somebody who changed the least could still be the most healthy patient in the group.

We based our assessments of change for the better or for the worse on the basis of change in patient variables as revealed through the psychological tests alone. Change in either direction did not occur uniformly across the patient variables; the variables could not be considered as equal units with respect to one another, nor did we expect them to contribute equally to overall change in any particular patient. For example, change in ego strength for some patients could change their life circumstances and their overall intrapsychic functioning, which would greatly overshadow the fact that they may not have changed at all with respect to, say, honesty or sublimation. In other words, we could not simply summate the changes in the patient variables; rather, from the implicit configurations of variables and the pictures of the patient which came to our mind from reading the descriptions of them by way of the test write-ups of the variables, we judged the degree to which things had changed overall for the better or worse. Our judgments did, in fact, correlate highly with those made by two groups of nontest clinicians who used all sources of information—patient, therapist, family, and others. These high correlations implicitly support the idea that people fall into recognizable gross groupings and that treatment goals and achievements can be assessed reliably by people with like training and theoretical background.

One group of nontest clinicians rated patients as better or worse on the basis of paired comparisons which resulted in a ranking of patients.* The test findings on the issue of better or worse correlated with paired comparison at the 1% level of confidence ($p = .72$). The other set of ratings, called "global change," by Ann Appelbaum and Leonard Horwitz as part of the Project's Prediction Study (1968), resulted in five rank-ordered groupings of patients.† These judgments correlated with the test findings on the issue of better or worse also at the 1% level of confidence ($p = .76$).

FINDINGS AND DISCUSSION

The patients were distributed on a 7-point scale as follows, with plus standing for change for the better, and minus standing for change for the worse:

$$+ + + + = 3 \qquad - = 3$$
$$+ + + = 3 \qquad - - = 3$$
$$+ + = 15 \qquad - - - = 2$$
$$+ = 5$$

As can be seen, 26 patients changed for the better, and 8 patients changed for the worse. These data leave unanswered the intriguing question of the relationship between intrapsychic change and life change. While the research testers did not know what changes had occurred in the patient's life, they occasionally speculated about such possibilities. For example, with one patient they thought that the small changes observable on the tests might make for large changes in her life. With another patient the testers thought large changes in his test productions might go unnoticed by those in the patient's environment except to the most careful observers. One may be reminded here of Eissler's report (1963) of a patient he considered to be a therapeutic failure on the basis of the technically incomplete treatment, although the patient herself considered the treatment had apparently made substantial beneficial changes in her life and considered the treatment a success. It is easy to imagine how such apparent discontinuities could occur. Take, for example, a patient whose small intrapsychic change

*A systematic comparison of the paired comparison findings with those of the tests is available in Chapter 7.
†The global change ratings are used as the criterion for the comparison of the usefulness of tests with other psychiatric information reported in Chapter 7 and in the writeup of the patient variable, honesty.

led to his being able to hold a job for the first time. This, in turn, provided a basis for self-esteem and made for vastly different life conditions, each providing a basis for change in other life circumstances as in geometric progression. With another patient, caught up in the throes of a psychosis, considerable intrapsychic changes occurred, and yet he was still unable to function fully outside the hospital. He might remain in the day hospital or night hospital, perhaps beginning to learn a trade. To his family and friends in a distant city, he would still be, after psychotherapy, a "hospital patient." (For a distinction between life goals and treatment goals see E. Ticho, 1972.) One has to keep open the possibility that the tests (and our theory) fail to account for growth possibilities, as they fail to account for genius (G. Ticho, personal communication). A patient may not have achieved intrapsychic change, as measured in the tests, but may have changed and grown in significant ways in nontest behaviors; also a patient may show improvement on the tests not apparent in nontest behaviors. This is less likely than the reverse, but it happens.

In every instance, even including those patients who had changed the most for the better, the research testers commented upon the patients' remaining difficulties. Sometimes the difficulties were specifically noted with respect to the stress of termination. It may well be, at least for some patients, that the stress of termination, which provides its own difficulties—the loss of the psychotherapist, being on one's own, having to believe one is better in order to justify one's investment—is an artifact which beclouds the extent and kind of changes which may have occurred. Finally, one still has to consider that the best of psychotherapies does not result in a "finished product." The model of unqualified cure is inapplicable. What model does fit the facts of psychotherapy better?

One such model is implicitly offered by Freud (1937), who notes that the human condition is one in which a substantial amount of unhappiness is expectable. Another, but not a contradictory model to this one, is that psychotherapy leaves people with substantial difficulties to be worked on in self-analysis in interaction with the "real" world, a world which he may have been slighting under the implicit expectation that his work in the special world of psychotherapy would take care of problems sooner or later. It may be that self-analysis is an indispensable part of the treatment (see G. Ticho, 1967). One may conceive of the end of psychotherapy less as an ending point than as the starting point in a graph of a new ascending line of life. It may provide small departures from the line which signified life at the beginning of treatment. But the difference between the two may widen steadily as the trajectory lengthens through the years. Finally, one must recognize that, at least with samples of difficult patients such as ours, some or all residual difficulties may be unavoidable under the best of therapeutic circumstances.

SUMMARY

1. Despite the complexities obscured by such gross words as better or worse, the test judgments showed high reliability with two other independent assessments of the same question made on the same patients.

2. Twenty-six patients changed for the better, and eight patients changed for the worse.

3. These data stimulate questions about the relationship between intrapsychic change and life changes, and between life change and change as reflected in the tests. How lasting are any kinds of changes? Can we at any one point account fully for change for the better in non-test life behaviors, or predict such changes in the future solely on the basis of test findings or present theoretical understanding of intrapsychic processes?

CHAPTER 5

Profile of Change:
Factor Analytic Study
of Patient Variables

INTRODUCTION

Factor analytic and clinical approaches to data which have been brought into juxtaposition with one another result in a meeting between two ways of thinking about people and data—ways usually uncomfortable to practitioners of both. The nomothetic–idiographic, the actuarial versus clinical debate is old and yet still with us. For our purposes, the major problem is that one can make clinical sense out of innumerable combinations of variables which result in what appear mathematically to be discrete factors. This, of course, is illustrative of both the strength and the weakness of the clinical approach. The elasticity of clinical thinking makes it possible to understand the innumerable combinations of intrapsychic variables which make up personalities, variables as dissimilar from one another as are their owners' thumbprints. These combinations do exist in real life. Yet a factor analytic study of such data in no way confirms that the *post hoc* explanations for the factors which we offer are reflected in real life. They could be made to sound plausible whether they existed in the particular instances or not. This is simply another manifestation of the problem we encountered throughout the Project which stemmed from our ambitious objective of treating clinical data, in part, statistically. The reader may judge the plausibility of the clinical thinking which explicates the various factors recorded in the following section.

221

FINDINGS AND DISCUSSION

A factor analysis of 21 patient variables was employed in order to elicit patterns of change. Patients were rated on 3-to-5-point scales for this purpose. The variables somatization, sublimation, and extent of desired change were not included because of the small number of patients written about in these respects, and the variable transference paradigms was not included because it did not lend itself to scaling. The ratings were intercorrelated, and the correlations then subjected to factor analysis.

Five factors were isolated in a factor analysis of principal components. The criterion for a defining loading was taken to be .40 or better. Factor 1 appears to be a general factor, with the loadings for all variables exceeding .40 except for conscious guilt, which had a loading of .36.

A normal varimax rotation, also using .40 as the criterion of a defining loading, yields the following patterns or profiles on each of the five factors:

Factor 1. Less depression, less unconscious guilt, better affect organization, better self-concept, better interpersonal relations, better ego strength, better patterning of defenses, better anxiety tolerance, change for the better in anxiety, less symptoms, change for the better in thought organization, change for the better in IQ, and overall change for the better. Strikingly absent from this long list are the variables insight, psychological-mindedness, externalizing, and conflict resolution. Apparently, despite substantial change, patients who conform to such a pattern are still looking outside themselves for the source of their difficulties, have not developed the attitudes of mind which are often held to be the mutative agents in expressive treatments, and have not resolved their conflicts. This kind of change, then, is suggestive of what might be described as successful supportive treatment. If one looks particularly at the six variables which most likely entail structural change (ego strength, anxiety tolerance, thought organization, affect organization, patterning of defenses, alloplasticity), one sees that all but one (alloplasticity) are loaded positively about .40 (changed for the better) in successful supportive treatment. This may be surprising to those who believe structural changes are possible only through expressive treatment (see Chapter 3).

Factor 2. More honesty, less externalization, and less alloplasticity. Here we have a pattern of change in the direction of more honestly looking inward for the source of difficulties coinciding with

less action directed outward, a recognizable and expectable development among patients with a dissembling, action-oriented "character
disorder." Yet those people who conformed to this pattern did not
show any changes for the better in an overall way, nor did they show
evidence of structural change or resolution of conflicts through insight
and psychological-mindedness. Thus, it appears that they were only
able to take initial steps toward change and improvement. Initial steps
are particularly susceptible to being rated as having changed, on the
basis of how much change was necessary to begin with. If people have
a lot of room for improvement in these respects, they may be easily
rated as having changed, although not having been able to make the
further changes that would have resulted in their being judged as having changed in an overall way for the better. Overall change was
loaded only on Factors 1 and 3 where it went along with structural
change (whether the treatment seemed to have been expressive or not,
as indicated by the other changes loaded on these factors).

Factor 3. Greater ego strength, greater anxiety tolerance, increased
psychological-mindedness, increased insight, increased resolution of
conflict, and better overall change. Here we have a pattern of changes
suggestive of successful expressive psychotherapy associated with
overall change for the better. Two of the structural change variables,
ego strength and anxiety tolerance, were also loaded as changed for
the better. It may be a bit surprising that even more of the structural
change variables were not loaded on this kind of change. The meaning
of this is difficult to estimate since the variables may have had a restricted range because the patients representing this kind of change
were not, as compared to the rest of the group, functioning so badly to
begin with. The same might be said for the fact that externalization
was not loaded as changing for the better. The relatively most healthy
and psychologically-minded patients, for whom this kind of change
was most likely possible, would not be expected to externalize a great
deal even at the beginning of the treatment.

Factor 4. Less conscious guilt, less unconscious guilt, and better
affect organization. This list suggests a probable change for the better
in mood but not a particularly impressive one, especially since there
was no change for the better with respect to the unpleasant affects of
anxiety and depression. In this pattern of change, one can picture patients benefiting somewhat from the fact that another person has involved himself with them, perhaps indicating to the patients that they
were not as "bad" as they may have felt, but changing little beyond
that. Only one structural variable, affect organization, was loaded as

changed for the better. Overall change for the better was not loaded. Thus, these seem to have been changes which were the results of strictly supportive treatments of limited effectiveness.

Factor 5. Better quality of interpersonal relations, better self-concept, better IQ, less secondary gain, and increased resolution of conflict. Better relations with one's self and others along with resolution of conflict and less use of symptoms for secondary gain is a pattern one might associate with success in expressive treatment. Yet absent from this list are increases in psychological-mindedness and insight. This apparent contradiction or discontinuity may perhaps be dispelled by the absence, also, of indications of structural change. It leads to the hypothesis that improvements in living, becoming less a "patient," and even resolving of conflict may be possible with superficially expressive treatment. Putting Factor 5 alongside Factor 1, we have a pattern of change with and without structural change, which occurs in the absence of noteworthy changes in insight and psychological-mindedness. Both of these patterns point toward nonexpressive components as being mutative, such as perhaps interpersonal relationship factors.

Using .70 or above as indicating a considerable amount of communality, all but 3 of the 21 variables overlapped considerably with the other variables. This fits with the conception of the variables as partaking somewhat of abstractions. For example, one would certainly expect that a change of ego strength would also involve a change in anxiety tolerance and patterning of defenses. Symptom change and conscious depression were just short of the .70 criterion. The only variable which was substantially below the criterion was IQ (.4735), indicating a fair amount of uniqueness. This fits with our understanding of the changes in IQ (see Chapter 3), i.e., that a change in intelligence for the better had a tendency to occur irrespective of changes in other aspects of the person.

SUMMARY

A factor analysis of 21 patient variables yielded the following patterns:

Pattern A. Change for the better in most variables, including structural ones, but without change for the better in psychological-mindedness, externalization, and conflict resolution. This pattern is suggestive of what might be described as successful supportive treatment.

Pattern B. Pattern change in respect to more honestly looking inward for the source of difficulties along with less alloplasticity. This was as far as it went; just what was usually regarded as the beginning steps toward a more comprehensive change for the better.

Pattern C. Overall change for the better in the context of increased psychological-mindedness, insight, and conflict resolution—a pattern suggestive of successful expressive psychotherapy.

Pattern D. A mild change for the better with respect to some moods and feelings, but little beyond that.

Pattern E. Change in ways suggestive of a superficially expressive treatment, without structural change, and the implication that nonexpressive aspects of treatment, probably interpersonal relationship factors, were mutative.

A great deal of overlap occurred statistically among most variables.

CHAPTER 6

Patterns of Change

INTRODUCTION

The purpose of our investigation was to determine what patterns of change emerged from the statistical analysis of 34 patients as represented by change in each of 18 patient variables. As with the factor analytic study (see Chapter 5), clinical thinking which elaborates the statistical results may be plausible but not necessarily definitive or a guarantee that groupings are other than chance or artifacts. We do believe, however, that plausibility counts. Fellow clinicians will not find it difficult to think about change according to the patterns suggested here, or perhaps to recall their own patients who seemed to have changed in similar ways. Furthermore, unlike the factor analytic study, the patterns in this study can be tied to qualitative appraisals of the patients themselves so that the statistical relationships can be validated against the overall understanding of these patients.

FINDINGS AND DISCUSSION

Five-point scales of change were based on the statistical analysis of 34 patients as represented by change in each of 18 patient variables. (Six variables could not be used because of too few cases.) These scales referred to change which reflected improvement, no change, or worsening. The judgments were made with respect to the overall personality of each patient. Thus, rather than "more" or "less" being scored in an absolute way corresponding directly to improvement or worsening, the score depended on the use to which the increase or decrease was put, in our judgment, in the total personality configuration. For example, increased anxiety might, in one patient, reflect an improvement, e.g., a more realistic recognition of difficulties which enabled a therapeutic process to be sustained and change to come about. In another patient, more anxiety might be considered worse, e.g., signal anxiety had given way to primary anxiety or panic.

The 34 profiles of change were clustered using Ward's (1963) hierarchical grouping method* as programmed by Veldman (1967). The solution with 10 groups was chosen for interpretation.†

Group A. Four patients became worse in 13 variables: depression (mean 1.5), ego strength (mean 1.2), patterning of defenses (mean 1.2), alloplasticity (mean 2.2), anxiety (mean 1.0), symptoms (mean 1.5), overall change (mean 1.5), affect organization (mean 1.0), anxiety tolerance (mean 1.8), externalization (mean 2.0), quality of interpersonal relations (mean 2.0), honesty (mean 2.2), thought organization (mean 1.5). These patients were unchanged in four variables: psychological-mindedness (mean 3.2), conscious guilt (mean 2.5), self-concept (mean 2.7), unconscious guilt (mean 2.8). They improved in one variable: insight (mean 4.0). That so many variables changed for the worse suggests that when people do badly in psychotherapy almost everything is worsened. That psychological-mindedness was an exception, remaining unchanged and in fact very slightly improving, and that insight in fact did improve gives one pause. Although there is high congruence between insight and overall change for the better in this study, these data indict the assumption that insight, in and of itself, is in all instances desirable. With all other variables worsening, including key structural variables such as ego strength, a likely explanation is that "insight" was accrued through the breakdown of defenses and adaptations, without the integration and overall strengthening of the

---

*This method looks for a set of natural groups among N Ss each measured on K different variables. It proceeds hierarchically starting with each S as a group and combining groups in such a way that the total "error" in a grouping is minimally increased with each combination. The method is essentially descriptive, providing no statistical tests and associated probabilities and no judgments as to a permissible amount of error. Choice of the grouping to be studied is made by inspection of the errors for successive groupings, looking for a substantially larger increase in error which would indicate that the previous grouping would be the choice.

†We shall make use in this discussion of the general dimension of "loosening" and "tightening" as descriptive of change, a dimension used in describing changes in IQs (Chapter 3) and in some of the analyses of single variables. Loosening includes greater availability of ideas to consciousness, more affective experience (including anxiety, depression, and guilt), and greater inclination to action and alloplasticity. Tightening refers to increased constriction and tighter controls over action, affects, and ideas.

personality which ideally follows from insight. A qualitative look at the test findings of these cases reveals just that. These people's personalities had "loosened." In every instance there was greater turbulence, openness of ideas and feelings, along with inability to control and modulate these for beneficial effect. These were classical instances of people who did not have the wherewithal to manage usefully the self-examination and disequilibrium which are the hallmarks of the expressive aspects of psychotherapy. On the basis of this evidence, they would have been better off intrapsychically if they had not entered psychotherapy, or if, in the course of their psychotherapy, they had been able to make the expressive aspects commensurate with their ability to absorb and helpfully use these.*

All four of these patients were described as showing paranoid-projective thinking. Three showed blatantly primitive oral conflicts, while the fourth was described as having oral conflicts underlying prominent difficulties in clarifying sexual identity. In every instance autoplastic capacities had failed to stem the tide of increasing alloplasticity. Their insight was mainly of the sort that allowed these patients to see themselves more clearly as patients, "sick" people, and in one instance attention was called specifically to the self-flagellating use to which this insight was put. How was it that insight was considered to have improved at all? The one step on the scale toward improvement merely reflected the judge's recognition that if a person identifies himself as a patient, when he has been a person inclined to externalize, this is a necessary beginning toward beneficial change. That is, indeed, how insight was originally defined in the Project. Here, and elsewhere in this study, improvement in insight along with absence of a quantitatively similar improvement in psychological-mindedness points either to a general worsening or to beneficial change brought about through other means than expressive psychotherapy, e.g., corrective emotional experience, borrowed ego strength.

Group B. In this group ($N = 3$) there was some improvement in externalization (mean 4.0), in quality of interpersonal relations (mean 4.3), a slight improvement in honesty (mean 3.7), a slight worsening of affect organization (mean 2.3), and a moderate worsening of symptoms (mean 2.0). All other variables hovered around the unchanged judgment. Because of the small number of people and the small amount of change, generalizations from these data are difficult to make. However, these data do lead to the speculative hypothesis that

---

*This finding calls for a more refined definition of insight—one that would take into account such issues as the person's capacity to be concerned, to feel responsible, and to act constructively upon what he "sees" about himself. (See S. Appelbaum, 1975, 1977.)

as people localize matters more within themselves they tend to take pressure off other people, with resulting improvement in their interpersonal relationships. The honesty finding is probably an expression of lessened externalization, and a franker recognition of these patients' participation in what has happened in their lives, with less need to dissemble, excuse, and blame. With all three patients the change in externalization was associated with a decrease in projection, and this provides a plausible way of understanding their improved interpersonal relationships. That symptoms became worse, as did affect organization to some extent, provides a variation of the observation made in Group A: Taking greater responsibility, as implied in the lowered externalization and projection, puts more pressure within, resulting in greater symptomatic expression rather than overall improvement.

Group C. In this group two people hit the top of the scale in overall change for the better (mean 6.0), achieved a substantial amount of improvement in insight (mean 5.5), alloplasticity (mean 5.0), anxiety tolerance (mean 5.0), patterning of defenses (mean 5.0), and a moderate amount of improvement in ego strength (mean 4.5), psychological-mindedness (mean 4.5), anxiety (mean 4.0), symptoms (mean 4.5), externalization (mean 4.5), thought organization (mean 4.0), honesty (mean 4.0), quality of interpersonal relations (mean 4.5), self-concept (mean 4.5), and unconscious guilt (mean 4.0). (Unconscious guilt was scored on only one patient.) Only conscious guilt (mean 3.0) and depression (mean 3.0) remain unchanged, while only one variable, affect organization became worse (1.0). Through inadvertence the latter judgment was restricted to only one patient. This one instance provides data to support the classical assumption that when a phobia is analyzed, as it was with this patient, it is replaced by affect, in this instance hostile feelings. With generalizations restricted only to these two cases, one sees that there was either moderate or substantial improvement almost across the board. Conscious guilt and depression were not prominent features in either instance, and so it is not surprising that these variables failed to change.

Group D. In this group three people achieved substantial overall change for the better (mean 5.0) along with substantial improvement in anxiety tolerance (mean 5.0) and insight (mean 5.3); moderate improvement in depression (mean 4.3), ego strength (mean 4.0), patterning of defenses (mean 4.0), psychological-mindedness (mean 4.3), anxiety (mean 4.0), symptoms (mean 4.0), affect organization (mean 4.3), quality of interpersonal relations (mean 4.3), self-concept (mean 4.0), and thought organization (mean 4.0). Two variables remained unchanged, honesty (mean 3.3) and unconscious guilt (mean 3.0). On one variable, externalization (mean 2.0), two patients did worse in the sense that it had increased (inadvertently one patient was not assessed on this variable), and on one variable, conscious guilt (mean 2.3), they did slightly worse. Thus, this is a somewhat tempered or modulated version of the pattern of high overall change for the better associated with high change for the better in most other variables. That externalization increased may at first glance seem contradictory to our other data as well as to the clinically plausible understanding that scribing blame to others, particularly with reference to one's symptoms or difficulties, is generally lessened in a treatment whose focus of cause is on the self. These two cases, however, offer another clinically plausible pattern. Both of them were classified at the start of treatment as showing minimal or insignificant use of externalization, and this aspect of themselves was part of the personality pattern whose effects had brought them into treatment. They were both people who turned inward to a fault, in the direction of excessive fantasy, depression, inhibition, and self-recrimination. Thus, distributing causes or blames in a more equitable manner provided relief for them, and taken in the context of change for the better in other variables points to fundamental change for the better. (That this understanding was not taken into consideration in the original scoring is an inadvertent violation of our usual practice of having scores represent an overall judgment of better or worse rather than more or less.) In one instance increased guilt was associated with greater insight, so that what had been unconscious guilt feeding into depression became consciously experienced with less depression.

Group E. This group of five patients showed moderate improvement in patterning of defenses (mean 4.0), insight (mean 4.4), anxiety (mean 4.2), symptoms (mean 4.0), affect organization (mean 4.4), and thought organization (mean 4.4). There was a tendency toward moderate improvement in alloplasticity (mean 3.6), self-concept (mean 3.6), externalization (mean 3.6), and quality of interpersonal relations (mean 3.8). All other variables were unchanged. All five patients were described as generally improving through "tightening," particularly featuring lowered anxiety, often through constriction and suppression. And in each instance this improvement was described as vulnerable to reversability, as being unreliable or unstable. The general picture is of lack of change in a fundamentally reorganizing way. Rather, change is tied to relationship aspects of the therapeutic interaction. These patients were described as "borrowing" ego strength in lieu of showing fundamental improvement of ego strength. (As noted under the analysis of ego strength as a separate variable, the research testers made an explicit discrimination between ego strength as an index of current behavioral functioning and ego strength as a derivative of structural properties.) These patients seem to have had a corrective emotional experience, to have been influenced by the presence of a figure whom they experienced as good, on whom they could rely, and whom to some extent they internalized. They showed increased insight, but without an increase in psychological-mindedness. They seemed to have been "given" the insight rather than having developed it. Insight was usually described as restricted as to content, and qualified as to usefulness.

In addition to constriction and general tightening, one patient showed increased somatization, thus affirming the assumption that bodily symptoms can absorb anxiety. Though she was "worse" in the sense that she had symptoms where there were none before, the symptoms contributed to the general betterment of total personality functioning.

Group F. There was only one patient in this group.* He achieved a moderate degree of overall change for the better (4.0); a substantial change for the better in only one variable, depression (5.0); moderate degrees of change for the better in patterning of defenses (4.0), anxiety (4.0), symptoms (4.0), affect organization (4.0), and thought organization (4.0); and worse in alloplasticity (2.0), honesty (2.0), and externalization (1.0). In some respects this single patient was much like the five patients of Group E for he, too, had changed primarily on the basis of the supportive aspects stemming from the introjection of a benevolently experienced therapist, and was living with the aid of "borrowed ego strength." His change was not considered as vulnerable as was change in the other group, however, as he had developed a much more coherent characterological reorganization. This had resulted in lowered anxiety, had helped overcome depressive feelings, and permitted better functioning and more pleasant self-experience in general. Although he was functioning in a borderline psychotic way before treatment, he now had a much more smoothly functioning character disorder. His difficulties were ego syntonic. He was, if anything, more smug about them, and felt euphorically fulfilled, with problems being localized in others rather than within himself. Whether this was a benefit to society or those who came in contact with him interpersonally is doubtful but, from the restricted point of view of his functioning and self-experience, he had changed some-

---

*Despite there being only one patient who showed this pattern, the term *group* is appropriate since it refers to a group of variables.

what for the better. From this standpoint, the shift in externalization was to his benefit. But from the standpoint of establishing a balanced understanding of reasons and causes of events, the understanding of which in some people could lead to a higher level of integration than shown by this patient, the shift in externalization was a worsening.

Group G. As with Group F, there was only one patient in Group G. This patient showed a moderate overall change for the better (mean 4.0) on the basis of moderate changes for the better in externalization (mean 4.0), quality of interpersonal relations (mean 4.0), thought organization (mean 4.0), anxiety (mean 4.0), insight (mean 4.0), psychological-mindedness (mean 4.0), and patterning of defenses (mean 4.0). Much worse was conscious guilt (mean 1.0), depression (mean 1.0), affect organization (mean 1.0). Worse also were unconscious guilt (mean 2.0) and symptoms (mean 2.0). This patient, a basically narcissistic character, had been caught up in an acute struggle against decompensation into borderline-paranoid ego functioning. In contrast to the Group F patient, who seemed to have installed a new character based on a relationship with the therapist, this patient's narcissistic aims remained the same, although her tactics were different. She was in considerable internal distress, which she used in a "poor me" masochistic fashion. She seemed more in transition than the patient in Group F, and indeed the point was made that she may continue to show movement. A somewhat uncontrolled variable in this is that she is basically a closed person, and on both sets of tests created the impression that things were masked or hidden, perhaps an expression of a masochistic need to confuse others no matter what the cost to herself.

Group H. The two patients in Group H were judged as remaining the same. They showed moderate improvement in only one variable, insight (mean 4.0), and showed a worsening of depression (mean 2.0), patterning of defenses (mean 2.0), anxiety (mean 2.0), anxiety tolerance (mean 1.5), self-concept (mean 2.0), and thought organization (mean 2.0). The scoring of overall change as neither for the better nor for the worse is a rather generous scoring. There is at least the implication with both of these patients that changes were for the worse. Contributing to the overgenerous appraisal is, perhaps, the fact that there was a degree of unclarity about how to understand these patients. One of them had been tested initially elsewhere, in a way different from most of the patients in this study. The other patient was so constricted on testing at termination that the research testers were forced to speculate more than usual. The question was also raised as to whether the initial tests on this patient had been read incorrectly as reflecting greater capacities than she indeed had. What was reasonably clear with both patients, however, was that change had resulted in increasingly maladaptive behaviors and increasingly maladaptive configurations of personality variables. What seemed in one patient as mainly a problem in control of affects came to be seen, or became in real life, a pressure upon the ego to regress and dissolve. The patient could see or sense this, to the point that he needed to create distance as an ego-preservative measure. (This led the research tester to speculate that this patient's subsequent suicide was an attempt at active mastery in the face of the threat of passive dissolution of self.) The other patient responded to greater self-knowledge and to the emergence in consciousness of conflicts with a different kind of distance. She withdrew behind a brittle, but pervasive, constriction. Neither patient had sufficient psychological-mindedness and ego-resilience to integrate an increased sense of immediacy of conflictual parts of themselves, as promoted by the treatment. Yet, neither gave way to florid ideation and burgeoning of affects along with considerable regressive movement, as did the patients in Group A. Instead, both found an alloplastic escape, one in suicide (after termination of treatment), and one in precipitious termination of treatment.

Group I. The six patients in this group showed a substantial overall change for the better (mean 5.7), the second highest of the 10 groups. Six variables changed substantially for the better: affect organization (mean 5.3), anxiety tolerance (mean 5.7), insight (mean 5.7), psychological-mindedness (mean 5.1), patterning of defenses (mean 5.0), and ego strength (mean 5.0). Eight variables changed moderately for the better: conscious guilt (mean 4.7), anxiety (mean 4.0), symptoms (mean 4.3), unconscious guilt (mean 4.8), self-concept (mean 4.8), and thought organization (mean 4.5). Two variables showed a slight tendency to improvement: alloplasticity (mean 3.8), and honesty (mean 3.6); and one variable remained unchanged: depression (mean 3.3). This group had the greatest improvement in both psychological-mindedness and insight. Such a pattern implies that the treatment of these patients was expressive, and that they were sufficiently well chosen for this kind of treatment as to benefit from it. As noted with Group C, when things go well, almost all variables seem to improve.

In all of the six cases in Group I the claims for improvement were modest, more of degree than of kind. In particular, core neurotic conflicts were described as improved rather than resolved. As noted elsewhere in the test findings, any ideas that people may have that psychotherapy, at least with such patients as these, can change a person qualitatively and direct him toward unlimited horizons of joy and fruition are wrong. Yet, the consistent note struck with these patients is that the differences, qualified as they are, are likely to have made a substantial difference and improvement in their way of life.

All of these cases were described as having achieved a "tightening" of the personality, in particular, as having overcome storms of affect and the symptoms and behaviors driven by these affects. This was achieved, in all instances, by an increase in ideational skills. The increase of insight plus a similar increase in psychological-mindedness offered evidence of change through classical expressive means even though the conflicts into which there was insight could not be considered resolved. A particular way of viewing the consequences of increased ideational capacities in this group was that the ego became more in control of situations, could function more adaptively and effectively, rather than having to submit and falter in its functions. A quantitative measure of this qualitative remark made by the research testers is the considerable improvement in IQ shown by these patients.

Another way that change in these patients was conceptualized was through affects being used as signals rather than overcoming capacities for adaptation. Such affects as anxiety and depression diminished in the sense of their being "symptomatic," but increased in the sense of their being more tolerable and presumably as stimuli toward understanding. One might consider that these patients became more in touch with themselves, more capable of assessing and experiencing the human condition, including its unpleasant aspects. Thus, their "mental illness" can be thought of as a kind of withdrawal from self, reversed during treatment even though at some painful internal cost. Indeed, several of these patients were described, simply, as "more human."

Group J. The seven patients in this group showed substantial overall change for the better (mean 5.4), only a shade less than did Group I (5.7). In common with Group I, and with Group C as well, all of the variables changed substantially for the better. Two variables changed substantially: insight (mean 5.1) and anxiety tolerance (mean 5.6). The rest of the variables changed moderately: self-concept (mean 4.9), patterning of defenses (mean 4.7), quality of interpersonal relations (mean 4.6), ego strength (mean 4.4), unconscious guilt (mean 4.3), thought organization (mean 4.3), affect organization (mean 4.0), externalization (mean 4.1), symptoms (mean 4.3), honesty (mean 4.0), and psychological-mindedness (mean 4.0). Alongside these overall similarities, there were some instructive differences: Patients in Group J improved moderately in psychological-mindedness (mean 4.0) while patients in Group I improved substantially in psychological-mindedness (mean 5.1). Patients in Group J showed a less pronounced improvement by way of ideation. Only two patients were considered to have primarily followed the ideational route toward change and, in all but one of the patients (including these two), insight was qualified as to restricted range and depth, or both. This relative diminution of the importance of the pattern "ideation-psychological-mindedness-insight" as a means of change, is further supported by remarks about three of the patients: Their insights were relatively superficial, even though two of them were in analysis. One of these patients was described as having changed primarily through borrowed ego strength, largely as a means of pleasing and being sustained by what, to him, was a powerful, benevolent therapist. A more consistent finding running through this group is their ability to move from anxiety as a potentially disorganizing experience to its use as a signal, with implications for ego mastery and control over their internal and external fate. The vicissitudes of this shift were different from one patient to another, as may be seen in the distribution of these patients on the dimension of loosening and tightening. One patient was considered to have improved through a loosening of his personality, three were considered to have improved through a tightening of their personalities, and three were considered to have loosened in some respects. Two of the last showed a loosening, in their becoming less rigid and better able either to express impulses or recognize their internal world, bleak as it might be, along with a tightening in their organization of thought as seen through the diminution of breakthroughs and interruptions in thought patterns. The third showed a tightening in the sense of giving up alloplastic, addictive behavior, and a loosening in the sense of a markedly increased experience of anxiety, along with increases in conscious guilt, depression, and affective warmth, and a proliferation of ideation.

This survey of patterns of change reveals that there are many routes to change, and that "more" or "less" of a particular factor is usually an insufficient explanation or description. The specification of change requires reference to the function of that change in that particular personality, its interlockings with other factors, and whether and what effects the more or less change has.

The concept of change coming about through a shift in controls over anxiety was conspicuous in these routes of change, and in each instance required individual specification. These data provide the following schema: An existential fact of life seems to be the need to control vulnerability to primary anxiety, some variety of panic. With some patients, this eventuality had become fact; with others, it was sufficiently close to becoming a fact as to require defense through such extreme maladaptive means as deviations in thinking or impulsive, often ultimately self-defeating actions. Except perhaps in some temporary emergency situations, which require wholesale discharge of energy, experiences of primary affect are undesirable; they are painful and have disruptive effects on intended, adaptive work. These data suggest that psychotherapy can help patients develop controls over the emergence of primary affects especially anxiety, and in addition can "tame" such experiences so that they serve as a signal for defensive and adaptive mechanisms to be brought into play. Ideally, such signals should operate with minute quantities of energy, or so quickly that the person is unaware of them. Many of these patients did not operate so silently, but rather were experienced as miniatures of primary affects. Thus, a frequent finding was that although people were spared through psychotherapy, disorganization of ego functioning, and intense discomfort, they nonetheless lived with an increase of anxiety or depression. Often coincidental with this was an increase of something that might be called "humanness," being in touch with all aspects of themselves, a facing of existence, sometimes expressed as their having become more sober, reflective, philosophical-minded. Indeed, neurotic suffering seemed to have been replaced by human misery.

SUMMARY

1. Scales of change for better or worse in each of the 18 patient variables yielded the following "natural" groups:

Group A (N = 4). These patients "loosened" in the sense of greater turbulence, openness to ideas and feelings, but were unable to control and modulate these for beneficial effect. They developed insight, but not in such a way that the insight could be used in an integrative, controlled fashion. From this evidence, these patients would have been better off intrapsychically if they had not entered psychotherapy, or if the expressive aspects of their psychotherapy had been commensurate with their ability to absorb and helpfully use them.

Group B (N = 3). These patients localized matters more within themselves, taking pressure off others; as a result they improved their interpersonal relationships.

Group C (N = 2). These patients showed an across-the-board moderate to substantial improvement in the functioning of intrapsychic variables.

Group D (N = 3). These patients showed a similar but attenuated pattern to that of Group C—high overall change associated with high change for the better in most variables.

Group E (N = 5). These patients generally improved through "tightening," lowering their anxiety often through constriction and suppression. Rather than changing in a fundamental and reorganizing way, their changes seemed tenuous and closely tied to the relationship with the therapist. Their increased insight, without an increase in psychological-mindedness, suggests that they had been "given" insight by the therapist rather than having developed it themselves.

Group F (N = 1). This patient resembled patients in Group E, but his change was not considered as vulnerable since he had developed a more coherent characterological reorganization, even though it was based primarily upon the introjection of a benevolently experienced therapist.

Group G (N = 1). This patient was much like the Group F patient, having overcome a decompensation into borderline ego functioning, but more on the basis of propping up her narcissistic character rather than reorganizing it.

Group H (N = 2). These patients remained the same, or perhaps got a bit worse; they had to find ways to take distance in order to preserve remaining ego functions.

Group I (N = 6). These patients showed overall change for the better in the context of most variables changing for the better. Their substantial improvement in psychological-mindedness and insight suggested that they had received and benefited from the expressive treatment. In general, these patients achieved a tightening of the personality by way of increasing ideational skills, a concomitant of which was to be able to use affects as signals rather than allowing affects to overcome their capacities for adaptation.

Group J (N = 7). These patients were much like the patients in Group I, though with somewhat less increase in ideational skills.

2. There are many routes to change; simply specifying more or less of a particular factor or quality is usually a less valid way of indicating change then showing how it interlocks with other factors in a particular patient's personality.

3. One way to categorize patients is with reference to degree and qualities of their dealing with the possibility of primary anxiety as an existential fact of life. Our data suggest that psychotherapy can help patients develop controls over the emergence of primary affects (especially anxiety) so that these serve as a signal for defensive and adaptive mechanisms. The price paid for such controls may be to live with a low-level or increased experience of anxiety or depression in the context of a sober, reflective, increased "humanness."

CHAPTER 7

Psychological Tests and Paired Comparison Analyses

INTRODUCTION

In the Quantitative Study of the Project (Kernberg *et al.*, 1972, pp. 3–85) an attempt was made to do a statistical analysis while preserving the clinical nature of the variables. The method used was a modification of the Fechnerian Method of Paired Comparisons. In this chapter we will examine the comparability between the psychological test ratings of patient variables and the ratings derived from the paired comparison method which was based on nontest clinical information.

FINDINGS AND DISCUSSION

As can be seen in Table 16, the Pearson r correlations between the psychological test ratings and paired comparison analyses are quite low. Only four variables—symptoms at .61, ego strength at .56, conflict resolution at .58, and global change at .71—are above .50, all of these being significantly different from zero (<.001). There are a number of plausible explanations for the low correlations between tests and paired comparisons on the other variables:

1. Since the nontest clinicians used the tests in making their ratings of the variables along with the other sources of information, there

Table 16. Psychological Test Ratings vs. Paired Comparison Scaled Scores

				Termination		
				r corrected for		
Variable	r	p_2	N	coarse	p	p_2
5 Change in anxiety level (−)	−.44	<.01	34	−.47	.54	<.01
4 Change in extent environment suffers (alloplasticity)	.24	n.s.	34	.26	.26	n.s.
5 Change in severity of symptoms (−)	−.61	<.001	34	−.65	.59	<.001
5 Change in externalization (−)	−.32	<.10	32	−.34	.32	<.10
5 Change in patterning of defenses	.40	<.05	34	.42	.42	<.05
6 Change in anxiety tolerance	.36	<.05	33	.38	.35	<.05
4 Change in insight	.43	<.05	34	.47	.44	<.05
5 Change in ego strength	.56	<.001	34	.59	.56	<.01
4 Change in quality of interpersonal relationships	.21	n.s.	32	.23	.22	n.s.
7 Global (overall) change	.71	<.001	34	.73	.72	<.001
4 Change in motivation (extent of desired change)	−.18	n.s.	8	−.20	−.63	n.s.
Conflict resolution	.58	<.01	28	.63	.63	<.001

may have been a divergence in test and nontest findings, and they chose to base their judgments to a greater extent on extratest sources of information (evidence supporting this explanation is offered in Chapter 8).

2. The basis of judgment was different. Raters making the paired comparison judgments did not make them on the basis of change. Rather they made fresh write-ups of the variables, and the difference between the write-up at initial and the write-ups at termination—the change between the two—was done statistically. Thus, these judges were doing a somewhat different task from that of the research testers, who were explicitly rating change between their initial and termination test assessments. The one variable, global change, that was rated with respect to change by *both* test and nontest judges achieved the highest correlation (.71).

3. The judgments of change based on the psychologist's test judgments of the variables could have been in error. The psychologist's statements were not always specifically couched with reference to change. When they were not, the research psychologist had to compare the two and come up with statements of change himself.

4. The nontest clinical group included different judges at initial

and at termination. This was done in order to avoid contamination of judgments, but at the same time it possibly introduced differences due to the presumed imperfect reliability between the two sets of judges.

5. It may be that with many of the variables, and certainly with some of them, the research testers and the paired comparison judges had different understandings of the variables. This possibility gains some credence from the fact that change in severity of symptoms and global change, both little based in theory, achieved the two highest correlations between test and nontest judges. The write-ups of some variables make clear the different conceptions of what was being measured. For example, the paired comparison judges were working with a variable named "change in extent environment suffers," which is not an intrapsychic variable. The variable used by the research testers, and compared with it here, was an intrapsychic variable, alloplasticity, only a part of whose effect may be consequences suffered by the environment. Another such variable was named "motivation" by the paired comparison judges and "extent of desired change" by the research testers who judged further changes desired by the patient at termination, a probable limited aspect of motivation and capacities for motivation in general. The correlation of these two sets of measurements was slight.

6. Perhaps these low correlations in such a relatively small sample could be due to a small number of patients contributing so large a deviation which resulted in the nonsignificant finding for the group. As a partial test of this possibility, rank order correlations were computed. In only three instances, extent environment suffers (alloplasticity), change in quality of interpersonal relations, and change in motivation (or extent of desired change) was there no significant difference, and so it seems that the low correlations likely reflect a fairly pervasive and substantive difference.

One piece of fortuitous information helps dispel the possibilities that differences in judges and method made for these differences, and is suggestive that differences are due primarily to the material judged. On one variable, conflict resolution, a paired comparison study was based on the test findings. Correlation of these paired comparisons and of the research psychologist's judgments of the tests is the highest correlation of all the variables ($r = .85$), significantly different from chance at $p < .001$. Thus, there is the strong implication that the differences in judgments of change are due primarily to the different kinds of information yielded by the tests as compared to the nontest sources. This issue surfaces again in Chapter 8.

SUMMARY

1. In a comparison of psychological tests and nontest paired comparisons, only symptoms, ego strength, conflict resolution, and global change were above .50.

2. Plausible explanations for the generally low correlations include: (a) In the instances of divergence in test and nontest information, the judges chose regularly to base their judgments on extratest information. (b) While the psychologists made their judgments on the basis of change between initial and termination tests, the paired comparison judges simply separated write-ups at these particular times, with the comparison being done statistically. (c) Either the research tester inferences or the extrapolations by the research psychologist could have been in error. (d) Different paired comparison judges were used at initial and at termination, which could have introduced poor reliability. (e) The research testers and the paired comparison judges had different understandings of variables which nonetheless were compared with one another. (f) In principle, low correlations could have been due to a small number of patients contributing so large a deviation which resulted in a nonsignificant finding for the group. This possibility was, however, dispelled through further statistical analysis.

3. A high correlation between paired comparison and research psychologist judgments was found on the one variable, conflict resolution. On this variable, the paired comparison study was based on test findings. Thus, there is the strong implication that differences in judgments of change were due primarily to the difference between the examination with psychological tests and that part of the psychiatric examination which did not include the use of test findings. This corresponds to the data noted in Chapter 8, suggesting that differences in demonstrated predictive power between the psychological test investigation and the psychiatric investigation stemmed from the fact that the psychiatric investigation was not being persuaded by the test findings available to it.

Comparing the Usefulness of Tests with Other Psychiatric Information*

INTRODUCTION

While writers of test reports vary a good deal in how explicit they are in making their predictions, all useful statements in psychological test reports carry at least an implicit prediction. To the clinically sophisticated reader, even a simple diagnostic label carries a gross prediction, e.g., the patient with hysterical neurosis is likely to get better with appropriate treatment, while the patient with paranoid schizophrenia is not as likely to improve. The test report may include the statement that a patient uses a certain pattern of defenses, which is at the same time a prediction that he will behave in certain ways, and that if these ways are interfered with he will be anxious unless he finds some other means of controlling anxiety. The report may include the statement that the patient feels in a particular way about himself, which is a prediction that if one responds to him on this basis he will feel understood. The report may include the statement that a prominent transference paradigm for the patient is of a certain kind, which at the same time is a prediction that if we offer him a relatively neutral figure, he will sooner or later experience that figure in the transference way described.

*Dennis Farrell contributed as judge and in drawing conclusions from data.

In our view, the true measure of "the validity of tests" is how well the psychologist who uses them is able to make useful clinical predictions. The aim of this chapter is to assess the ability of the testers (1) to arrive at a correct diagnostic understanding, (2) to make treatment recommendations and predictions on the basis of this understanding or "diagnosis," and (3) to learn which variables lend themselves most and least to accurate predictions and are best suited for analysis by way of tests. To accomplish this task, we compared the test findings with nontest psychiatric information.

STUDY I

Method

Uncontaminated by knowledge of the patient's treatment and outcome, Judge 1 (S. Appelbaum) went through the write-ups* done at initial by the tester and the research psychiatrists. Both write-ups were done according to the same research form (Form B), which required separate comments about each variable. Both write-ups were based on information that was gathered by others in regular clinical practice: The research tester's judgments were drawn from tests administered by others; the psychiatrists' judgments were based on psychiatric and social work examinations, hospital observations, and the clinical test report which was based on the same tests the research psychologist was using for his independent research inferences from tests.

Judge 1 assigned each single variable a score representing the degree of congruence between tester and psychiatrist. In addition to scoring each patient variable, he scored global diagnostic understanding, treatment recommendations, and specific predictions. Scale scores were "1" for agreement, "2" for partial agreement, "3" for disagreement. Inability to make the comparison, usually because testers and psychiatrists addressed themselves to different phenomena, were denoted by "(- - - -)." Sometimes, a variable was not commented upon by tester or psychiatrist, occasionally through apparent oversight, but usually because one or another did not believe that his data could yield a valid judgment.

In addition to scoring each variable numerically, Judge 1 included

---

*These write-ups were done mainly by Research Tester Siegel and Research Psychiatrists Robbins and Wallerstein.

qualitative statements about explicit disagreements where they existed. For example: conscious guilt—score of "3"; "tester says that the patient is consciously guilty over her sexual promiscuity and masturbation, and is less guilty over her hostility"; psychiatrist says the patient seems to be without conscious guilt."*

The 22 patient variables settled upon in the original design of the Project are:

Anxiety	Insight
Symptoms	Externalization
Somatization	Ego strength
Depression	Intelligence
Unconscious guilt	Psychological-mindedness
Conscious guilt	Sublimation
Alloplasticity	Honesty
Core neurotic conflicts	Extent of desired change
Self-concept	Secondary gain
Patterning of defenses	Quality of interpersonal relations
Anxiety tolerance	Transference paradigms

Deleted from this list are such variables as patient's physical health, adequacy of finances, etc., about which tests could say nothing. As we shall see, even with respect to the variables attended to, there was a good bit of variation in how well the variable lent itself to being judged by way of the tests. Two more variables, thought organization and affect organization, were added by the testers since, on the basis of clinical experience, these variables were known to lend themselves well to scrutiny by way of the tests, and because they were thought to be important in diagnostic and predictive understanding. While the research tester wrote a specific statement about each of these as he did with all the others, the psychiatrists did not, and Judge 1 was therefore forced to extrapolate where possible from the psychiatrists' remarks about other variables.

Two more variables, treatment recommendations and treatment predictions, were included in Research Form C, designed to capture recommendations and predictions. These variables were done on each patient by the psychiatrist, but on only four patients by the tester. Just as he extrapolated with respect to thought organization and affect or-

*These somewhat abbreviated qualitative remarks should not be subjected by the reader to too close an analysis. We are sure that the psychiatrist would agree that this patient and probably all people have conscious feelings of guilt which are more or less intense under various conditions. What is meant here is that conscious guilt is a small factor relative to the diagnostic understanding of the patient, as a person in general, and her presenting difficulties in particular.

ganization in making judgments of the psychiatrist's view on these variables, Judge 1 extrapolated from the Form B write-ups, where possible, the tester's opinion on the variables treatment recommendations and treatment predictions.

These procedures were simply to disclose the extent of agreement between tester and psychiatrist. But who was right, and how did it happen? To answer this we selected a criterion, a measure of what *did* happen to the patients presumably as the result of the treatment. The criterion for each patient was a write-up done by Drs. Ann Appelbaum and Leonard Horwitz as part of their section of the Project (1968). These write-ups, based on all sources of data except that of the research testers, provided an overview of the diagnostic process, treatment, and nonpsychiatric life of the patient from initial through termination through follow-up. They were written to provide a criterion by which the accuracy of formal predictions done at initial could be measured. Therefore, they are well suited to our purposes of assessing test findings and predictions in the sense of their telling generally "what happened," although they do not necessarily address themselves specifically to the particular issues which emerged as disagreements between the tester and the psychiatrist. Thus, some degree of extrapolation, varying with patient and clinical issue, was necessary.

All the data reported above with respect to the extent of agreement were read by Judge 2 (Dennis Farrell), who until now was unacquainted with any of the research material or patients. He was asked to make a judgment on a scale of agreement and disagreement between the tester and criterion, and between the psychiatrist and criterion with respect to the following questions: (1) global diagnostic understanding, (2) treatment recommendations, (3) specific predictions. Further he was to note which of the patient variables were crucial to correct inferences in global diagnostic understanding, treatment recommendations, or specific predictions. In making his quantitative assessments, Judge 2 used a 5-point scale going from 1, referring to agreement, in half-steps to 3, referring to disagreement. In addition, he wrote a qualitative description for each patient of the particular differences between the tester and the psychiatrist, especially attempting to trace the sources and paths of inference and evidence. These write-ups provided the basis for the discussion of the quantitative results, and for the generalizations and hypotheses noted later in the chapter.

The following are examples of the kinds of information judged and the kinds of judgments made. A treatment recommendation scored 2, for partial agreement: Here the tester sees no contraindication to psychoanalysis but (for reasons remarked upon in the write-ups of the particular variables) is mildly skeptical about its suitability and likely achievements, while the psychiatrist is enthusiastic about psychoanalysis being the treatment of choice and about the extensive gains expected from it. Judge 1's write-up of treatment prediction for this situation is as follows: "Tester predicts there will be significant limitations to what can be gained in psychoanalysis, and this stems directly from his disagreement with the psychiatrist about the nature of conflicts. Tester predicts that oral conflicts will be prominent and that they will be the prime reason for the setting of limits to what can be expected from psychoanalysis. 'From the point of view of being able to resolve deep-seated unconscious conflict, ego strength in the form of ability to give up thoroughly ingrained, subtly expressed impulse-defense configurations may be lacking . . . significant pregenital fixations perhaps covered by phallic features. I would suspect, in view of this, that he is a less ideal treatment case for psychoanalysis than the clinical picture might show.' The psychiatrist says that it may be a long analysis specifically because of the unavailability of affect, and the patient may remain a predominantly anal character, but 'he can be happy, successful individual . . . will achieve structural change.' Thus, the psychiatrist looks optimally for the 'oedipal conflict not having to be buried behind anal defenses' while the tester emphasizes pregenital, particularly oral, difficulties."

In a further treatment prediction, the tester says, "I would risk the prediction that transference will be strong, quickly established maybe one of the principal forms of resistance of the treatment. 'Quite a long time before the patient can view his transference feelings in such a way that he will become able to analyze them.' The psychiatrist's remarks about the transference paradigms stem from his remarks about the variable, *quality of interpersonal relationships*. Rather than a quick but in some respects affectively unmanageable transference, as predicted by the tester, the psychiatrist sees a bigger problem in the patient's being able to involve himself affectively. Rather, the psychiatrist predicts that the patient will be 'polite, obedient, unobstrusive, correct, etc., instead of involving himself affectively!' The tester further comments that the transference may provide a certain amount of gratification, at least enough to sustain a long analysis, but that it may remain stickily unresolved. It seems that the tester and psychiatrist are making predictions of fundamental differences with respect to the transference, and the score on this variable is 3."

Findings

The following data are used to answer the question of how well the tester and the psychiatrist agreed at termination on the 24 patient variables, plus treatment recommendations and treatment predictions, regardless of the accuracy of the judgments.

By adding the occurrence of scores reflecting agreement on all variables studied here, one gets evidence of a simple and clear likelihood that tester and psychiatrist will agree, and that the greater the disagreement the less often it occurs (1 occurs 122 times, 2 occurs 8 times, and 3 occurs only 28 times). As we shall see, however, this gross test of agreement masked a great deal. The differences that did occur between tester and psychiatrist had important implications.

The following data are used to help answer the question of the relative degree of agreement between the tester and the psychiatrist on each patient variable. Table 17 shows the average agreement for each of the variables. Through oversight or inability to assess it, the number of judgments of each variable was not always the same.* Thus, the total for each variable was divided by the number of times it was judged.

A noteworthy finding is that the variables least agreed upon were treatment recommendations and treatment predictions. In some settings such disagreement could stem from widely varying availability and belief in treatment modalities. But in the setting where this research took place, where general agreement and homogeneity in understanding of treatment prescriptions exist, this discrepancy most likely reflects fundamental differences in diagnostic appraisal, at least as these are related to the making of treatment recommendations. Data further bear this out.

Listed below is the ranking of the patients on the basis of the degree of agreement between tester and psychiatrist on them. Again, the lower the number the higher the agreement.

Average Agreement on Patients between Tester and Psychiatrist

1.1	1.5
1.1	1.5
1.2	1.5
1.3	1.6
1.4	1.6
1.4	1.8
1.5	

Mean = 1.41

We turn now to the question of which, the tester or the psychiatrist, was more correct in his judgments.

---

*The amenability of each variable to analysis by way of tests, alone, is reported in the single variables analyses, Chapter 3.

Table 17. Average Agreement of Tester
and Psychiatrist on Patient Variables

Patient variables	Average[a]
Intelligence	.8
Extent of desired change	.9
Somatization	1.0
Honesty	1.1
Secondary gain	1.1
Insight	1.2
Unconscious guilt	1.2
Anxiety	1.2
Thought organization	1.3
Self-concept	1.3
Alloplasticity	1.3
Conscious guilt	1.3
Symptoms	1.3
Anxiety tolerance	1.4
Transference paradigms	1.4
Externalization	1.4
Quality of interpersonal relations	1.5
Psychological-mindedness	1.5
Core neurotic conflicts	1.6
Ego strength	1.6
Depression	1.7
Patterning of defenses	1.7
Treatment recommendations	1.8
Treatment predictions[b]	1.9
Sublimation	[e]
Affect organization	[d]

[a] The lower the number the greater the agreement.
[b] Varying numbers of predictions were made per patient total-
ing 42 scoreable judgments for the group.
[c] Only one case scoreable for the tester.
[d] No scoreable cases for the psychiatrist.

Analysis of variance of the data on global diagnostic understanding, treatment recommendations and specific predictions reveals
that the tester is significantly more often in agreement with criterion
than the psychiatrist ($p < .001$) across all three questions. No significant differences among the three questions occurs for the tester and
criterion comparison or psychiatrist and criterion comparison or their
combination.

Means for each question and all questions added together for the
tester and criterion and psychiatrist and criterion are noted in Table 18.

There were 3.8 variables *per patient* (number of variables cited as
crucial divided by N) considered crucial in the tester's coming to more

Table 18. Means

	Global	Treatment	Predictions	Σ
Tester and criterion	1.62	1.69	1.85	1.72
Psychiatrist and criterion	2.27	2.46	2.46	2.40
Σ	1.94	2.08	2.15	2.06

correct judgments than the psychiatrist. (In some cases crucial variables were not cited.) The mean number of variables considered crucial to correct judgments, considering only those instances where there was a crucial variable cited, was 3.4. That these many variables were so considered is unsurprising considering the overlap and high correlation among some variables.

Those variables judged to be crucial in four or more cases (above the mean) along with the number of times they were so noted are:

> Ego strength= 8
> Transference paradigms= 7
> Core neurotic conflicts= 6
> Quality of interpersonal relations= 5
> Patterning of defenses= 5
> Self-concept= 4
> Psychological-mindedness= 4

Thus, the most useful variables in making correct predictions were a mixture of structural, dynamic, and interpersonal ones.

STUDY II

Method

A test report based on the same set of tests on which the research tester based his inferences, written under the usual clinical conditions at the Menninger Foundation, was included in the diverse sources of information on which the psychiatrist made his judgments. If the research tester was more accurate than the psychiatrist, two possibilities present themselves: One, the clinical test report was as correct as the tester; but it conflicted with other sources of information available to the psychiatrist, was ignored by the psychiatrist, or for whatever reason did not play a determining factor in the psychiatrist's conclusions. The other possibility is that the clinical test report was as incorrect as the psychiatrist was. If so, it was not "tests" but a particular tester which made the difference. If the psychiatrist was more accurate than the research tester, then the clinical test report may have been more accurate than the research tester, or it may have been as inaccurate and ignored.

To help answer these questions a comparison was made between the clinical test report and the psychiatrist. The method was identical to that used in the comparison between the tester and the psychiatrist. The same judges and the same 13 patients were used. The same 5-point half-step scale was used, with "1" standing for agreement, "3" standing for disagreement, and (----) standing for situations where "1," "2," or "3" score judgments could not be made, usually because different issues were addressed. Note was taken of those instances when "(----)" appeared in conjunction with scale scores as well as when they appeared alone. One big difference between the clinical test report and the psychiatrist comparison and the tester and psychiatrist comparison is that the clinical test reports are just that—reports, rather than research forms. They do not address themselves to each of the patient variables designated in the research. While some of these variables would be crucial to any such clinical document and were reported as such, some were not mentioned at all or mentioned only skimpily. In clinical test reports a further selection of which variables to write about is often made according to the issues faced by the psychiatric team at a particular time. Consequently, an "X" category was used to refer to instances where either clinical test report or occasionally the psychiatrist was not addressed to the variable in question to a degree that made a judgment possible. The judge was fairly strict in keeping to a minimum his inferences about what the psychologists may have thought but did not write about particular patient variables. The rough test he used was whether a different assessment of a particular variable could have been made on the basis of what was written. If so, he scored the variable "X". With respect to treatment recommendations and treatment predictions, however, he extrapolated a bit more freely since he did the same with these questions when such material was not directly available from the research tester either.

Thus, this comparison gives us some information about what variables are most often, as well as most usefully, written about in clinical test reports, and also provides in an indirect way a comparison between test reports done for research purposes and those done in usual clinical practice.

It was possible to compare the research tests and the clinical test report indirectly by comparing mean ranking of agreements on each patient between them. However, such agreement would come about spuriously if the clinical test report and the research tester were in agreement or disagreement about different cases. It was possible to make a more direct comparison by comparing the clinical test report with the criterion and comparing those findings with research tests and criterion.

Judge 2 (Farrell), who did the comparison of the research tester and psychiatrist with criterion, compared the clinical test report and criterion according to the same method.

Findings

Extent of gross agreement between the clinical test report and psychiatrist is reported in Table 19. As there was between the tester and psychiatrist, there is a simple and clear likelihood that clinical test report and psychiatrist will agree, and the greater the disagreement the less often it occurs (1= 87, 2= 61, 3= 5).

The following data are used to help answer the question of the relative degree of agreement between the clinical test report and the psychiatrist on particular patient variables. It was necessary to report averages because of the unequal numbers of times particular variables were judged. (To obtain the average we divided the total points assigned the variable by the number of patients.) The variables were ranked from lowest score meaning greatest agreement to highest score meaning greatest disagreement. However, the average in itself failed to solve the comparison problem because there was such great variability in the number of patients for whom a particular variable was judged. (The average reached on the basis of none or very few instances is sufficient to generalize.) Thus, the X column reports the number of times the variable could *not* be judged so that by inspection the reader may see the size of the sample on which the average ranking was based. The (----) column is also included as a rough measure of the degree to which a variable lent itself to apposite comparisons. Low number of (----) would presumably reflect high agreement between the clinical test report and the psychiatrist in understanding what the variable measures, assuming the variable was addressed frequently at all.

Those variables written about (no more than twice) by the clinical test reports are sublimation, secondary gain, alloplasticity, honesty and unconscious guilt. These variables require knowledge of the patient's life apart from tests (sublimation, alloplasticity), value judgments (sublimation, honesty), or theoretical inferences far removed

Table 19. Average Agreement on Patient Variables
between the Clinical Test Report and the
Psychiatrist ($N = 13$)

Patient variables	Average	X	(− − − −)
Sublimation	0	13	0
Secondary gain	0	13	0
Alloplasticity	0	12	1
Somatization	1.0	9	1
Depression	1.0	2	0
Anxiety tolerance	1.0	8	4
Externalization	1.0	9	1
Honesty	1.0	12	0
Intelligence	1.1	2	2
Symptoms	1.1	5	1
Conscious guilt	1.2	7	1
Anxiety	1.2	2	0
Extent of desired change	1.2	8	1
Core neurotic conflicts	1.3	0	0
Self-concept	1.3	3	0
Insight	1.3	4	2
Transference paradigms	1.4	1	0
Quality of interpersonal relations	1.4	0	3
Unconscious guilt	1.5	10	1
Patterning of defenses	1.5	2	1
Psychological-mindedness	1.6	5	3
Treatment recommendations	1.6	1	1
Ego strength	1.7	0	0
Treatment predictions	1.7	8	2
Affect organization	2.0	4	6
Thought organization	2.2	1	3

from test data (unconscious guilt) because they are difficult to assess on the basis of tests. That the testers did not attempt to assess them is reassuring evidence that they stuck loyally to test data alone for their inferences. By the same token, most of those variables written about at least 12 times by the clinical test reports (core neurotic conflicts, treatment recommendations, ego strength, treatment predictions, affect organization, and thought organization) are classically amenable to portrayal through tests.

Recalling that "1" refers to agreement and "2" refers to partial agreement, let us take every variable on this list above the average of 1.5 as referring to those variables about which there is the greatest disagreement. There are six such variables: psychological-mindedness, treatment recommendations, ego strength, treatment predictions, affect organization, and thought organization. These are listed below alongside the five variables averaging more than 1.5 in the previous comparison between the tester and the psychiatrist. (It might be recalled that Xs were not an issue in the tester and psychiatrist comparison since for the most part each of the variables was written about by both of them.)

Clinical Test Report and Psychiatrist	*Tester and Psychiatrist*
Psychological-mindedness	Depression
Ego strength	Ego strength
Treatment predictions	Treatment predictions
Affect organization	Patterning of defenses
Thought organization	Core neurotic conflicts
Treatment recommendations	Treatment recommendations

Three variables are on both lists: treatment recommendations, treatment predictions, and ego strength. One implication that can be drawn from this is that treatment recommendations and treatment predictions are both based to a great extent on assessments of ego strength, and it is here that both the clinical test report and the tester were inclined to differ with the psychiatrist. One would guess that the usual clinical recognition of tests as a highly sensitive way of ascertaining ego strength (usually a relative lack of it, which one might expect in this group of patients) is formally supported here, and that this occurs whether the report is written on the clinical firing line or under research conditions. But whether this occurs for the clinical test report correctly cannot be known until the clinical test report is compared to criterion.

Since thought organization is an aspect of ego strength, and especially of the way ego strength seemed often to be defined by the clinical test report, it is not surprising that thought organization, too, groups itself along with treatment recommendations and ego strength as a major disagreement between the clinical test report and the psychiatrist. That it did not appear in this light in the comparison between the tester and psychiatrist may be an artifact. As mentioned, thought organization was not one of the original patient variables about which the psychiatrist wrote. Along with affect organization, it was adopted by the tester as an addition to the original list. Such comparisons as the judge was able to make were gathered from the psychiatrist's remarks on other variables. Even so, in two instances, the judge could make no comparison judgment at all, and in three instances the score was (----). Thus, the overall comparison between the tester and the psychiatrist on thought organization is based on only

eight cases. The smallness of this sample and the degree of extrapolation necessary for any judgment to be made at all probably conspired
to make the comparison of this variable less valid than the others. The
same line of reasoning and conclusion applied to affect organization.
With an average of 2.0, this too was one of the most disagreed-upon
variables between the clinical test report and the psychiatrist, but it
was dealt with only nine times.

Psychological-mindedness is an exceptionally ambiguous term as
it is discussed clinically (S. Appelbaum, 1973), and this ambiguity
may have been responsible for the disagreement between the clinical
test report and the psychiatrist. It may not have been so much dis-
agreed about by the tester and the psychiatrist because of their having
the benefit of the researcher's written definition.

The data show the comparability with respect to patients of the
clinical test report and the psychiatrist.

Average Agreement on Patients between the Clinical Test Report and
Psychiatrst ($N = 13$)

1.1	1.6
1.2	1.6
1.2	1.6
1.2	1.6
1.3	1.8
1.4	1.9
1.5	

Mean $= 1.46$

The mean average ranking for the tester–psychiatrist comparison
was 1.41. A t test (for correlated measures) comparing the mean reveals that these means are not significantly different. The data in Table 20 compare the clinical test report and the criterion. Analysis of
variance of the data on global diagnostic understanding, treatment
recommendation, and specific predictions reveal that the clinical test
report is significantly more often in agreement with criterion than the
psychiatrist ($p < .01$). The research tester had achieved an even greater
level of significance of difference from the psychiatrist ($p < .001$), but

Table 20. Means

	Global	Treatment	Predictions	Σ
Psychiatrist and criterion	2.27	2.46	2.46	2.40
Clinical test report and criterion	1.58	1.96	1.96	1.83
Σ	1.92	2.21	2.21	2.12

an analysis of variance comparing the research tester and criterion with the clinical test report and criterion revealed no significant difference between the research tester and the clinical test report. Global diagnostic understanding was the question on which the research tester and the clinical test report agreed with criterion significantly more often than on the other questions. Thus, the research tester and the clinical test report were in agreement with each other and in agreement with criterion significantly more than the psychiatrist was.

Noted below are the variables considered by the judge as crucial in coming to correct judgments. The mean number of crucial variables *per patient* was 3.5. The *mean times* a variable was considered crucial was 3.8. Again, if one takes those variables judged crucial in four or more cases (above the mean) in coming to correct predictions, the list includes with numbers of instances: ego strength = 8, core neurotic conflict = 7, transference paradigms = 6, patterning of defenses = 5, thought organization = 5, and psychological-mindedness = 5.

STUDY III

Method

The findings from Study I and Study II were based on only 13 cases. But since the clinical test report did assess more correctly than the psychiatrist, just as the research tester did, and the research tester and the clinical test report did not differ significantly, we were justified in adding the 26 cases on which there was a clinical test report but no initial research tester study. Now with an N of 39, the same procedure was followed with the same judges as on the above comparisons.

Findings

Clinical Test Reports at Initial

The data comparing the clinical test report and criterion are shown in Table 21.

An analysis of variance reveals, again, a significant difference ($p < .01$) between the clinical test report and criterion and the psychiatrist and criterion. It further reveals no interaction with respect to global assessment, treatment recommendations, or treatment predictions. Thus, with three times as many cases, the superiority of the test finding over the psychiatric examination is demonstrated.

Table 21. Means ($N = 39$)

	Global	Treatment	Predictions	Σ
Psychiatrist–criterion	1.87	1.94	2.14	1.98
Clinical test report–criterion	1.58	1.64	1.78	1.67
Σ	1.78	1.79	1.96	1.82

For the second series of 26 patients, the mean number of times per patient that a variable was considered crucial was 4.8. The mean time a variable was considered crucial was also 4.8. When these 26 cases are combined with the first 13, the mean number of times per patient becomes 4.3 and the mean time a variable was considered crucial becomes 6.5. Again, taking all those above the mean as being most critical in coming to correct judgments for all 39 patients, the following list of variables results (in rank order of importance and with number of times they were considered crucial in parentheses):

> Ego strength (27)
> Transference paradigms (19)
> Core neurotic conflicts (18)
> Patterning of defenses (16)
> Thought organization (13)
> Quality of interpersonal relations (11)
> Psychological-mindedness (9)
> Alloplasticity (7)
> Self-concept (7)

The variables considered by the judge as crucial in the clinical test report's coming to correct judgments for the first series of 13 cases are:

> Ego strength (8)
> Core neurotic conflicts (7)
> Transference paradigms (6)
> Patterning of defenses (5)
> Psychological-mindedness (5)
> Thought organization (5)

The crucial variables in the whole series of 39 cases are:

> Ego strength (27)
> Transference paradigms (19)
> Core neurotic conflicts (18)
> Patterning of defenses (16)

The general comparability of these two lists supports the idea that there was nothing atypical about one or another of the series of cases in this respect, and suggests that the superiority of the clinical test report over the psychiatrist in both series may have come about in similar ways.

As noted before, the variables considered crucial by the judge in the research tester and psychiatrist comparison (on the first 13 cases of course, the only ones on which we have data from the research tester) are:

> Ego strength (8)
> Transference paradigms (7)
> Core neurotic conflicts (6)
> Patterning of defenses (5)
> Quality of interpersonal relations (5)

Again, there is great comparability which further supports the idea that there was nothing atypical in the first batch of 13 cases as compared to the second batch of 26. This comparability further suggests that correct conclusions came about by attention to approximately the same variables. As noted previously, these crucial variables were the ones about which there was most disagreement between the research tester and the psychiatrist and the clinical test report and the psychiatrist. Thus, it is quite likely that these variables led to the test's superiority over the psychiatric examinations.

DISCUSSION

Having ascertained that both research tests and the clinical test report were significantly more correct than the psychiatrist was in global diagnostic understanding, treatment recommendations, and treatment predictions, we are thereby presented with several questions and issues. At first one might be tempted to generalize that tests are "better" than the psychiatric examination in making such judgments. This generalization would be faulty for a number of reasons. To begin with "tests" do not exist in the abstract, but rather include a variety of devices or tools, given singly or in combination. Particular individuals administer, read, and make inferences from them. In the first 13 cases researched here, Richard Siegal's judgments based on a particular test battery were compared to the judgments of Drs. Wallerstein and Robbins, who used information obtained from other people in their own ways. If Wallerstein and Robbins had conducted their own examination, the results might have been different. Dr. Siegal made his judgments in ways different from his usual ways of working clinically: He was forced by the research design to study the variables intensively enough to write a paragraph about each one, he was not under the usual time pressures of nonresearch clinical responsibilities, and, finally, he knew that his conclusions were going to be checked as to their correctness. One cannot say that he would have obtained different conclusions if he had made his judgments in the usual clinical setting, and one cannot assert that the research conditions had no effect on his judgments. For example, they could have aided him by encouraging thoroughness and by providing ample time. Or these conditions could have disrupted his accustomed process of inference by encouraging misleading complexity. That his results were duplicated by the clinical test report, however, which *was* written under ordinary clinical conditions, does suggest that these differences did not make for a difference.

Could a less talented and experienced tester than Dr. Siegal have done as well? The success of the clinical test report does not help much with this question. In six cases, the clinical test report was written by one or another of the research testers themselves. Thirty reports were written or supervised by staff members, most of whom were associated with the Menninger Foundation's Post-Doctoral Training Program, and all of whom were homogeneous with respect to locally used theory of personality testing and practice in general. In short, the clinical test reports were written by testers who were probably better trained and more experienced than the general run of testers. Such efficiency might not be available elsewhere.

What does emerge clearly from these data is a rather no-nonsense, pragmatic view of tests in which a handful of key variables reported upon in relatively brief documents get the job done. Of course, these data allow this conclusion only with respect to answering the specified gross diagnostic and predictive questions. The data shed no direct light on the effectiveness of these test approaches with respect to other and finer questions which may be asked of the tester. Such questions may require more minute and extended analysis and reporting. But, practically speaking, the issues researched here are the major questions asked of tests, and probably do make the greatest difference for key treatment decisions.

It is not surprising that the test assessments of ego strength were most often crucial to correct conclusions. The test battery used, with its systematic progression from structured to less structured stimuli and including a variety of tasks, was designed to afford a view of the efficiency of mental structures, a chief ingredient of ego strength. The Rapaportian tradition in which the testers were trained strongly emphasizes ego psychology, and the series of patients included a good many people with the kinds of underlying ego incapacities which are often held to be especially well discernible through the use of tests. Patterning of defenses is also highly correlated with ego strength. But inferences about dynamics and interpersonal relations—core neurotic conflicts and transference paradigms—were also instrumental in arriving at correct conclusions.

In 10 instances, the largest single source of error resulted because the psychiatrist ignored the clinical test report's findings of the severity of the patient's difficulties. In those few cases that did better than the psychiatrist and the clinical test report expected, both had tended to overlook the patient's assets, particularly the patient's apparent potential for introjecting the therapist as a good object. It may be that the testers were accurate not only because of the battery of standardized tests but also because they were less involved with patients' personalities than were the psychiatric examiners, and therefore less subject to "countertransference" or other interpersonally misleading effects. The psychiatrist seems to have been subject to constant errors, either seeing fewer difficulties or believing overoptimistically in the efficacy of treatment, or both.

While the clinical test report's assessment of ego strength was its major tool in making correct predictions, the psychiatrist was particularly silent on the "thought organization" aspect of ego strength. The grave implication that can be drawn from this is that inadequate attention to thought organization, which is often thought to be best assessed on the basis of tests, can lead to many diagnostic errors, at least for such patients as were in this sample. On this basis alone, then, there is strong evidence for the inclusion of psychological testing in diagnostic and predictive processes.

That the clinical test report demonstrates its superiority over the psychiatrist despite the psychiatrist having the clinical test report's information at his disposal is disheartening. A great deal of time, labor, and expense failed to produce the results, and was therefore wasteful to the institution, presumably injurious to the morale of the workers, and failed in the primary task of promoting the welfare of the patients. The unvarnished fact of the matter is that major questions about these patients would have been better answered if the examinations had consisted solely of testing.

How did it happen that the psychiatrist had the information at his disposal but did not use it? Conceivably the test reports were written so badly that they failed to communicate their findings (Appelbaum, 1970b, 1972a). But in only one instance did Judge 2 report that the psychiatrist seemed to have misread or misunderstood the clinical test report. One might argue that Judge 1, being an experienced tester, was able to read the correct conclusions from "between the lines." However, he used a local clinical standard of understanding in his judgments, one that was no more sophisticated than could be expected from a psychiatrist who is also a senior clinician. Further, the questions investigated were of a sufficiently gross kind as to yield information that was ascertainable without much subtle drawing of inferences. A much more tenable explanation is that in the minds of the psychiatrists nontest data were more compelling and convincing. Faced with disagreements between such data and the tests, they erroneously chose to believe nontest information.

In general, these data bespeak the need for much better integration of diagnostic data by testing and nontesting approaches, with special attention perhaps to the need for reconciliation of differences where disagreement occurs. For in these disagreements there may well lie important diagnostic and predictive information. An obvious moral to be drawn is that we may be struggling with an artificial schism in diagnostic thinking between "psychiatric" and "clinical psychology" approaches, based perhaps on unfortunate, narrowly conceived professional differences rather than substantive ones. Even if the interviewer does not himself give the tests, formal training in understanding and appreciating their value might allow him to make better use of them. By the same token, it is likely that experience in psychiatric interviewing, and especially in conducting the kind of treatment procedures assumed in the predictions, would further increase the effectiveness of testers and extend the range of issues with which they are effective.

SUMMARY

1. On 13 cases fully worked up by the research testers, the tests were significantly more often in agreement with an external criterion than were all psychiatric findings, with respect to global diagnostic assessment, treatment recommendations, and specific predictions. Those variables judged to be crucial in coming to correct conclusions in four or more cases (above the mean) along with the number of times they were so noted were: ego strength = 8, transference paradigms = 7, core neurotic conflicts = 6, quality of interpersonal relations = 5, patterning of defenses = 5, self-concept = 4, psychological-mindedness = 4.

2. A comparison of the clinical test report on the same 13 cases noted above revealed that the clinical test report, as was the case with

the research testing, was significantly more often in agreement with the external criterion than was the psychiatrist's. Those variables judged critical in four or more cases (above the mean) in coming to correct predictions along with the number of times they were so noted were: ego strength = 8, core neurotic conflicts = 7, transference paradigms = 6, patterning of defenses = 5, thought organization = 5, and psychological-mindedness = 5.

3. In view of the comparability of the research testing and the clinical testing, 26 cases on which there was a clinical test report but no comparable research study data were added to the 13 fully worked-up cases, making an N of 39. A comparison of testing in general with psychiatric findings revealed the tests to agree significantly more often with the external criterion than did the psychiatrist on the same three questions: global diagnostic impression, treatment recommendations, and specific treatment predictions. Those variables considered crucial (above the mean) in coming to correct decisions along with the number of times they were so noted were: ego strength = 27, transference paradigms = 19, core neurotic conflicts = 18, patterning of defenses = 16. Comparison of crucial variables suggests that both sets of testers came to the correct conclusions by exploiting approximately the same variables, and that these variables were the ones about which there was disagreement between the testers and the psychiatrist.

4. The largest single source of error was in the psychiatrist's ignoring the clinical test report's findings of the severity of the patient's difficulties; ego strength was the most crucial variable in both sets of test conclusions.

5. Faced with disagreements between the test findings and the other data at his disposal, the psychiatrist evidently chose to believe nontest information.

CHAPTER 9

Follow-Up Study

INTRODUCTION

The relative absence of studies of patients years after the completion of treatment is well-known, and the need for such studies hardly requires extensive discussion. Even when the goal of treatment is the removal of symptoms, it would seem necessary to know whether the symptoms have stayed removed, or been replaced by other symptoms or behaviors. When the goal of treatment is to bring about changes in the shape and quality of a life as contrasted solely to removal of symptoms or other limited treatment goals (E. Ticho, 1972), learning of the effects of treatment can, by definition, only come through an assessment of the person's continued life.

For practical purposes, we chose the arbitrary point of 2 years for follow-up assessment. Even so, we were unable to test some patients because of their unavailability. We simply had to countenance the ambiguity of such situations as raised by the research tester who wrote that one patient's continued changes for the better were tenuous, and that an assessment of her might be quite different if she were seen after the follow-up period. One can raise the question whether a 2-year follow-up point is ever long enough. Indeed, one of the questions implicitly asked and answered below was whether there would be substantial changes at all after only 2 years. Whether these changes are definitive as to symptom goals or life goals is more difficult to answer.

Both termination and follow-up testing were available on only 28 patients (11 males, 17 females). Full research forms were filled out by the research testers on 8 of these. On the remaining 20, data were gathered by the research psychologist from brief interim documents,

summaries, and "work sheets" done by the research testers prepara-
tory to their projected elaborate and differential Form Bs. These documents usually did not include comments about each intrapsychic variable, but were adequate for most central purposes of this research.
Having to use these kinds of documents instead of extensive research
forms, however, did limit some single variable comparisons, and prevented the statistical pattern analyses done at termination from being
repeated.

Our quantitative analysis of follow-up data resulted in our learning how much patient variables had remained the same, changed for
the worse, or how much and which patients changed for the better.
We also compared those who changed for the better at follow-up with
those who changed for the better at termination. We then made qualitative descriptions of three groups of patients: (1) those who had done
worse from initial to termination but had done better between termination and follow-up, (2) those who had done better between initial
and termination but had done worse between termination and follow-
up, and (3) those who had done better between initial and termination
and had done still better between termination and follow-up. In the
course of these descriptions, we offer a brief analysis of the vicissitudes of ideation, a major issue in verbal and insight-oriented psychotherapy.

FOLLOW-UP FINDINGS

Unless otherwise specified all the following findings of change
refer to the period between termination and follow-up.

The same research psychologist (S. Appelbaum) who did the initial to termination ratings rated the same intrapsychic variables, the
overall question of improvement or worsening, made notations as to
whether the patient's situation was considered tenuous. All these data
are recorded in Table 22. "Q" refers to those instances where the research psychologist could not make a judgment as to change in the
variable, usually because of the absence or nature of the data. A question mark refers to his inability to decide whether a change in the
variable was for the better or worse. "S" reflects the judgment of
sameness, or no change. As in some previous analyses of data, "increase" and "decrease" refer to extent, which may or may not be the
same as better or worse.

Sufficient cases were available for Chi-square tests of 12 of the 27
variables and categories rated. Observed as against expected frequen-

cies were tallied with respect to how much the category or variable in question had changed for the better, changed for the worse, or remained the same. (Tenuousness was rated as to presence or absence.) The following variables changed for the better to a significant degree: anxiety ($<.0005$), patterning of defenses ($<.025$), thought organization ($<.005$), intelligence ($<.05$), alloplasticity ($<.025$), overall change for the better ($<.0005$), and tenuousness of change ($<.0005$). It is difficult to say whether these variables were more changeable than the others, as it could be that they were more easily ascertainable on tests than others and thus were written about more, or it could be that they were written about more often because the testers found them most useful. One should note, however, that these variables tend to be structural. Core neurotic conflict and quality of interpersonal relations had sufficient cases to be included in the analysis, but did not change significantly more often than would be expected by chance. This finding, at least tentatively, gives rise to the hypothesis that the dynamic and object relations aspect of personality change only during psychotherapy while structural change may occur during and after psychotherapy has ended. In this context psychic structure might be likened to an engine which, when new, requires use under various conditions in order to achieve the efficiency designed into it. This finding accords with Wheelis's (1950) views of the role of continued action as a means of bringing about change.

A comparison of termination and follow-up change in intrapsychic variables, and overall change of patients for the better, expressed in percentages, is available in Table 23. As was done in the termination single variable analyses, a distinction was drawn between those variables in which change is, by definition and directly, judged to be for the better, and those variables whose change in quantity could represent either a change for the better or for the worse is indirect based on "all other things being equal." Thus, all other things being equal, the lowering of anxiety reflects a change for the better, but as we have seen throughout these analyses, in particular instances it does not.

The figures enclosed by parentheses refer to the equivalent figures at termination. The roughly comparable changes in patterning of defense, thought organization, and intelligence* correspond to the roughly comparable overall change for the better between termination and follow-up over the same period. Lessening of anxiety seems to have substantially occurred across the group of patients at follow-up

---

* Intelligence refers to comments particularly made by the research testers on this issue, not simply to IQ. An analysis of change in IQ with the almost identical group of patients was reported in Chapter 3.

Table 22. Change in Patient Variables and Overall Change between Termination and Follow-Up

	Increase	Decrease	Total	Better	Worse	?^a	Q^d	Same
Anxiety	7 (B-2^a, W-4^b, ?-1)	10 (B-10, W-0, ?-0)	17	12	4		1	0
Symptoms	3 (B-2, W-0, ?-1)	4 (B-3, W-0, ?-1)	7	5	0	1	1	3
Somatization	2 (B-2)	0	2	2		2		1
Depression	6 (B-1, W-4, ?-1)	5 (B-4, W-0, ?-1)	11	5	4		3	2
Conscious guilt	1 (B-0, W-0)	4 (B-4, W-0)	5	4		2	1	3
Unconscious guilt	1 (B-0, W-1)	2 (B-2, W-0)	3	2	0		3	4
Alloplasticity	4 (B-3, W-0, ?-1)	4 (B-4, W-0, ?-0)	8	7	1		1	4
Core neurotic	—	—		5	5	1	3	4
Self-concept	—	—		3	2		2	2
Patterning of defenses	—	—		10	4		5	1
Organization of thought	—	—		11	4		2	

	Better	Worse	Q	Same	Total		
Organization of affect	—	—	3	3		3	1
Anxiety tolerance	—	—	6	1		0	6
Insight	3 (B-1, W-1, ?-1)	0	1	1		4	4
Externalization	4 (B-1, W-2, ?-1)	2 (B-1, W-0, ?-1)	2		2	1	2
Ego strength	—	—	6	1		2	4
Intelligence	—	—	6			2	6
Psychological-mindedness	—	—	1			2	3
Honesty	—	—	1			2	2
Extent desired change	—	—	2			3	3
Secondary gain	1 (B-0, W-1, ?-0)	1 (?-1)		1		1	3
Quality interpersonal relations	—	—	6	2		3	2
Transference paradigms	—	—		1		2	
Sublimation	—	—				1	1

	Better	Worse	Q	Same	Total
Overall better or worse	15	7	4	2	=28
	Yes	No			
Tenuous	12	2	1	2	=15

[a] B = better
[b] W = worse
[c] ? = unable to judge "better" or "worse"
[d] Q = unable to judge change in variable

Table 23. Comparison of Follow-Up and Termination Significant
Change for the Better of Intrapsychic Variables and Overall

Indirect judgment (less anxiety, less alloplasticity)			Direct judgment (better or worse for each individual)		
Percentage of patients changing for the better	T→U	I→T	Percentage of patients changing for the better	T→U	I→T
Anxiety	75	(47)	Patterning of defenses	66	(77)
Alloplasticity	58	(30)	Thought organization	73	(80)
			Intelligence	50	(54)
			Overall change for the better	68	(75)

as compared to termination, which may reflect an artifactually elevated anxiety due to the termination itself, or may be a consequence of the generally strengthened improvement in structure noted at follow-up. Improved structure seems a plausible explanation for so many more patients improving in alloplasticity at follow-up as well.

Let us look more closely at the finding that at termination 75% of the patients were considered to have changed for the better and 24% for the worse, while at follow-up 68% were considered to have changed for the better and 32% for the worse. At follow-up only 2 of 23 patients were judged to have remained the same; thus, patients did not remain stable intrapsychically. Even without ongoing treatment considerable change occurred. The preponderance of change is for the better just as it was at termination. This suggests that psychotherapy sets a process in motion which continues even when the treatment *per se* is ended.

But did the same people continue to change in the same ways: Were the changes at follow-up simply continuations of changes noticed at termination? Of 28 patients examined at follow-up, 10 had improved at termination and had improved still further at follow-up.

No patients had done worse at termination, and still worse at follow-up. Five had changed for the worse at termination but had reversed themselves and changed for the better at follow-up. As can be seen from the analysis of the "tenuous" category, the changes in all five of these patients were judged as being tenuous. Seven patients were judged as having improved at termination but took a turn for the worse at follow-up. Four patients changed for the better at termination with changes not assessable with respect to better or worse at follow-up. Two patients had changed for the better at termination and had remained the same at follow-up. Thus, most patients continue to change after termination. It seems that psychotherapy sets a process in motion which continues after its termination; the direction of that continuation, in interaction with life events, may well be different from that at termination. To judge from these data, neither long-term congratulations nor long-term despair is in order at termination.

Unlike the single variable analyses, the occasional inability to assess change was usually not due primarily to the absence of the data. Rather, some patients had changed in ways which, by their nature, were difficult to categorize as being for the better or for the worse. For example, one patient was described, in part, as follows:

> The most striking change in this period has been the emergence of more spontaneous, less controlled affect. This has its adaptive aspects in an increased ability to experience and accept her need for close interpersonal relations. At the same time, however, her expression of passive oral needs is likely to be somewhat arbitrary. In addition, the spontaneity of her affect life would seem sometimes to tend towards lability and irritability. To the extent that this greater affective freedom takes the place of the depression we saw originally, it is of course a welcome change, but one cannot help but wonder to what extent affect outbursts and lability may cause difficulty for the patient and those in her environment.

The "same" category should not be taken to mean that the patients were identical, or even that no changes were discussed by the research testers. Rather, the changes were slight and counterbalanced by other changes leading to the conclusion that the overall difference did not make much of a difference in functioning. For example, with one patient the research tester noted "an increase in ideational activity in an attempt (for the most part fairly successful but at times falling short) to bind anxiety . . . impulse control seems a little more adequate, alloplasticity has diminished—although we would not imply any basic increase in anxiety tolerance over the two years that have elapsed since we last saw this patient." Change in this patient was summarized by the research tester as follows:

> The test picture at Follow-up continues to emphasize the slight decrease in alloplasticity that was seen at Termination; it reemphasizes the tenuousness of the patient's current state of equilibrium and its reliance upon external environmental supports; it underscores the slight increase in effectiveness of controls; and, in general, when compared with the Termination and Initial test studies, continues to point up the patient's need for some kind of long-term supportive (possibly expressive) therapy.

More than one-fourth of the patients offered some variation of the idea that their difficulties were "something to live with." Since this kind of statement is not directly inquired for in the course of the test battery, and was not an *a priori* issue for investigation, its appearance in the test write-ups suggests its prominence in the posttreatment psychology of these patients. Naturally, its specific meaning carried the imprint of the person in whom it appears. For example, one patient put it in a rather worldly, sophisticated context; another made it sound resigned, if not masochistic; another gave it a burned-out, orally dissatisfied quality; and still another experienced it as resignation that nothing could change aspects of the human condition, and the feminine condition in particular. Continuing investigations of self-analysis such as that by G. Ticho (1967) should be able to shed further light on what seems to be the generally underemphasized and under-researched state of mind of patients after they have completed such a major attempt at life or symptom change as psychotherapy.

This finishes the quantitative analysis of the follow-up data. Let us now look qualitatively at some of the changes occurring from termination to follow-up. Of particular interest might be those five patients who were judged as having changed for the worse at termination but as having improved at follow-up. Before drawing some generalizations, it will be helpful to abstract the general dimensions of change in these patients, individually, at follow-up.

One patient was working hard at suppressing and constricting dereistic, bizarre, paranoid ideas from expression. Substantially he seemed the same person as at termination—full of guilt, exploitive toward women, suffering with oral conflicts, living a life of slow suicide. He was simply managing better, without much change in ego strength, settling in and acclimating himself to a paranoid schizophrenic orientation, without letting it cause him or others as much trouble as before.

One patient was less projective at follow-up, more self-aware, and thus better able to adapt herself to tasks. Some of this increased control was through constriction of the personality, especially by way of reaction formation and denial. She seemed to feel less orally deprived, somewhat less angry toward men, but her conflict over sexual identification was unimproved. Apparently she was better able to take advantage of external gratification and thus seemed generally happier. But her heightened self-awareness led to some self-doubt, with the implication that a sense of aging and decline would be especially hard for her to manage. After the abortive explosion of feelings during her truncated analysis, this patient was making the best of it largely through denial. She was more sociable and compliant, and less driven by turbulence and fear from stirred-up conflicts, especially oral-passive ones, which she experienced as less threatening and better integrated into her character. Such a stance would not be expected to lead toward further change, but rather was a reinstitution of her pretreatment self.

One patient was no longer as psychotic as he was at initial and termination. He was better able to concentrate and attend, to organize himself, and to use his intellect. For example, he showed a substantial increase in IQ; he had a much better sense of the boundary line between inner and outer as part of generally improved reality testing and strengthened ego activity vis-à-vis impulses; and his awareness of his underlying psychosis seemed expressed in a resigned, burned-out attitude. The research tester said, ". . . insight . . . is not the causative agent [of change]."

One patient was somewhat better able to concentrate and organize herself toward the task at hand and this was reflected in a considerable rise in IQ. She had much insight, but little conflict resolution. To be useful to her insight required self-esteem based on a good oral relationship. She was intermittently and sporadically capable of feeling and benefiting from such a relationship and at termination may well have performed poorly on the tests in the shadow of the loss of the psychotherapeutic relationship. The variability and tenuousness of her better organization was noted at follow-up. Despite her sporadic ability to feel better about herself and function in accordance with this, she nonetheless showed more depression at follow-up than she did at termination.

The changes for the better in all five of these patients were described as being "tenuous."

From the results and added information at follow-up, one can see that because the termination of psychotherapy, itself, is a stressful time, termination may be a poor point at which to measure the results of change. Measured at termination, treatments may appear less successful than they might at a less situationally stressful time. This possible artifact was emphasized with two patients. With one, termination seemed to function as a trigger to her specific difficulty in maintaining herself in the face of loss. She was subject to sharp dips in functioning whenever her self-esteem was threatened, which was one implication for her of losing the psychotherapist. It remains moot, from the standpoint of the tests, as to how much the disturbance noted at termination was due to the loss of a needed relationship, from which she may have recovered at follow-up. Another patient took the termination tests in a period of "drying out" from an alcoholic binge, which probably exaggerated the remorsefulness noted by the testers at that time.

Thus, there is reason to believe that for some patients poorer functioning at termination as compared to initial and follow-up may be due to the stress of termination, in a sense an artifact of the overall process of change.

Follow-up testing, too, seems to have a specific influence for some people. The research tester commented on this about one patient: She seemed "more matter of fact, more taciturn, less eager to discuss herself and try to make a good impression than she was at termination." He continued, "This is frequently found, as matter of fact, when testing people two years after their termination. This patient seems not to be so pressed to put her best foot forward; she does not have to strain so much to prove herself as she did at termination."

Now to return to those patients who did worse at termination and changed for the better at follow-up. None of them did better at follow-up on the basis of developing further insight with which to resolve neurotic conflicts. It may be that self-analysis leading to conflict resolution is possible for people who have a high degree of psychological-mindedness. Such people can process continued internal and external events of life with the skills and information they have learned in psychotherapy. But it was clear at termination that none of these patients had achieved that degree of psychological sophistication.

Three patients had changed for the better primarily through becoming less disorganized in their intrapsychic functioning. In other words, at follow-up they were less psychotic than they had been at termination. Two of them were better able to concentrate and were therefore more adaptively practical, as could be seen quantitatively in their improved IQ.

Three of the patients showed a narrowing of awareness, a tightening up of the personality. One of these showed effortfully suppressed dereistic, bizarre, paranoid ideas. Another showed constrictiveness based on reaction formation and increased reaction formation and denial. A third constricted herself through heightened denial.

Although it is difficult to separate structural management of impulse from the intensity of drive and conflict, it did seem to the research testers that three of the patients showed less peremptoriness of need, and felt less orally deprived and less threatened by the conflictual aspects of passive yearnings, with such yearnings being more integrated into the character. They experienced less threat from primary process derivatives and catastrophic anxiety.

To summarize, these tenuous changes for the better in no instance reflect definitive improvement, or definitive resolution of conflict. Rather, they reflect helpful shifts in defensive alignments, a tilting of the balance in favor of better functioning of structures as against the demandingness of impulse. One can hardly feel sanguine about such changes; for example, one of the patients despite changes for the better was considered still to have as dire a prognosis with respect to suicide or homicide as he had at termination.

Only one of these patients was described as being generally more happy. Strikingly, a kind of bleakness accompanied the improvements noted. Hardly any mention was made of hopefulness for further change. Rather, the emphasis was on resignation, making the best of a bad situation, settling down with what is possible rather than hoping for what might be possible. With one patient his increased cogwheeling with reality seemed to have led to a sense of the existential absurdity of that newfound reality for him, suggesting that his psychosis was an attempt to avoid such a recognition.

Another group of patients ($N = 7$) of special interest are those who had improved at termination but had gotten worse at follow-up. In general, only one of the seven had taken a severe turn for the worse. She had received only one year of treatment and was judged as being substantially more troubled at follow-up than she had been at initial. The other patients could be judged as having changed for the worse, on balance or in small degree from the improvement point they had reached at termination.

Again, before drawing some generalizations, it might be helpful to abstract and record dimensions of change in these patients at follow-up.

With one patient the change from termination to follow-up is best seen in the context of change from initial testing. At that time she was seen as an alloplastic, addictive character disorder with low anxiety and affect tolerance. At termination, after only 1 year of treatment, she was better organized, better able to concentrate, more realistic about herself, showed evidence of internalization of conflict rather than acting upon one or another arm of conflict, and showed a beginning development of insight along with self-concern and commitment to change for the better. At follow-up, despite attempts at constriction, suppression, even conscious withholding, she showed many evidences of an insidious paranoid disintegration of thought (a new element in the picture) along with ineffective use of the alloplastic-denying characterological pattern noted at initial. In effect, she was more troubled at follow-up than she had been even at initial.

One patient maintained, even added to, significant gains she had achieved at termination, one example being a continued dramatic rise in her IQ. From termination to follow-up she had increased ideational activity, with less pervasive need for repression, and consequent heightened precision of thought. However, despite the increase in ego strength, controls, and other emerging capacities, she was in greater distress at the time of follow-up, particularly from conscious anxiety, than she was at termination. This seems to have been caused by the revivification (possibly through her recent marriage) of an incompletely resolved hostile identification with mother, with malevolent aspects of women and related sexual disturbance breaking through repression and reaction formations and becoming thinly and awkwardly denied. This case illustrates the at least occasional difficulty in linking intrapsychic change to psychotherapy independent of knowing concomitant and reverberating environmental change. Voth and Orth (1973) in another Project publication, do link changed behavior with environmental change.

At follow-up one patient was more ideational and less repressive, and in general dealt with conflicts more internally than she had previously. Coincident with that shift was heightened anxiety, possibly intensified depression covered with strained denials, and recourse to increased alloplasticity, all of this with respect to hetero- and homosexual urges and conflicts. She was less able to maintain a feminine identification.

One patient at follow-up resorted to many of the same strained denials, reaction formations, and obsessional vacillations and doubting that were characteristic of him at the time of initial testing. He found it more difficult to maintain the behavioral manifestations of vigorous assertive masculinity of which he was capable at termination. He had not, however, gone all the way back to the beginning. Now he was more anxious, and less able to make believe that he was not in conflict, dissatisfied, and depressed. He seemed to be paying, with this discomfort, for some continuing capacity to be assertive, masculine, and grown-up. (There was some question as to whether the follow-up testing had been influenced by the stressful situational circumstances at the time, namely a hospitalization of his wife.)

One patient, while not slipping back to becoming the depressed, phobic, mildly paranoid person that he was at the time of initial testing, at follow-up had slipped back from the point of farthest advance noted at termination. In particular, he was more severely anxious, and was forced to adopt a more pervasive use of avoidance, particularly toward anything to do with sexual themes. Rather than the somewhat counterphobic, hypermasculine stance he had taken at termination in reaction to his view of women as cold and depriving, at follow-up while avoiding women sexually he accepted solicitous, maternal care from them. His present tenuous adjustment rested upon the continuation of external dependency ties.

One patient at follow-up was more vulnerable to intense anxiety and severe periods of apprehension, self-doubt, and depression than she was at termination. The intellectualization, reaction formation, and denial with increased anxiety tolerance noted at termination, which had replaced her reliance on repression, had not been consolidated—all this despite her having much insight not only into her conflicts but into the formal aspects of her functioning. A new configuration at follow-up was masochism and guilt, stemming particularly from her strong masculine, competitive wishes. The research tester wrote, "Much more than is usual for patients at follow-up, she is a person still very much in a state of flux."

One patient had become more ideational in this respect and less constricted. However, such ideation was mildly deviant, and seemed connected with an increasing struggle to control anxiety and depression especially. Depression arose from the uncovering of deep-seated oral deprivations, and showed itself in a lack of purpose, goals, and satisfactions. Intrapsychically she did not show as much of a shift for the worse as the other patients in this group. Her worsening seemed specifically tied to an increasing recognition of a reality that was increasingly unhappy and unfulfilling as the 2 years passed.

VICISSITUDES OF IDEATION

Although the balance between "support" and "expressiveness" varies from patient to patient, any psychoanalytic psychotherapy deals primarily with ideas. One might expect, therefore, that ideation would increase during psychotherapy, and, when it does not, that is usually an indication of a marked incapacity of the patient to have accomplished the developmental tasks inherent in the manipulation of ideas (assuming competence of the therapist). There would seem to be less reason, on the face of it, for ideation to increase in the years following termination of psychotherapy. But with 4 of the 7 cases who had done better at termination and worse at follow-up, that is indeed what happened (ideation increased in 12 of the 28 cases at follow-up). Thus, it seems that for some people ideational facility, once launched, can have a kind of life of its own, not only maintaining itself, even in the absence of regular exercise of it in psychotherapy, but increasing.

For some people increased ideation seems to be a mixed blessing. In all four patients who did better at termination and worse at follow-up in a setting of increased ideation, increased ideation was accompanied by increased anxiety, depression, or both. Such a result is not entirely unexpected. Most emotional disturbances are an attempt to blunt the sharp edges of reality, to substitute wish for fact, to narrow an awareness which is experienced as unpalatable. As these coping mechanisms and styles are examined in psychotherapy, and yielded in the strengthening of secondary process, a limbo can occur between consolidated solutions and ways of life. Some people can probably never fully stabilize or adequately use ideation as a primary means of defense and adaptation. Others, even while reaping the benefits of better organization of their thinking and problem-solving capacities, become increasingly aware of the deprivations in their lives. Increased ego functions may be an inadequate substitute for these, and fail to lead to adequate substitutes from the external world either. Psychotherapists would do well to take into consideration what the poets have been telling us all along, that some people need their illusions. Psychotherapists should also consider the possible overall usefulness, as well as the disadvantages, of secondary gain.

All this should hardly be taken to imply that psychotherapy should not be entered into, or that all illusions and secondary gains should be let stand as it. But it does suggest that a sober estimate should be made of the balance of expectable gratifications given up and gratifications received. Choices should be made as to whether and how much of what should be examined, and the conscious expectations of the patient should be clarified, confronted, and brought into a realistic context during the course of the treatment.

By contrast, of the 10 people who had done well at termination and still better at follow-up and for whom ideation was in some respects disadvantageous, 3 showed an increase of ideation at follow-up and 4 showed better organization, control, and general use of ideation—a total of 7 out of 10 who exploited ideation for continued improvement. Again, the rich get richer. These were people who by and large had good ideational capacities and they exploited these during the psychotherapy.

Of the remaining three, the judgment on this issue could not be made in one instance, and in two instances ideation was not a prominent feature of their continued improvement. Thus, ideation, psychological-mindedness, and insightfulness in the right person made up the cutting edge for substantial and maintained gain in psychotherapy; in the wrong person they make up the dangerous edge (S. Appelbaum, 1975, 1977).

In two instances mention was made of a revivification of conflicts as instrumental in reversing the intrapsychic direction toward improvement of these patients. On one instance, this was assumed to have been triggered environmentally by the patient's getting married. In the other, a conflict was revivified in the absence of a clear environmental trigger. Ideally conflicts should be sufficiently resolved in the course of psychotherapy so that the danger and extent of revivification is minimal. This may or may not be possible under ideal circumstances, but in this population of patients it was not possible. This could be, and often was, predicted from the beginning, and was borne out by the data at termination and follow-up on conflict resolution, insight, and psychological-mindedness. Rather, with many of these patients the therapeutic strategy was by design or inadvertently to increase the patient's ability to deal with conflicts through less deleterious means than they formerly employed. These seven patients, despite the gains they showed at termination, evidently remained sufficiently vulnerable to their conflicts, in conjunction with life events, so as to, on balance, have gone downhill since termination.

Now, what of the 10 patients who had improved at termination and had continued their improvement through follow-up? What can we learn about the changes they made? And do their changes alter the rather grim tone of changes and current status of patients thus far reported?

The following brief summary statements of change in individual patients were made at follow-up. The quotations are from the research testers.

1. This inhibited, constricted patient who "loosened up" slightly at the time of termination had loosened up slightly more at the time of follow-up. He showed more ideational freedom, particularly a tolerance for conscious hostile fantasies, and "a slight—and the minuteness of this change needs to be emphasized—increase in affective experience. Behaviorally I would expect there to be very little overt change in this patient. In terms of his being withdrawn, shy, seclusive, and timid, the tests describe a man very similar to the one we examined at termination and only slightly changed from the individual seen at initial."

2. With this patient, "While cognitive functioning has not improved in efficiency or strength since the termination testing, there are some changes which are noteworthy . . . ideational functioning seems more prominently used as an anxiety-binding measure." Along

with the increased ideational activity, however, were exacerbated phobic symptoms. "One could say that now the patient is more neurotic—in contrast to a previous picture of a more characterological disturbance." Also, along with the increased ideational activity were increased defense and conflict around the expression of hostile wishes which stimulate unconscious guilt now seen as "a significant feature of the patient's problems." The patient is "now slightly more self-assertive, slightly less afraid of punishment, slightly less afraid of and troubled by depression." She offered clear evidence of superego conflict in regard to sexuality, tended to derogate men at the same time that she showed "a greater capacity for and interest in 'love,' particularly a greater capacity for passivity or a greater acceptance of her oral yearnings and dependency." These changes seem to have come about through a diminution in denial and a more "realistic acceptance of the human condition . . . a growth in both ego strength and anxiety tolerance. . . . I want to be careful in this report not to mislead the reader into thinking that the changes between termination and follow-up have been major. They have not. I have tried to describe the direction of the changes and the areas in which they occur but want to make it very clear that the changes are quite small but still hold some significance. They are perceptible, there have been changes which suggest that some working through has occurred, but the changes are quite small. . . . The kinds of insights she has could be termed simply *descriptive.*"

3. One patient went from being a late adolescent with an exhibitionistic symptom to a more neurotic person struggling to become a man. He did this to a large extent on the basis of taking conventional manlike actions, staking out an autonomy in real life with respect to inner promptings and psychiatric treatment in general. "The changes are not many but seem to be of some significance. What might be described as basic or far-reaching restructuring in his personality organization has not occurred . . . though the changes as seen through the tests are striking in some ways." The follow-up tests did, however, contradict the termination tests' inference that there had been an important increase in the ability to sustain intimate relationships—". . . his detachment and uninvolvement would need to be even further emphasized now."

4. One patient came to treatment suffering with clear-cut phobic symptoms and was regarded as a loosely organized, ideationally fluid, impulsive, and generally infantile person. By the time of termination repressiveness had given way to greatly increased ideation, but this ideation was arbitrary and autistic. At follow-up, while maintaining

much of her newfound ideational freedom, she showed a much greater regard for conventional reality, was less given to sweeps of disorganizing anxiety and rage, and showed movement in the direction of settling down, with less psychological disturbance. Sexual fantasies were less disturbing, competitiveness with men had lessened along with increased acceptance of her femininity. "Despite the movement in the hoped for direction, she remains quite vulnerable to psychological stress and, as time goes on, reality blows or misfortune or reverses of one sort or another could easily mobilize the affect-ridden, repressive, phobic picture which characterized her previously."

5. One patient originally considered schizoid, with deviant fantasies and difficulty relating herself emotionally to people, showed excellent gains at termination. "Genuine conflict resolution of significant proportions . . . reorganization and strengthening of defenses . . . anxiety tolerance and ego strength materially increased . . . major changes in affect organization . . . greater involvement in object and interpersonal relations . . . reality testing has improved . . . fantasy no longer substitutes for involvement in the object world." At follow-up the changes were described as a consolidation of changes noticed at termination: ". . . intellectual functioning continued to improve, reality testing has grown more reliable (in the sense that there is less deviant ideation), resolution of oedipal sexual conflict has continued, and there has been a continued growth in self-esteem."

6. One patient had shown a good deal of improvement at termination through a pervasive tightening up of both ideational and motoric control, allowing better reality attunement and less vulnerability to regressive impulse expression and affective experience. Follow-up testing showed a continuance in the same direction. "However, such changes, far-reaching though they may be in the patient's capacity for everyday reality adaptations, rests rather heavily on a strained, effortful combination of constriction, denial, and avoidance . . . far more than is true for most patients that we see, I should say that this young man relies rather heavily on external environmental support in his efforts at self-maintenance . . . one still sees ample evidence of continuing vulnerability to disorganization."

7. One ruminative, pedantic, intellectualizing patient had made changes for the better in his sterile pattern at termination, and at follow-up had made similar changes which even "outstripped those seen at termination." He had become more able to permit himself forthright and direct human interaction, which brought in its wake an increase in the frequency and intensity of conscious anxiety. Although there were no significant changes in the degree of insight between ter-

mination and follow-up, he experienced himself and others as having a much wider range of emotions, people becoming more "sad, anxious, lonely, frustrated, seeing themselves as lacking in certain crucial respects. Indeed, what seemed to be this man's impenetrable narcissistic armor now seems to have many realistic chinks in it and he, we should infer, experiences from time-to-time periods of saddened, somber self-scrutiny. He has a degree of self-awareness that was unmatched on either of the two psychological studies. This seems like a curious result of treatment that he should be free to be sad and depressed about himself, but when we see this rigid man whose affect seemed much in the nature of a caricature having moved in the direction of much more life-like experiences, then one can respect the meaning of this change and what it means for this patient. Perhaps he may, at some future date, return for treatment."

8. One patient's acute turbulent borderline psychotic quality had decreased in prominence at termination and an infantile, immature, character-disorder quality had become prominent. At follow-up the termination changes had been confirmed and increased; for example, he became more efficient, less anxious, and more confident in his use of denial. He seemed to have become relatively comfortable with his deviant, infantile, immature approach to reality. "However, this is a man whose adjustment rests very heavily upon external supports and, as one might expect, cut off from the kind of unilateral, gratification-demanding, relationships that he sets up with women, he could quickly revert to the angry, borderline-psychotic state that we saw him in at the time of initial study."

9. One patient at termination had largely overcome a subtle but substantial decompensation in ego functioning. At follow-up she had become more ideational, and generally more accurate in her thinking and perceiving, slightly less alloplastic although maintaining alloplasticity as her most prominent support, and evidently continuing her homosexuality. Nonetheless, she entertained slightly more favorable possibilities of being a mature, "feminine" woman, was less overtly cynical, suspicious, and guarded, and her "object ties seem a trifle less superficial and she seems somewhat more able to enter into more lasting interpersonal relations."

10. One patient, "when first tested, was confused, disorganized, and openly psychotic. Two years ago she relied rather heavily on suppression, denial, constriction, isolation, and avoidance to deal with ever-present threatening affect and fantasy. Now, what seems to have occurred is a slow, gradual strengthening of repression, making less necessary her desperate reliance on the defenses and maneuverings cited above . . . a slow, undramatic consolidation . . . a satisfactory

equilibrium, but one, however, which is not without its points of weakness and strain. One still needs to keep in mind the possibility that with not too great an increase in psychological stress this woman could revert to the disorganization and confusion that characterized her first set of psychological tests."

DISCUSSION

The reports of these patients at follow-up are disappointing from the standpoint of achieving anything like ideal life goals or achievement goals, or inspiring confidence that changes are solidly entrenched. Even those patients who did best are often described as having made tenuous adjustments and being particularly vulnerable to life or internal stresses, or as wanting to return for treatment. Only one patient who did better at termination and even better at follow-up was described as having made extensive and well-consolidated changes. She was also the only patient who was said to have achieved conflict resolution.

Another disquieting note in these findings is a kind of hydraulic principle in action. At least in the absence of definitive conflict resolution, changes and improvements in one aspect of intrapsychic functioning coincided with increased difficulty in other aspects. A frequent occurrence in several of these patients, for example, was that along with increased ideation, there came increased anxiety, if not increased or new symptoms.

Another new concomitant to some patients' intrapsychic change was a depressive-sounding mood or attitude. A frequent paradigm was for ideation to increase, perceptions to become more accurate, and action as a means of dealing with anxiety and feelings less relied upon. The result for some people was a depressingly clear view of what they took to be the human condition. In at least one patient such realizations occurred, not because impulse and action had been preventing them, but because hyperideation had been used to stifle feeling and concern for others and, except for narcissistic interests, in himself. We are reminded of Freud's (1917) observations of heightened awareness of melancholic patients, their "keener eye for the truth."

Are we presented with a kind of nasty joke, that neurosis is a kind of pleasure, and that a dedication to reality is a sorry end? Are we caught up in a kind of Greek tragedy in which despair wins out inexorably by one means or another? It is not an untenable position. However, other positions are possible. One of these is derivable from Kübler-Ross's (1969) specification of the stages patients go through after learning of their impending death. One might consider that these stages are applicable to all loss experiences, when stimuli are too traumatic to be absorbed in other ways. One of the distinctions Dr. Ross makes is between "resignation" and "acceptance." Resignation follows stages of denial and rage and is tinged with defeat—the fight has gone out of the person, he feels overcome by superior forces. Acceptance, on the other hand, while hardly joyful is without these meanings—one has not been overcome or whipped, there never was a fight in those terms. Rather one took a ride on a carousel, and the music wound down. It may be that without definitive conflict resolution these patients developed a state of mind more like resignation than acceptance. It remains an open question whether psychotherapy, at least with patients such as these, can ever do more. But perhaps tests of this were and are insufficiently made. It may be that psychotherapists have not been as explicit as they could be, in their thinking and in their consequent work with patents, in working through conflicts as they impinge on this termination state of mind, themselves perhaps not always aware of a wisdom greater than knowledge. It is one thing to "destroy" illusions, and and another to create new ones in their place. Working through a neurosis should be abetted and extended by working through the new reality so that its helpful potential can be made available, so that it too can be safeguarded from new illusions, including *dis*illusions.

We should also be aware, in this context, that by virtue of change itself, patients may be asking questions of themselves and taking on challenges which before treatment were merely abstractions. When someone is psychologically concerned, for example, about the next meal on the table, he is not meaningfully asking questions about his place and contributions to mankind and succeeding generations. These new issues lead to new challenges, new realizations, new questions, new recognitions of distances between what is hoped for and what seems achievable, and new awesome responsibilities. In the course of helping the patient overcome the old and symptomatic disequilibrium, treatment may also help him to a new disequilibrium with its own complement of depression, anxiety, and other symptoms.

In evaluating these findings, we must remind ourselves that we are dealing solely with test findings. As far as we know there is no solid, comprehensive research (using tests as we do) comparing the relationship between test findings and life changes. Informally, we believe there is a tendency for the outward manifestations of changes in extratest behaviors—overcoming of symptoms, ability to hold a job, marriage—to outstrip changes as reflected in tests. There are striking instances, however, of tests suggesting important changes which are not reflected in key areas of life functioning. That even small life changes can make a good deal of difference in the quality of the patient's life and that of those around him should be taken into consideration.

We need also to remind ourself that no one should entertain the probability of achieving ideal life circumstances with this population of, by and large, severely disturbed people. Most patients who come to Topeka for treatment have already tried and failed at treatment elsewhere. The "best" patients in our community tend to be professional staff and members of their families, and these were excluded from this study for reasons of confidentiality. As particularly demonstrated in Chapter 7, the predictions made for these patients during the initial examination, especially by the psychological testers, were realistically accurate about the limitations of what could be accomplished.

As evaluators of the results of psychotherapy, we must recognize the limitations of our sphere of investigation. We need to respect the difficulty in tracking down the qualities of existence, the elusiveness of one person's ability to know the life of another, the boundedness of our means of investigation (no matter how skillful we may be) and of the concepts with which we work (no matter how well conceptualized and intellectually elegant they may be). We need, further, to consider what alternative possibilities there might have been for these patients. Surely, if the alternative to the amount of change for the better seen here was for them to continue to live as they had been, then many of these treatments could well be considered "successes." Whether there were other alternatives, whether totally different interventions would have been more helpful, whether the professional time expended on these people was justifiable are large questions, steps removed from these data, which will be addressed in the following chapter.

SUMMARY

1. Single variable analyses which, in contrast to termination findings, were based to a larger extent on clinical test reports than on research test forms, revealed that primarily structural variables changed significantly for the better: anxiety, patterning of defenses, thought organization, intelligence, alloplasticity. Overall changes for the better were highly significant but so were judgments of the tenuousness of these changes. Such dynamic and object-relation variables as core neurotic conflict and quality of interpersonal relations did not change significantly.

2. Although the preponderance of change is for the better to a

degree that approximates the change at termination, slightly less than a third of the patients had continued to change at follow-up in the same way that they had changed at termination, with others showing marked shifts in direction of change between termination and follow-up. Some patients had changed for the worse at termination but had reversed themselves and changed for the better at follow-up. Some patients had changed for the better at termination, but had taken a turn for the worse at follow-up. Based on these data, neither long-term congratulations nor long-term despair seemed to be in order at termination of psychotherapy.

3. An attitude of difficulties being "something to live with" was fairly prominent in the posttreatment psychology of these patients.

4. The changes in patients who had done worse at termination and better at follow-up were all described as tenuous. In none of the patients was the change brought about through insight, but rather was in the nature of helpful shifts in defensive alignments, tilting of the balance in favor of better functioning of structures as against the demandingness of impulse.

5. A number of patients who had done better at termination had slipped back, although not as far back as at initial. In several instances ideation had increased, even between termination and follow-up. This was a mixed blessing, opening up new intrapsychic and probably new external situations which carried their own new sources of distress. These patients were confronting the sharp edges of reality which were once blunted by emotional disturbance and finding it hard going.

6. By contrast, of those who had done well at termination and still better at follow-up, most patients showed an increased exploitation of ideation for continued improvement. It seems that for some patients psychotherapy provides the two-edged sword of ideation which can be grasped by them with a minimum amount of danger and for maximum beneficial use. Nonetheless, even these patients fell short of achieving anything like ideal life goals, nor do they inspire confidence that their changes were solidly entrenched. Changes in one aspect of intrapsychic functioning often coincided with increased difficulty in other aspects. Although these patients were able to contend with life better because of the changes they had accomplished, they seemed to have entered new existential modes. They faced new challenges, suffered keen disappointments, asked questions for which as yet there were inadequate answers.

CHAPTER 10

Overview and Conclusions

PERSONAL AND PERSONNEL

The Project as a whole took more than 20 years to complete and cost more than $1 million. It was the first, and remains the only, research into long-term psychotherapy and psychoanalysis with intensive, elaborate examinations before, immediately after, and 2 years after treatment. Its objectives, in our opinion, continue to be important. Thus, there are good reasons for a careful, candid retrospection.

We consider the many researches purporting to examine change in psychotherapy based on treatments measured in months to be a travesty with respect to their stated goal; they measure, if anything, the effects of brief psychotherapy, which should be measured in its own right rather than equated with long-term psychotherapy. At the same time our experience shows that in attempting to assess people over the natural course of long-term psychotherapy, many pitfalls occur. For example, two of the major Project researchers died in the course of this work; others moved geographically, some dropping their participation, others limiting theirs and working at the disadvantage of isolation from the rest of the group. Still others in the Project changed their interests and priorities, altering, dropping, or increasing their participation. Each one of these vicissitudes added to the instability, and consequent inefficiency, of such a long and complex study. One can hardly expect a large group of people to maintain enthusiasm and interest in one area of inquiry and one research design over a period of many years.

It has long been bemoaned that clinical research suffers when it is done by researchers with inadequate clinical sophistication or by clinicians without adequate research sophistication. On the basis of our experience one would have to append to this general problem the specific difficulties in doing research with fragments of time, as practicing clinicians are forced to do. Such fragmentation may exact a toll from clinical work, but it is especially damaging to research work. Research ordinarily does not have the built-in structure of, for example, a 50-minute hour or an appointment for diagnostic testing which most of us find beneficial to continued high productivity over a long period of time. And research thinking is often so complex that it is difficult to put the research aside and pick it up as bits of time may allow.

Such issues as these should hardly dissuade one out-of-hand from undertaking large, long-term research projects. But surely these considerations require a sober, realistic weighting in the making of such a decision. Research planning should require not only sufficient initial manpower, but provision for alternate and expanded manpower as time goes on.

RESEARCH DESIGN (WITH RESPECT TO TESTS)

One of the hoped-for yields from research is that findings will be understandable, generalizable, and usable by others in the broad clinical and scientific community. Toward that end one should use concepts upon which there is general agreement, or specify such concepts conceptually to a point of refinement that allows shared understanding of them. Such an approach is especially difficult when using clinical concepts, since clinical language is typically imprecise, and varies from community to community and from one theoretical persuasion to another. A number of the intrapsychic variables used here cannot be assumed to mean the same thing to all readers as they did to members of the Project. Worse, they did not always mean the same thing even to different members within the Project itself, as noted in this work—apples and oranges sometimes *were* compared. An egregious example was the different understandings of "externalization" held by the research psychologists and the paired comparison teams. The Glossary (Wallerstein, *et al.*, unpublished manuscript) offered by other members of the Project was an attempt to achieve a common understanding of terms, as are the conceptual analyses of each variable offered here. Such an agreement should have been achieved from the beginning. Clinicians working together can accommodate to "clinical language," learning each others' predilections or particular uses of various terms, getting the correct meaning from the context, or simply by asking. Not only is this impossible when communications are with distant readers, but the collection, judging, and organization of data is dependent upon homogeneous classification. Without a high level of agreement as to what is being so classified, research findings designed to depend on such classifications may be of little value.

An allied issue is raised by the high intercorrelations of the variables, which is a quantitative proof of what one notices in ordinary clinical work. How does one assess ego strength, for example, without at the same time assessing the effectiveness of defenses, alloplasticity, thought and affect organizations? One intensive analysis of psychological-mindedness (S. Appelbaum, 1973), often spoken of as a single thing, quality, or talent, delineated psychological-mindedness into a wide array of structural and content variables. To some extent, then, our separation of variables was artificial, the separate word creating the illusion of discreteness. Also, the intercorrelations among our intrapsychic variables were not perfect. In clinical work and in research it is often useful to separate one factor or element from another. This may be done for heuristic purposes, for experimental manipulation, and because such separations correspond operationally to some life behaviors. But the mischievous effects of such separations should be minimized by explicit definitions of each element as it is isolated for the task at hand.

In most instances the research testers did not give the initial tests. While there is fairly good uniformity in the administration of tests at the Menninger Foundation, there still are differences between students and staff, and among staff members. Thus, the research testers were comparing tests done in some respects differently from the way they might have done them themselves, and they were comparing patients whose tests were administered by a variety of testers. (In two instances the tests were administered elsewhere and in substantially different ways from the termination and follow-up batteries which were administered at the Menninger Foundation.) One cannot overlook, also, the substantial problems in having to make minute, precise observations based on someone else's handwriting, complete with idiosyncratic shorthand and recorded under the time pressure of testing. All these practices may have introduced error, and certainly are a departure from the naturalistic method espoused by the research design. It is reasonable to assume that had the tests been given by the research testers, the validity of test inferences would have been even higher than they were shown to be here.

Another departure from the naturalistic objective, and one likely to have lessened validity, is the practice throughout the Project, and especially on the part of the research psychologists, of analyzing variables separately. Many clinicians do this in the course of their daily work, or at least try to, but the synthetic and interlocking nature of personality and the adventitious way most data are collected quickly forces configuration and organization of variables. Some of this did happen in the thinking of both the research testers and research psychologists as they went through the single variables. It remains an open question as to just how pure the single variable analyses were, whether done in the original judgments from the tests or in the research data analyses, and how much and in what way such judgments may have been influenced by configurational promptings based on clinical sophistication and by the accumulation of knowledge of previously analyzed variables.

Another departure from naturalism which may have lessened validity was the "blindness" of research testers and research psychologists. The research testers had not seen the patients while doing their analyses of the initial tests, and by design at no point knew extratest information. The research psychologists never saw the patients, and even as this is written do not by design know anything about most patients other than what they could not avoid learning from the test data. Such a procedure maximizes the use of the test data, and avoids inimical influences on the process of drawing inferences and generalizations from test data. At the same time, it deprives this work of the possible benefits from being able to integrate test and nontest data thereby enriching conclusions. It especially limited speculation about causes of observed changes. For example, with respect to the exacerbation of conflicts over the feminine role in one of our patients at followup, one is at a disadvantage in understanding this exacerbation without knowing that the patient had married after termination (a piece of information introduced by the patient in the course of follow-up testing).

REMARKS ON FINDINGS

Often throughout this communication we found ourselves concluding that the rich get richer, while the poor tend to get poorer, stay the same, or become only a little more prosperous. In other words, the more a patient has to work with psychologically to begin with, the better he will do. Thus, many of our findings by implication corroborate the theoretical understanding that the central ingredients of personality are difficult to change after their early development. People tend grossly to continue as before. At the same time, some people, fundamentally and severely disturbed as they were, did benefit, at least in ways commensurate with their intrapsychic starting points. Such findings certainly fly in the face of any assumption that psychotherapy is like a medicine whose effects can be expected to be more or less the same for anybody who gets it. Rather, they underline the need for diagnosis prior to treatment. Adequate diagnoses would lead to better decisions as to who should get treatment and who should not (especially when treatment facilities are limited), what kinds of treatment interventions would benefit one person or another, and what goals and goal-linked strategies would be commensurate with patient capacities.

Since the inception of this research, social and political conditions have developed in such a way that some people may find our conclusions about the need for diagnosis offensive on antidemocratic grounds. We think this an unfortunate and inappropriate crossing of the boundary between politics and science. On the basis of the data reported here, treating all people as "equal," however much it may conform to egalitarian philosophies, is likely to do them a disservice, hampering those with greater capacities and unduly pressuring those with less. Expertise need not be elitism.

Another important facet of this reminder of the idiographic nature of clinical work is our repeated conclusion that the meaning of change, and an assessment as to whether it is beneficial or harmful, depends on who has the change, the personality context (and often the social context) in which the change occurs. For most of the intrapsychic variables one simply has to know the use to which they are put, and the alternatives to them, before being able either to attach a value to change for research purposes, or to strive for such change for treatment purposes. Again, such a point of view leads to a call for adequate diagnosis not only of the person but of his situation in life, its opportunities and limits; and not only before treatment begins, but during treatment, as new uses and meanings arise in the flux of personality change. As patients change in psychotherapy, we in a sense continually work with "new" patients. If diagnosis is helpful with the patient as he first presents himself, then by the same token it should be helpful all along. Diagnosis, in this sense, may or may not refer to psychological tests. Rather, testing may be an adjunct used at particular points in the ongoing diagnostic–therapeutic process.

In several data analyses the principles which we labeled "loosening" and "tightening" were useful ways of organizing data. Such principles reflect the truism that some people need greater access to their thoughts and feelings while others need greater controls over their thoughts and feelings. This is probably the single most important reason why change cannot be judged in the abstract, why it requires reference to the starting point and goal of each person.

Factor analysis, and other quantitative analyses of change, resulted in configurations of variables which were clinically plausible and recognizable. Such comparability serves as a kind of external criterion, implying support for the subjective, qualitative clinical ways of thinking.

Several sources of data, notably Factor 1 in the Factor Analysis (Chapter 5) and groups of variables involved in change (Chapter 3), support the conclusion that substantial change, even some kinds of structural change, can come about in so-called supportive treatments in the absence of marked change in those variables central to expressive treatments, e.g., insight, conflict resolution, psychological-mindedness. It would be most unfortunate, however, if the findings offered here should be taken to mean that one might as well offer patients supportive treatment as expressive treatment since structural change occurs anyway. We have no data to suggest that the end result of such change is as good as change brought about through expressive treatment, or even equal to it. Indeed, our finding that those with good capacities to begin with (often put in expressive treatment) did better in an absolute sense than those with poor capacities to begin with (often put in supportive treatment) implies the reverse. In assessing the finding of structural change one has to bear in mind the considerable psychopathology in these patients, which allowed, for some of them, only the option of supportive treatment. Structural change for them turned out to mean that shattered egos were put back together, that a general tightening of controls was instituted, that better organization and adaptation of basic functioning occurred. Such changes are more easily measured than the minute structural changes of patients who are pretty well organized to begin with, and may even result in greater and more striking changes in extratest life. *Structural change,* as with so many clinical and metapsychological terms, requires specification if it is to refer to agreed-upon, homogeneous phenomena. The finding does suggest, however, that at least the structural changes noted here are not as elusive as they sometimes are made to sound in clinical discussions.

One implication of this finding is to encourage further thought about the effects of the interpersonal relationship between patient and therapist, as done in our Project by Horwitz (1974) and by many others in various contexts. From one point of view this finding could provide a fresh corrective to the sometimes-held fantasy and practice that psychotherapy should be offered only to the "good" patient—which usually means someone of high intelligence, capacity for psychological-mindedness, and not "too sick." (However, see below for a restatement and assertion of the argument that psychotherapy should be offered to only "good" patients.)

Test findings were shown to be more valid with respect to predicting the results of treatment than nontest findings, directly, in the comparison of tests and other psychiatric information (Chapter 8) and, indirectly, in the test and paired comparison data (Chapter 7). Assessment of ego strength seemed to have been the chief source of difference between the nontest clinicians and the tests, as it often is in clinical practice. Certainly, in this sample of severely disturbed persons, assessment of the ego was a key issue. In clinical contexts where ego strength is not such a key determinant, the comparative differences reported here may be less crucial. Also, the psychiatric predictions made at initial were based on the gathering of data by a good many generally junior clinicians while many of the testers were senior (although the organization and predictions made from these were done by senior clinicians). The results may be limited by these considerations.

The finding that the relatively brief clinical test reports were as valid as the extensive research analyses of the data with respect to gross, but usual and practical, central questions was gratifying. It implied that these questions can be answered effectively by a variety of testers under the time pressures and conditions of usual clinical work. The extensive finding and reporting of test inferences in the research documents (see Chapter 2) would, to be sure, make the answering of many questions not answered in the clinical test report possible. At the same time the finding of equal validity raises the question of how much time, expense, and effort should be expended in test report analysis and in reporting. Beyond a certain point, the accumulation of information is not only useless but may be counterproductive in needlessly complicating those questions that could be answered with less data. With respect to the clinical contexts in which the tester's work will be inserted, every bit of information offered runs the risk of boring or confusing the reader or listener even while it is designed to clarify, interest, and be helpful. Such risks are minimized by pertinent and relevant selection of information which are determined by practical needs based on the goals of the examination. Extensive collection and intensive analysis of data (as used illustratively here, and as practiced by the research testers in this research) might in some instances be better restricted to the mind of the test analyzer than put on paper. Categorizing data in test reports is one way of avoiding discursiveness while forcing the tester to attend to central issues (Appelbaum, 1972a).

REMARKS ON THE OUTCOME QUESTION

Consistent with the goals and design of this study, the outcome findings reported here are of limited generalizability. No attempt was made for these patients to represent the general population of people to whom long-term psychotherapy is offered, nor was any attempt made to select cases that could be expected to do well in psychotherapy. The way patients were selected certainly worked against the possibility of demonstrating a movie fade-out view of psychotherapy—the cured person walking off in the sunlight of unlimited personal horizons. For example, 17 of the 42 patients were hospitalized sometime during their treatment. As previously noted, less disturbed people, often the "best" cases potentially available, were members of the professional community in Topeka and were, for reasons of confidentiality, systematically excluded from the research.

It is also plausible that patients at termination reacted to the meanings of termination to them and from the expectable emotional flurries accompanying any significant changes in life circumstances. Finally, at termination and even at a 2-year follow-up point, one has no way of assessing the degree to which a therapeutic process has been set in motion by the treatment which, aided by self-analysis or improved life circumstances, may lead to greatly improved life later on. Such improvements may be only partially accounted for or knowable on the basis of changes revealed in tests at the points of examination. The variability in changes demonstrated at follow-up implies this possibility. In other words, we need to recognize that accurate assessment at any given point need not be the same as accurate prediction of the long-term and ultimate effects of psychotherapy, especially as these may interact with unpredictable life events. Relevant here is the work of Voth et al. (1962) on the situational variables part of the Project.

The words improved and better have a comforting sound, especially to people whose professional lives and self-esteem are substantially organized according to judgments of their patients with such words. However, with this population, "improved" as measured by tests referred to limited and often tenuous gains. With a view toward the professional, humanitarian, and societal future, we might well ask ourselves about the worth of such treatment enterprises as recorded here.

From the standpoint of most of the patients, these treatments were probably worth having if compared with no interventions at all in their troubled lives. But can we be sure that there are not better alternatives for patients such as these? In recent years many alternatives to long-term psychotherapy have been offered—ranging from brief psychotherapy, drug-and-other stimulants, to purely affective and purely interpersonal experiences, family and other field approaches, counseling, guidance, and environmental manipulations. Splits between these activities and between competing theorists have hampered full investigation and judgments of all of them, and possibly in finding still other ways of intervening helpfully (S. Appelbaum, 1976). As a general tendency, those with the most extensive and intensive training in human psychology, best learned through the practice of long-term psychotherapy, have devoted proportionally less of their expertise to these problems than have those with less training. The findings reported here should encourage improving the treatments offered and emphasize the importance of correct diagnostic and predictive selection of patients most likely to benefit greatly from long-term psychotherapy, and in putting more effort into finding and evaluating alternative means of helping people. Finally, if political arguments between competing schools could be put aside then attention and energy toward understanding the processes, causes, and conditions of change could be released (Strupp, 1975).

What implications are there for the helping professions and for society in the findings of this study? It has become almost fashionable to question the fairness of offering long-term psychotherapy largely to wealthy people. The position has also been taken that limited professional resources might best be used for those in a position to influence other people, such as school teachers, behavioral scientists, and others with potential power and influence. Our findings are consistent with the belief that well-functioning people are likely to be just the ones who can make maximal use of psychotherapy. While some severely disturbed people, perhaps surprisingly, were helped considerably, the best endowed patients were helped most. The social gain in treating the latter, if a choice must be made, is obvious. The alternative is to claim that the gains reported here represent an optimal social and professional use of skilled and limited expertise.

These are difficult issues. They give an awesome responsibility to diagnosticians and to the makers of treatment decisions. One can argue that severely disturbed people can do more social damage than those merely functioning below their potential, who can get along anyway. It is alien to many of our democratic values to have "experts" decide who should get what, even more alien for many people than letting such decisions be decided by wealth. The deployment of resources on a strictly functional basis runs counter to the professional–medical ethic of providing care for anyone who needs it and asks for it, and it is distasteful simply on humanitarian grounds to withhold the promise of alleviation of pain. But can we in good conscience fail to pursue these and other implications? Distasteful, disturbing, or challenging as they may be, these questions call for the establishment of priorities among our values, including those values of thinking objectively and of providing the greatest good for the greatest number.

Whether in its social implications or with respect to its intrinsic findings, this research should not lead to despair and ought not lead to complacency.

SUMMARY

1. Our personal experience should serve as a reminder of the expectable difficulties in a research that covers a long period of time, and as a warning that such a design should include plans for these eventualities.

2. Naturalistic research must recognize and accommodate the frequent contradictions between the language and methods of clinical practice and those employed in formal research.

3. In our study, a consistent finding was that the better endowed patients did better in psychotherapy than those less endowed—the "rich-get-richer" phenomenon. An important moral to be drawn from this is that an adequate diagnosis is needed prior to treatment—diagnoses leading to better decisions as to who should get treatment and who should not, what kind of treatment intervention would benefit one person or another, and what goals and goal-linked strategies would be commensurate with patients' capacities.

4. Our data support the clinical recognition that for many clinical purposes people should be thought about in idiographic terms. Assessing of any element in their personality is dependent upon the context in which it occurs and the use to which it is put.

5. "Loosening" and tightening" were often useful ways of organizing the data of change, implicating each person's starting point and consequent goal.

6. Serving as a kind of external criterion, quantitative studies agreed with clinical sense, thus supporting ways of thinking about patients developed informally among clinicians, and the adequacy of our research methods to represent clinical reality.

7. The best endowed patients, receiving expressive treatment, did best in an absolute sense, but some disturbed patients nonetheless showed structural change in that they became better organized with respect to fundamental ego capacities. Structural change, without further specification, may be an inadequate term to refer fully, and with correct implications, to changes among parts of the psychic apparatus as these occur in patients with different capacities and different degrees of disturbance receiving different kinds of treatment. That such changes occurred in these disturbed patients, usually in the absence of insight, conflict resolution, and psychological-mindedness, should encourage a closer look at other mutative elements in the therapeutic process, perhaps relationship ones especially.

8. While the production of insight was associated with the best gains, for some patients it was associated with worsened functioning. Even among patients who benefited overall, it was often associated with increased anxiety and depressingly tinged perspectives. Insight seems to be a two-edged sword.

9. Test findings based on psychological tests were shown to be more valid than nontest findings in two independent studies, with assessment of ego strength being the chief source of difference. The brief clinical test report was just about as effective as the lengthy, detailed research analyses with respect to gross, but central and practical, questions.

10. As a group, these patients did not show definitive, glowing, solidly entrenched gains. Such a finding is no surprise to clinicians who know from experience the kinds of gains usually realized by a population as disturbed, overall, as this one was.

11. The changeability at follow-up as compared to termination implies that these temporal points may not be highly useful as predictors of the years to come, whether because of the special stresses at termination and follow-up themselves, or because it simply is too early to tell.

12. Within the sharp limitations of generalizability imposed by our research design and selection of patients, the findings encourage an emphasis on a correct diagnostic and predictive selection of patients most likely to benefit from long-term psychotherapy.

13. The modest gains noted cannot lead to complacency. They imply that, for some patients at least, the clinically informed worker

might well devote himself to finding alternative ways and mixtures of providing help. The politics of competing psychotherapies should be put away in favor of objective, functional research and actions.

14. The tendency for the best endowed people to gain more from psychotherapy than the less endowed raises, again, the social issues as to whether psychotherapy is best dispensed in a free market place, or whether the short supply should be devoted to those persons who are in an intrapsychic position to benefit most, and who would be likely to benefit society most.

References and Bibliography

Appelbaum, A. & Horwitz, L. A hierarchical ordering of assumptions about psycho-therapy. *Psychotherapy*, 1966, *3*, 71–80.

Appelbaum, A. & Horwitz, L. Correlates of global change in psychotherapy. Paper presented to the staff of the Menninger Foundation Psychotherapy Research Project, 1968 (unpublished).

Appelbaum, A. A critical re-examination of the concept "Motivation for Change" in psychoanalytic treatment. *Int. J. Psycho-Anal.*, 1972, *53*, 51–59.

Appelbaum, S. A. & Siegal, R. S. Half-hidden influences in psychological testing and practice. *J. Proj. Tech. Pers. Assessment*, 1965, *29*, 128–133.

Appelbaum, S. A., Coyne, L., & Siegal, R. S. Change in IQ during and after long-term psychotherapy. *J. Proj. Tech. Pers. Assessment*, 1969, *33*, 290–297.

Appelbaum, S. A., Coyne, L., & Siegal, R. S. Routes to change in IQ during and after long-term psychotherapy. *J. Nerv. Ment. Dis.*, 1970, *151*, 310–315.

Appelbaum, S. A. Science and persuasion in the psychological test report. *J. Consult. Clin. Psychol.*, 1970, 35, 349–355.

Appelbaum, S. A. A method of reporting psychological test findings. *Bull. Menninger Clin.*, 1972, *36*, 535–545. (a)

Appelbaum, S. A. How long is long-term psychotherapy? *Bull. Menninger Clin.*, 1972. *36*, 651–655. (b)

Appelbaum, S. A. Psychological-mindedness: Word, concept, and essence. *Int. J. Psycho-Anal.*, 1973, *54*, 35–46.

Appelbaum, S. A. The idealization of insight. *Int. J. Psychoanal. Psychother.*, 1975, *4*, 272–303. (a)

Appelbaum, S. A. Questioning the question: The effectiveness of psychotherapy. *Interamer. J. Psychology*, 1975, *1–2*, 213–225. (b)

Appelbaum, S. A. & Katz, J. Self-help with diagnosis (A self-administered semi-projective device). *J. Pers. Assessment*, 1975, *39*, 349–359. (c)

Appelbaum, S. A. A psychoanalyst looks at gestalt therapy. In C. Hatcher & P. Himelstein (Eds.), *The handbook of gestalt therapy*. New York: Jason Aronson, 1976, pp. 753–778.

Appelbaum, S. A. The dangerous edge of insight. *Psychotherapy: Theory, Research and Practice*, 1977, *13*, 202–206.

Barron, F. An ego-strength scale which predicts response to psychotherapy. *J. Consult. Psychol.*, 1953, *17*, 327–333.

Davis, J. D., Fisher, L., & Davis, M. L. "Therapeutic" interventions of clinicians in standardized interviews: A test of the social competition model. *J. Cons. Clin. Psychol.*, 1973, *41*, 16–26.

Ehrenreich, G. A. A psychoanalytic approach to the prediction of overt behavior from psychological tests. Unpublished doctoral dissertation, University of Kansas, 1956.

Ehrenreich, G. A. Assessing therapeutic results with psychological tests. Paper presented at symposium "Evaluation of Processes and Results of Therapies II," American Psychological Association Convention, August 31, 1957.

Ehrenreich, G. A. Toward a systematic conception of the structure and functioning of defense mechanisms. Paper read at the Topeka Psychoanalytic Society meeting, January 1958, unpublished.

Ehrenreich, G. A. & Siegal, R. S. Assessing intrapsychic variables with psychological tests in psychotherapy research (unpublished manuscript).

Eissler, K. R. Notes on the psychoanalytic concept of cure. *Psycho-anal. Study Child*, 1963, *18*, 424–463.

Freud, S. (1893–1895): Studies in hysteria. *Standard Edition*, 1955, *2*, 1–305.

Freud, S. (1917): Mourning and melancholia. *Standard Edition*, 1957, *14*, 237–260.

Freud, S. (1937): Analysis terminable and interminable. *Standard Edition*, 1964, *23*, 211–253.

Hall, B. H. & Wallerstein, R. S. Operational problems of psychotherapy research: II. Termination studies. *Bull. Menninger Clin.*, 1960, *24*, 190–214.

Harty, M. & Horwitz, L. Therapeutic outcome as rated by patients, therapists and judges. *Arch. Gen. Psychiatry*, 1976, *33*, 957–961.

Holt, R. R. Clinical and statistical prediction: A reformulation and some new data. *J. Abnorm. Soc. Psychol.*, 1958, *56*, 1–12.

Holt, R. R. Clinical judgment as a disciplined inquiry. *J. Nerv. Ment. Dis.*, 1961, *133*, 369–382.

Holt, R. R. Yet another look at clinical and statistical prediction: Or, is clinical psychology worthwhile? *American Psychologist*, April 1970, 337–349.

Horwitz, L. & Appelbaum, A. A hierarchical ordering of assumptions about psychotherapy. *Psychotherapy*, 1966, *3*, 71–80.

Horwitz, L. *Clinical prediction in psychotherapy.* New York: Jason Aronson, 1974.

Kernberg, O. Three methods of research on psychoanalytic treatment. *Int. Ment. Health Res. Newsletter*, Winter 1965, *7*, 11–13.

Kernberg, O. Borderline personality organization. *J. Amer. Psychoanal. Assoc.*, 1967, *16*, 641–685.

Kernberg, O. The treatment of patients with borderline personality organization. *Int. J. Psycho-Anal.*, 1968, *49*, 600–619.

Kernberg, O. Factors in the psychoanalytic treatment of narcissistic personalities. *J. Amer. Psychoanal. Assoc.*, 1970, *18*, 51–85.

Kernberg, O. Prognostic considerations regarding borderline personality organization. *J. Amer. Psychoanal. Assoc.*, 1971, *19*, 595–635.

Kernberg, O., Burstein, E., Coyne, L., Appelbaum, A., Horwitz, L., & Voth, H. Psychotherapy and psychoanalysis: Final report of the Menninger Foundation's psychotherapy research project. *Bull. Menninger Clin.*, 1972, *36*, 1–278.

Klopper, B., Crumpton, E., & Grayson, H. M. Rating scales for ego functioning applicable to diagnostic testing. *J. Proj. Tech.*, 1958, *22*, 70–81.

Kubler-Ross, E. *On death and dying.* New York: Macmillan, 1969.

Luborsky, L. Self-interpretation of the TAT as a clinical technique. *J. Proj. Tech.*, 1953, *17*, 217–223.

Luborsky, L. & Sargent, H. D. Sample use of method. *Bull. Menninger Clin.*, 1956, *20*, 263–276.

Luborsky, L., Fabian, M., Hall, B. H., Ticho, E., & Ticho, G. R. II. Treatment variables. *Bull. Menninger Clin.*, 1958, *22*, 126–147.

Luborsky, L. Clinicians' judgments of mental health. *Arch. Gen. Psychiatry*, 1962, *7*, 407–417.

Luborsky, L. The patient's personality and psychotherapeutic change. In H. H. Strupp & L. Luborsky (Eds.), *Research in psychotherapy* (Vol. 2). Washington, D.C.: American Psychological Association, 1962, pp. 115–133.

Luborsky, L., Chandler, M., Auerback, A. H., Cohen, J., & Bachrach, H. M. Factors influencing the outcome of psychotherapy: A review of quantitative research. *Psychological Bulletin*, 1971, *75*, 145–185.

Luborsky, L. Clinicians' judgments of mental health: Specimen case descriptions and forms for the health sickness rating scale. *Bull. Menninger Clin.*, 1975, *39*, 448–480.

Mayman, M. Psychoanalytic study of the self-organization with psychological tests. In *The proceedings of the academic assembly on clinical psychology.* Montreal: McGill University Press, 1963, pp. 99–117.

Meehl, P. E. *Clinical vs. statistical prediction: A theoretical analysis and a review of the evidence.* Minneapolis: University of Minnesota Press, 1954.

Menninger, K. Psychological aspects of the organism under stress: Part 1. The homeostatic regulatory function of the ego. *J. Amer. Psychoanal. Assoc.*, 1954, *2*, 67–106. Part II. The regulatory devices of the ego under major stress. *J. Amer. Psychoanal. Assoc.*, April 1954, *2*, 280–310.

Rapaport, D., Gill, M. M., & Schafer, *Diagnostic psychological testing: The theory, statistical evaluation, and diagnostic application of a battery of tests.* Chicago: Yearbook Publishers, 1945–46.

Rapaport, D., Gill, M. M., & Schafer, R. In R. R. Holt (Ed.), *Diagnostic psychological testing.* Rev. Ed. New York: International Universities Press, 1968.

Robbins, L. L. & Wallerstein, R. S. Orientation. *Bull. Menninger Clin.*, 1956, *20*, 223–225.

Robbins, L. L. & Wallerstein, R. S. The research strategy and tactics of the psychotherapy research project of the Menninger Foundation and the problem of controls. In E. A. Rubinstein & M. B. Parloff (Eds.), *Research in Psychotherapy.* Washington, D.C.: American Psychological Association, 1959, pp. 27–43.

Rosen, I. C. Choices in psychotherapy research. *Br. J. Med. Psychology*, 1965, *38*, 253–260.

Sarason, I. G. & Ganzer, V. J. Concerning the medical model. *American Psychologist*, 1960, *23*, 507–510.

Sargent, H. D. Rationale. *Bull. Menninger Clin.*, 1956, *20*, 221–278.

Sargent, H. D. Design. *Bull. Menninger Clin.*, 1956, *20*, 234–238.

Sargent, H. D., Modlin, H. C., Faris, M. T., & Voth, H. M. Situational variables. *Bull. Menninger Clin.*, 1958, *22*, 148–166.

Sargent, H. D. Methodological problems of follow-up studies in psychotherapy research. *Amer. J. Orthopsychiat.*, 1960, *30*, 495–506.

Sargent, H. D. Intrapsychic change: Methodological problems in psychotherapy research. *Psychiatry*, 1961, *24*, 93–108.

Sargent, H. D., Coyne, L., Wallerstein, R. S., & Holtzman, W. H. An approach to the quantitative problems of psychoanalytic research. *J. Clin. Psychology*, 1967, *23*, 243–291. (Also published as a separate Monograph Supplement, No. 23, July 1967.)

Sargent, H. D., Horwitz, L., Wallerstein, R. S., & Appelbaum, A. Prediction in psychotherapy research: A method for the transformation of clinical judgments into testable hypotheses. *Psychological Issues* (Vol. VI), No. 1, 1968, *21*, 1–147.

Schafer, R. *Psychoanalytic interpretation in Rorschach testing.* New York: Grune & Stratton, 1954.

Schlesinger, H. J. Diagnosis and prescription for psychotherapy. *Bull. Menninger Clin.,* 1969, *33*, 269–278.

Schlesinger, H. J. Interaction of dynamic and reality factors in the diagnostic testing interview. *Bull. Menninger Clin.,* 1973, *37*, 495–517.

Siegal, R. S. & Ehrenreich, G. A. Inferring repression from psychological tests. *Bull. Menninger Clin.,* 1962, *26*, 82–91.

Siegal, R. S., Rosen, I. C., & Ehrenreich, G. A. The natural history of an outcome prediction. *J. Proj. Tech.,* 1962, *26*, 112–116.

Siegal, R. S. & Rosen, I. C. Character style and anxiety tolerance: A study in intrapsychic change. In H. H. Strupp & L. Luborsky (Eds.), *Research in psychotherapy* (Vol. 2). Washington, D.C.: American Psychological Association, 1962, pp. 206–217.

Siegal, R. S. A psychological test study of personality change: The psychotherapy research project of the Menninger Foundation. *Int. Ment. Health Res. Newsletter,* Summer 1967, *9*, 2, 6, 7.

Siegal, R. S. What are defense mechanisms? *J. Amer. Psychoanal. Assoc.,* 1969, *17*, 785–807.

Siegal, R. S. Quantification and psychoanalytic research. *Bull. Menninger Clin.,* 1969, *33*, 146–153.

Strupp, H. H. & Blackwood, G. Recent methods of psychotherapy. In A. M. Freedman, *et al.* (Eds.), *Comprehensive Textbook of Psychiatry—II.* Baltimore: Williams & Wilkins, 1975, pp. 1909–1920.

Strupp, H. H. On failing one's patient. *Psychotherapy: Theory, Research and Practice,* 1975, *12*, 39–41.

Szasz, T. The problem of psychiatric nosology: A contribution to a situational analysis of psychiatric operation. *Amer. J. Psychiatry,* 1957, *114*, 405–413.

Ticho, E. A. Termination of psychoanalysis: Treatment goals, life goals. *Psychoanal. Q.,* 1972, *41*, 315–333.

Ticho, G. R. On self-analysis. *Int. J. Psycho-Anal.,* April 1967, *48*, 308–318.

Veldman, D. J. *Fortran programming for the behavioral sciences.* New York: Holt, Rinehart & Winston, 1967.

Voth, H. M., Modlin, H. C., & Orth, M. H. Situational variables in the assessment of psychotherapeutic results. *Bull. Menninger Clin.,* 1962, *26*, 73–81.

Voth, H. M. & Orth, M. *Psychotherapy and the role of the environment.* New York: Behavioral Publications, 1973.

Wallerstein, R. S. & Robbins, L. L. Concepts. *Bull. Menninger Clin.,* 1956, *20*, 239–262.

Wallerstein, R. S. & Robbins, L. L. Further notes on design and concepts. *Bull. Menninger Clin.,* 1958, *22*, 117–125.

Wallerstein, R. S. Helen D. Sargent and the psychotherapy research project. *Bull. Menninger Clin.,* 1960, *24*, 159–163.

Wallerstein, R. S. & Robbins, L. L. Operational problems of psychotherapy research: I. Initial studies. *Bull. Menninger Clin.,* 1960, *24*, 164–189.

Wallerstein, R. S. Report of the psychotherapy research project of the Menninger Foundation: January 1954–July 1961. *Int. Ment. Health Res. Newsletter,* December 1961, *3*, 12–15.

Wallerstein, R. S. The problem of the assessment of change in psychotherapy. *Int. J. Psychoanal.,* 1963, *44* (Part I), 31–41.

Wallerstein, R. S. The role of prediction in theory building in psychoanalysis. *J. Amer. Psychoanal. Assoc.*, 1964, *12*, 675–691.

Wallerstein, R. S. The goals of psychoanalysis: A survey of analytic viewpoints. *J. Amer. Psychoanal. Assoc.*, 1965, *13*, 748–770.

Wallerstein, R. S. The current state of psychotherapy: Theory, practice, research. *J. Amer. Psychoanal. Assoc.*, 1966, *14*, 183–225. (a)

Wallerstein, R. S. The psychotherapy research project of the Menninger Foundation: An overview at the midway point. In L. A. Gottschalk & A. H. Auerbach (Eds.), *Methods of Research in Psychotherapy*. New York: Appleton-Century-Crofts, 1966, pp. 500–516. (b)

Wallerstein, R. S. The psychotherapy research project of the Menninger Foundation: A semi-final view. In J. M. Shlien (Ed.), *Research in Psychotherapy* (Vol. 3). Washington, D.C.: American Psychological Association, 1968, pp. 584–605.

Wallerstein, R. S. & Sampson, H. Issues in research and the psychoanalytic process. *Int. J. Psycho-Anal.*, 1971, *52*, 11–50.

Wallerstein, R. S., *et al.* Glossary of the psychotherapy research project of the Menninger Foundation (unpublished).

Ward, J. H., Jr. Hierarchical grouping to optimize an objective function. *J. Amer. Statistical Assoc.*, 1963, *58*, 236–244.

Wheelis, A. The place of action in personality change. *Psychiatry*, 1950, *13*, 135–148.

Index